Big Brother and the National Reading Curriculum

How Ideology Trumped Evidence

Richard L. Allington
Author/Editor

HEINEMANN
Portsmouth, NH

Heinemann
A division of Reed Elsevier Inc.
361 Hanover Street
Portsmouth, NH 03801–3912
www.heinemann.com

Offices and agents throughout the world

The author and publisher wish to thank those who have generously given permission to reprint borrowed material:

"The National Reading Panel Report" by J. W. Cunningham in *Reading Research Quarterly*, 30. Copyright © 2001 by the International Reading Association. Reprinted by permission of the International Reading Association.

"Beyond the Smoke and Mirrors: A Critique of the National Reading Panel Report on Phonics" by E. Garan in *Phi Delta Kappan*, 82. Copyright © 2001 by Phi Delta Kappan. Reprinted by permission of Phi Delta Kappan.

Credits continue on p. 304.

Library of Congress Cataloging-in-Publication Data
  Big brother and the national reading curriculum : how ideology trumped evidence / [edited by] Richard Allington.
      p.   cm.
  Includes bibliographical references and index.
    ISBN 0-325-00513-3 (alk. paper)
    1. Reading—United States.   2. National Reading Panel (U.S.).
    I.   Allington, Richard L.
  LB1050 .B52 2002
  372.4'0973—dc21   2002009620

Editor: Lois Bridges
Production editor: Sonja S. Chapman
Cover design: Lisa Fowler
Cover photo: Scott Barrow Inc./Superstock
Compositor: House of Equations, Inc.
Manufacturing: Steve Bernier

Printed in the United States of America on acid-free paper

06   05   04   03   02   VP   1   2   3   4   5

Contents

Preface

One of the mixed blessings with being one of the "graybeards" band of scholars is that you remember what education was like thirty-five or more years ago. You recall how the federal government was going to eradicate illiteracy through the application of scientific research—primarily applied research done at federally funded regional educational laboratories. You remember that the best minds in the nation were working to develop code-emphasis (phonics) reading curricula that were scientific and effective. You remember the Wisconsin Design for Reading, the skills-tracking package from the University of Wisconsin; the Sullivan Programmed Readers from Behavioral Research Labs; the Miami and Palo Alto linguistic readers with their "Nan can fan Dan" sentences; the International Teaching Alphabet; Words in Color; Direct Instructional System for Teaching Arithmetic and Reading (DISTAR); plaid phonics; multisensory phonics; and so on. All of them were developed with federal funds. You also remember that we gave up on those research-based programs when they didn't pan out with improved reading achievement.

I feel like Bill Murray's character in the movie *Groundhog Day*—I'm seeing the same things happen over and over again. I awake every day now and have to remind myself that it isn't 1972. It's just that the same old ideas that were so popular in 1972 have returned as the next "new, new thing" for reforming American education. Phonics is back. The vendors have dusted off all those 1970s materials, stuck new covers on them, gussied up the artwork a bit, and put them up for sale. That the two most heavily promoted reading curricula have barely changed since 1970 seems to bother almost no one.

But it isn't just the recycled reading programs that make this feel like the early 1970s. It was the 1970s that brought us "performance contracting"—bidding out schools to for-profit vendors. Teachers were paid for student performance on tests. That didn't pan out. It was the 1970s that brought us large-scale minimum competency testing and the first accountability packages. It was, as Rowan (1990) notes, an era when "control" strategies were the education management fad of the day. We had pacing schedules to keep teachers on track to cover the materials. We had skills testing of every child, with scores turned into the central office for plotting. We even had a Right to Read movement that asserted that literacy was a civil right and promised literacy for all. But all those schemes didn't accomplish the Olympian goal of universal literacy.

There are days when I could swear that some sort of social amnesia is running rampant. How is it that so many folks cannot see that the new, new educational reform plans are but recycled bad ideas? Ideas we have tried before. Ideas that had their chance. Ideas that fell flat on their faces thirty years ago.

I did not plan to create this book. I planned to largely ignore the various policy promoters and entrepreneurs who are offering up these tired ideas as new solutions. I was just going to slide into retirement over the next few years.

When the *Preventing Reading Difficulties* report (Snow, Burns, & Griffin, 1998) appeared, I read it and yawned. As Catherine Snow (2001) herself has argued, "Nothing said in the report about reading instruction, for example, could not have been formulated by an experienced, thoughtful, reflective first-grade teacher with a few weeks' free time" (p. 236).

When the National Reading Panel (NRP) was formed I yawned again, if only because virtually all of the panel members were old (even older than me), and none were among the group of active reading researchers that most people in the profession would recognize. My dean joked that it was a cutting-edge panel— circa 1978. I testified to the panel that I thought their choice to focus only on experimental research was too narrow. And when the panel's 500-plus page report appeared, I read it and yawned.

But when I read Elaine Garan's *Phi Delta Kappan* article (Chapter 4), something set me off. Maybe I was just tinder for her sparks. Garan exposed the ideological distortions of what the research said and how these had affected the educational reforms being dumped on teachers. Maybe I wasn't ready to retire. I don't know why, but suddenly the need for this book loomed large in my mind. I had never considered myself a whole language kind of guy. In fact, I viewed the first edition of *Classrooms That Work* (Cunningham & Allington, 1994) as a cautionary tale about the exaggerations of research by whole language advocates. (The third edition opens with a cautionary tale about the exaggerations of the phonics advocates.) It wasn't until that book was branded a whole language manual (a nice oxymoronish twist) by California state representative Steven Baldwin and I was called a whole language conspirator by a member of the California state board of education that such thoughts even entered my head. Dick Allington a whole language guru?

Then I was invited to offer the keynote address at the Whole Language Umbrella (WLU) conference! The invitation was for me to talk about reading policy making in Texas and California. I recall wondering, "Me, at the Whole Language Umbrella?"

Bess Altwerger introduced me to the WLU audience, relating that when my name was brought up she had asked, "Is Dick Allington whole language?" It hadn't occurred to her either. She went on to note that many U.S. states had once had guidelines for determining a person's ethnicity on the basis of the race of a single long-ago ancestor, the so-called one-drop rule. She said she had decided that, using similar criteria, Dick Allington was probably a whole language person. I began my talk that day by noting that I too was unsure about my classification, but agreed that if it only required a single drop of blood, I was in fact a whole language person.

Of course I'm not really a whole language person. I disagree with Ken Goodman on at least as many things as I disagree with Marilyn Adams. But I do admire the spunk the whole language folks have demonstrated. When it comes to school reform, I know they are closer to the mark than the direct-instruction folks. The whole language folks understand the critical importance of teachers—expert, autonomous teachers—in the development of children's literacy. Dumbing down the curriculum and curricular materials through narrowly conceived accountability schemes and scripted materials didn't work in the 1970s and it won't work now. The whole language folks may miss the mark on occasion, but they're not nearly as off target as the direct-instruction gurus who are now trying to lead the reading mandate parade.

This book is my attempt to demonstrate that it isn't just whole language advocates who are having problems with the NRP report and the new education laws. I've framed the articles written by others with my own chapters, both extending their arguments and developing an additional evidence-based argument for reconsidering the direction of educational reform. As a researcher by vocation, I decided I could not simply sit on the sidelines and allow the ideologically based distortions of what the research says go unchallenged. I hope this book will move you, too, to get off the sidelines and into the game.

Cunningham, P. M., & Allington, R. L. (1994). *Classrooms that work: They can all read and write.* New York: Harper-Collins.

Rowan, B. (1990). Commitment and control: Alternative strategies for the organizational design of schools. In C. B. Cazden (Ed.), *Review of Research in Education: Vol. 16* (pp. 353–389). Washington, DC: American Educational Research Association.

Snow, C. E. (2001). Preventing reading difficulties in young children: Precursors and fallout (pp. 229–246). In T. Loveless (Ed.), *The Great Curriculum Debate.* Washington, DC: Brookings Institution.

Snow, C. E., Burns, M. S., & Griffin, P. (1998). *Preventing reading difficulties in young children.* Washington, DC: National Academy Press.

INTRODUCTION

*Setting the Stage for the
Federalization of American
Reading Instruction*

1 ■ Troubling Times: A Short Historical Perspective

Richard L. Allington
University of Florida

American education, and especially reading instruction, is once again under attack. In many respects, this attack isn't much different than earlier ones: The politicians and pundits unrelentingly bemoan the low levels of academic performance demonstrated by children and adolescents and criticize the recalcitrance of the education profession to address the problem. National reports concerning the failure of American schools to educate students well have been around for more than a century. Media reports on what high school or college students don't know have been an almost annual event for the better part of the past century (Bracey, 1997). Compelling narratives of personal illiteracy, even after years of school attendance, continue to appear in books, television documentaries, and promotional materials for various products, programs, and political movements.

So what's new? Why should anyone be concerned about *this* campaign to improve schools, teaching, and reading instruction? More attention to these things usually means more money to fund educational improvement attempts. It means that this time around, and Lord knows more money would help.

Whether or not the most recent attacks on reading education mean more money, I am concerned about the campaign to convince everyone that not only is there a reading crisis, but that those in the education profession have routinely ignored "scientific evidence" detailing the nature and form of effective reading instruction. I'm concerned that this supposed ignoring of the evidence is being used to justify an unwarranted federal intrusion for control of the reading curriculum.

I'm worried about this new push for "evidence-based" instruction because, as the articles in this volume demonstrate, the scientific evidence we do have about teaching and learning to read is now being selectively reviewed, distorted, and misrepresented by the very agents and agencies who should give us reliable reports of what the research says. I'm worried because ideology is trumping evidence at the moment and teaching and learning to read will be both be worse for it.

In this chapter I hope to situate the current state of affairs in the recent historical context. It's often my personal historical context, too, because I've now spent thirty-five years worrying and thinking about children who struggle in learning to read.

Thirty Years as Reading Researcher

For thirty of those thirty-five years I've worked as a reading researcher. I've conducted experimental, quasi-experimental, descriptive, correlational, and qualitative research studies, mostly on reading instruction in elementary classrooms and resource rooms. Most of those studies were funded by one governmental agency or another. Most were conducted in collaboration with colleagues who made me think about the problems we were studying in ways that would never have occurred me without their insistence.

I also worked as a professor, primarily teaching graduate courses to aspiring teachers of reading. I was a member of an author team that developed several reading series for one of the major textbook publishers. I authored or coauthored a number of professional books and lots of research and professional journal articles. I also helped raise five children, now grown.

In each of these roles I've relied on "what the research says" to guide my decisions. My teaching drew heavily on research, especially the research I was most invested in—my own. As a basal author I drew on the research about more effective lesson designs. When one of my sons had difficulty learning to read, the research helped guide my family's decisions about appropriate (and inappropriate) interventions. The books I've written or helped write have likewise drawn upon the research, and they have been far more successful than any of us involved had optimistically expected. My experiences suggest that the notion that educators have largely ignored the available research is simply wrong.

A few years ago, I decided that I wouldn't continue working for the basal publisher I'd worked with for over a decade. I made this decision primarily over the issue of author authority, of who would have the authority to make final decisions about the design of a program that would have had my name listed as an author. My concerns had been heightened by the passage of a Texas State Board of Education regulation requiring that all reading series submitted for adoption in the state must include texts that were 80 percent decodable. There was no research supporting this mandate—none. So I went public on the issue. (See Chapter 9 for more details on the lack of research.) A corporate vice-president, asserting that my public comments on this topic, and others, might harm sales—a hint of a gag order—essentially forced my decision to leave the author team.

The publisher was worried about losing its sales in Texas (and other states) if its series did not include the mandated decodable texts. And because those in the business of producing reading textbooks are judged more on their sales than on their reliance on the research, it had a right to be concerned. As it turned out, the publisher created decodable texts—as did virtually every other publisher—and made money in Texas and other states. But it made that money by ignoring scientific evidence at the behest of ideological policy mandates.

It is probably easier for a professor to stand on principle than it is for the publisher or editor of a basal series. Neither my regular paycheck nor my career were threatened by my terminating the relationship with the publisher. My experience with publishers over the years had led me to believe that they were keenly interested in producing reading programs that helped teachers develop children's reading proficiencies, and that they were interested in using research to design those programs. But instead, publishers have been essentially driven to produce what politicians and policy makers in the big textbook adoption states (California, Florida, and Texas) mandate, even when the mandates don't reflect the available research.

I admit it, I am not a strident anti-basalist. But over the years I have become more concerned that the purchase of basal reading series has the potential for producing unintended negative effects.

My primary concern is that in adopting a reading series, a school district's officials might think they have purchased a reading curriculum. They may also believe that they don't have to worry about teachers who aren't very expert in the teaching of reading, because they think teachers can just follow the instructional guides that accompany each series. But there is a long history of research that indicates that teachers, and teacher expertise, matter much more than which reading series a school district might choose. (I must point out that Peter Johnston first raised this issue with me, and it was only after those discussions that I began to understand Pat Shannon's [1989] arguments about de-skilling—but that's another story.) The reliable evidence on the importance of expertise in reading instruction is being routinely ignored, distorted, or misrepresented in policy talk and in the popular press (Shaker & Heilman, 2002). Even more pointedly, the reading achievement of American students is routinely misrepresented to the public (Bracey, 2002). Because it is the supposedly inferior (and even declining) reading performance of American students that is driving so much of the current reform agenda, it seems important to briefly review the status of American reading achievement.

The Status of American Reading Achievement

The National Assessment of Educational Progress (NAEP) data indicate that reading achievement has remained relatively stable for thirty years. Obviously, it is difficult to make an argument that things are getting worse. Have American schools been failing to teach children to read for a long time? Such questions are hard to answer with much precision, but the evidence that's available indicates that more kids read better today than at any point in our nation's history. To go back further than the NAEP data, we need to consider the test re-norming data, for instance. Test publishers re-norm standardized tests regularly. And every time publishers re-norm their reading tests, average reading achievement has risen. In other words, reading achievement has risen slowly but steadily since the turn of the century (Berliner & Biddle, 1996; Kibby, 1995). But more children attend school, and attend for more years, than they did in the early 1900s or in the 1940s. As a result, good reading is simply more common and low levels of literacy are less common. There is simply no evidence that American reading achievement has declined. None. Even the National Research Council (Snow, Burns, & Griffen, 1998) opened its *Preventing Reading Difficulties* report with the following assertion:

> *Current difficulties in reading largely originate from rising demands for literacy, not from declining absolute levels of literacy. (p.1)*

In fact, the reading achievement of fourth-grade students has inched up on each assessment since 1988. The achievement levels have risen primarily in states that have invested heavily in teacher development. There's little progress evident in the states that have invested heavily in testing and curriculum standards (Darling-Hammond, 1999).

NAEP PROFICIENCY LEVELS

Politicians are, nevertheless, relentless in their proclaiming that 40 percent of American fourth graders cannot read independently—and that more testing and more phonics will solve this rampant illiteracy. American students cannot read even simple texts with understanding, they say. Cannot read at all, they rant (Sweet, 1997). And, more recently, that 70 percent of urban fourth graders cannot read independently. This evidence means that

American schools are still failing, and American educators are inept, or ignorant, or both. *Something* must be done!

And once again, that something seems to be testing and accountability mandates that further shift educational decisions away from the classrooms, schools, districts, and even states, placing increasing authority at the federal level. But the NAEP scores have not dropped. Just the opposite—they have risen a bit in recent years. So how is it that 40 percent of kids cannot read?

First of all, it is simply not true that 40 percent of American fourth graders cannot read independently. It's just not true. Such a misleading notion may result from the fact that the NAEP proficiency levels—Basic, Proficient, Advanced—used to report reading performances are substantially flawed. Both the General Accounting Office (GAO) and the National Research Council (NRC) of the National Academy of Sciences (Pellegrino, Jones, & Mitchell, 1999) have recommended that their use be discontinued because the proficiency levels mislead the public and politicians.

Here's why. Achieving Basic proficiency at the fourth-grade level requires children to demonstrate an overall understanding of what they have read when they read texts that are appropriate for fourth-grade students. They must be able to summarize the basic story elements and make connections between the text and their own experiences (Williams, Reese, Campbell, Mazzeo, & Phillips, 1995, p. 4). In other words, kids who achieve the Basic level should have literal comprehension of grade-appropriate texts. To achieve the Basic level requires what has historically been considered on-grade-level reading performance. (To achieve the Proficient level a student must be able to read grade-appropriate texts and draw conclusions, make inferences, and make connections to their own experiences.)

All we really know about the students who fail to achieve the Basic level on the NAEP reading assessments is that they were not able to read fourth-grade texts with literal comprehension. That's it. It may be that they can read fourth-grade texts accurately but without comprehension. Or maybe they can read accurately and with comprehension, but so slowly that they fail to complete enough passages and tasks to achieve the Basic level score in the time allotted. They may not be able to read some of the words in a fourth-grade passage, but do fine when reading texts typically used in third grade (or second, or first). They may be able to read texts on familiar topics with comprehension, but have difficulty when reading about unfamiliar topics. At least, these are the sorts of things that NAEP informational materials suggest might be true of the 40 percent (actually it is 38 percent) of students who fail to achieve the Basic proficiency level.

What we do know is that it is patently false to suggest that these students are non-readers or that they cannot read independently or cannot read simple children's books.

Historically, half of school children read below grade level. Grade level has been defined as the average reading achievement level at any particular grade. As with any average, half the population is, by definition, above average and half is below average. But using average performance as a benchmark for elementary school reading achievement was seriously flawed. As achievement rose, so did the average, and so did the fourth-grade (or second-grade or sixth-grade) level of difficulty. So the NAEP folks decided to develop stable, or fixed, benchmarks. They then set three difficulty levels and labeled them Basic, Proficient, and Advanced. When these levels were first used a decade ago, a little more than half of fourth-grade students achieved the Basic proficiency level, which suggests that the Basic level was set somewhere near the traditional fourth-grade reading level. In other words, since about half of the kids scored above Basic and about half below it, Basic proficiency approximated what had historically been considered reading on grade level.

The problem seems to be in the use of the term *basic*. "Basic proficiency" has connotations of a dumbed down, of "minimal competence," of something less than on-grade-level reading achievement. For whatever reason, the press, the public, and, yes, the politicians, understood Basic very differently from the NAEP designers. This misunderstanding is one of the reasons that the GAO and the NRC recommended that the NAEP stop using those proficiency levels. But the ranking of American students on international literacy assessments also played a role.

THE INTERNATIONAL LITERACY STUDIES

Probably the best-kept secret in the reading world is the fact that the reading performance of American fourth graders ranked second in the world (Elley, 1992). American adolescents ranked lower, but right in the middle, in that assessment, and again ranked in the middle in the most recent assessment (fourth graders were not tested in the most recent round). In other words, early adolescents in the U.S. read as well as the average early adolescent in the international arena (Elley, 1992; NCES, 2001).

The fact that our elementary school children ranked quite a bit better than our adolescents indicated that reading instruction in middle schools and high schools could be improved. The rankings in the study where both elementary and adolescent achievement were measured indicate that American students demonstrated substantially less reading development between ages nine and fifteen than did students in most other nations (Allington, 2001). Given this information, I'm not sure why so much attention has been paid to K–4 reading instruction and so little to reading instruction in grades five through ten.

So the international comparisons indicate that our elementary schools are doing a good job teaching reading, compared to elementary schools worldwide, but that reading instruction in our middle and high schools needs improvement. I'll buy that. But, like the NRC and GAO, I won't buy the ideological sales pitch

---

Top Ten Nations Ranked by Fourth-Grade Reading Achievement

1.	Finland
2.	United States
3.	Sweden
4.	France
5.	Italy
6.	New Zealand
7.	Norway
8.	Iceland
9.	Hong Kong
10.	Singapore

Source: Elley, W. B. (1992). *How in the world do students read?* The Hague, Netherlands: International Association for the Evaluation of Educational Achievement.

that tries to convince me that lots of our fourth graders cannot read at all. I won't buy the argument that this indicates that more federal control of education is needed.

THE RICH/POOR READING ACHIEVEMENT GAP

What I do find enormously troubling is the difference in reading achievement exhibited by children from families of different income levels. The NAEP reading data provide strong evidence of the extent of the rich/poor achievement gap. For instance, twice as many (58 percent) poor fourth-grade students scored below the Basic proficiency level as students who were not poor (27 percent). Far fewer poor students (13 percent) achieved the Proficient level, compared to 40 percent of their peers from more advantaged families (Donahue, Voelkl, Campbell, & Mazzeo, 1999, p. 82).

We hear more about the problems of urban schools than we do about the rich/poor achievement gap. But more kids live in rural areas than in urban centers. We hear about the black/white achievement gap, but the rich/poor gap is larger. American schools have never found it as easy to educate poor kids as they do rich kids (indeed, poor kids don't fare well in most countries). So why has the problem so rarely been characterized as a problem of poverty? A problem of vastly uneven income distribution? Why is it a "school" problem as opposed to, say, a "wages" problem? Or an income problem, a salary inequity problem, or a social safety net problem? I'll leave such issues to my colleagues who have spent far more time considering them (Coles, 1998; Kozol, 1991; Shannon, 1998), but it does seem just too convenient that the failure of poor kids to fare as well as other kids is seen almost exclusively as a school problem by politicians and their corporate sponsors.

> [It] does seem just too convenient that the failure of poor kids to fare as well as other kids is seen almost exclusively as a school problem by politicians and their corporate sponsors.

I also worry about the troubling recent trend that has the reading achievement of the best readers rising, while the achievement of the poorest readers remains steady or declines (NCES, 2001). I worry that recent educational policies have resulted in decisions that are working to reverse a twenty-year trend of narrowing the gap between rich and poor children. As more and more testing takes place and more and more accountability policies are put into practice, the rich seem to be getting richer and the poor getting poorer. Raising average reading achievement in a school or district can be accomplished by raising the reading levels of any group of kids, as long as no group has its performance decline. Focusing greater instructional resources on the higher achieving students may be the most cost-effective method for raising average reading achievement levels. Moving a few more high-achieving kids into to the top reading category (the NAEP's Advanced, for instance) typically takes less effort than moving the lowest achieving students up to the target standard (the NAEP's Basic).

What I've learned from thirty years of doing research in high-poverty schools is that those schools could do better, but it would cost more. Schools in poor communities usually don't have funding that's on a par with schools in wealthier communities

---

In addition to proclaiming that 40 percent of fourth graders cannot read (or read independently, or read a simple book), powerful politicians and policy makers have recently asserted that the NAEP data show 70 percent of urban fourth graders fell below the Basic proficiency level. Imagine that, seven out of ten city kids cannot read well enough to achieve the Basic performance level. But wait! Once again, these folks who are so concerned with "scientific evidence" seem to have a difficult time getting their numbers right. The NAEP data show that 47 percent of the fourth-grade students in central cities failed to achieve the Basic level (Bracey, 2001). Not 70 percent—47 percent. The NAEP data also show that 60 percent of poor children, children eligible for free lunches, fail to meet the Basic level. There is that poverty problem again—more evidence that the most serious reading problem is the problem of teaching poor kids, most of whom do not live in big cities and most of whom are not members of an ethnic or linguistic minority. Most of whom are just poor.

Source: Bracey, G. W. (2001). The condition of public education. *Phi Delta Kappan, 83,* 157–169.

(Kozol, 1991). The U.S. educational system is structured such that wealthy communities have well-supported schools and poor communities have poorly supported schools. This spending pattern holds true even in large districts, where the highest-poverty schools typically employ the least experienced, least credentialed, and therefore the least expensive and least expert teachers. Schools serving many poor children, then, often have more limited capacity—less expertise—than other schools.

Even though schools in high-poverty communities have less money to spend and more limited capacity, there is some evidence that the instructional outcomes are often not very different from those achieved in many schools in better advantaged communities (Entwisle, Alexander, & Olson, 1997). That's hard to believe, but the evidence is both scientific and compelling.

The Baltimore Beginning School Study, funded by the National Institute of Child Health and Human Development (NICHD), gathered student reading achievement data from the beginning of grade one to the end of grade six. Researchers had randomly selected almost eight hundred students from schools in high-poverty and economically better-advantaged neighborhoods. Reading achievement was measured each fall and spring to allow comparisons during the school year and during summer vacation. The researchers concluded their longitudinal study by noting that "the achievement levels of children from poor socioeconomic backgrounds increase on par with those from favored economic backgrounds when school is open" (Entwisle et al., 1997, p. 152).

The researchers found that the reading of poor kids improved just as much as the reading of their wealthier peers, *during the school year*. Teachers and programs in the high-poverty schools were just as effective at developing literacy skills and strategies as those in schools in wealthier communities.

But every summer the poor kids' reading achievement experienced a setback. They tested lower in September, at the end of summer vacation, than they had in June (about three months lower). Children from more-advantaged homes experienced no similar setback. In fact, they typically tested a little higher in September than they had in June. Thus, every two or three years, this summer setback expanded the achievement gap by one additional year. By sixth grade the gap stood at more than two years.

Other researchers have studied this phenomenon and reported similar results (Allington & McGill-Franzen, 2001), but this research has largely been ignored in attempting to address the rich/poor achievement gap. The problem is poverty. The best indicator of whether children will improve their reading or suffer a setback during the summer months is simply whether they read during the summer. Rich kids read, poor kids don't. Rich kids have books in the home and bookstores in the neighborhood, and poor kids don't (Neuman & Celano, 2001). Purchasing books and magazines requires both opportunity and discretionary income. Both are in short supply in poor communities.

But summer setback has hardly ever been on the policy makers' agenda, even though the scientific evidence has been accumulating for almost thirty years (Allington & McGill-Franzen, 2001). Politicians, policy makers, and pundits have been more likely to name poor parenting, poor teaching, lack of initiative, or some other personal failing of the victims as the source of the reading achievement gap. Even among educators and educational researchers, such explanations were more common than interventions aimed at minimizing summer reading loss. The limited access that poor children have to books and magazines in their schools, neighborhoods, and homes has barely been on the federal agenda, or on the agenda of state and local reform initiatives. The negative portrayals of high-poverty schools led us to ignore what the scientific evidence suggests is the most critical factor in fostering the reading achievement gap—opportunity to read.

THE ADULT LITERACY SURVEY

The average citizen has been so steeped in negative information about the literacy performance of Americans, both children and adults, that even horrendously inaccurate information on reading achievement is seldom questioned. The best recent example of this phenomenon comes from the National Adult Literacy Survey (NALS). That 1993 report, issued by the National Center for

Educational Statistics (NCES), indicated that 47 percent of American adults were largely illiterate, scoring in the two lowest levels of literacy. One of five adults scored in the lowest literacy band. Imagine that! Almost half of the adults studied could not interpret information from a simple newspaper article. No more evidence was needed that our schools were failing. The political calls for educational reform, accountability through more testing, and higher standards poured forth. Something had to be done and, obviously, educators could not be trusted to know what to do. Neither could local school boards or local educational leaders. Thus, federal educational reform began to focus on mandates for the adoption of "proven programs" and schoolwide, systemic reform. The educational system was broken.

But in a reanalysis of the very same adult literacy data, researchers discovered that the original statisticians "misread the data" (Baron, 2002). A correct reading of the evidence indicates that fewer than 5 percent of American adults were illiterate. Two-thirds of that group never completed high school, and a quarter were immigrants. So much for the notion that U.S. schools have failed to produce a literate population. But have you read the headlines announcing the reanalysis? Probably not, unless you read *Education Week* or the *Chronicle of Higher Education*. In fact, the week after the new analysis was announced, enclosed with my utility bill was a pamphlet noting that "more than four of ten American adults" have serious reading problems.

The most interesting bit about this fiasco is how many of us—yes, us: you and me and our educator colleagues—bought the original report hook, line, and sinker. Same goes for the news media. We should be expert enough, and they should have been cynical enough, to ask: Where do all these adult illiterates live? Think about it, half the population unable to read a newspaper. Where are these folks? How could we have believed that half of the folks sitting in church with us were illiterate. Couldn't read the Bible or the hymnal! That half the folks at the local high school play or concert were illiterate. Couldn't read the program. That half the folks at Home Depot couldn't read the labels or the signs. But we bought it. The public bought it. Probably even the politicians bought it. What's worse is that the same phenomenon is still occurring: It is the worst news about schools that most often makes the news, that drives our thinking about teaching and learning to read and what needs to be done.

CONCLUSION

I'll grant that American schools could be improved, and that we could improve children's reading proficiency, but it seems to me it that it's almost time for a national celebration of what we have accomplished to this point (at least in our elementary schools). I'll grant that the rich/poor achievement gap is a terribly pressing problem and that we must develop school programs that do more to address it. I'll even grant that there's a body of research that might guide us in these efforts. But I will also argue, just as the National Research Council did, that

> *If we have learned anything from this effort, it is that effective teachers are able to craft a special mix of instructional ingredients for every child they work with. (Snow, et al., 1998, p. 2)*

In other words, I will argue that we have compelling scientific evidence that it is teachers and their expertise that matter the most in solving both problems—evidence that seems largely ignored in the current policy-making environment.

No Such Thing as a Proven Program

The early evidence about the primacy of the teacher effect came from the First Grade Studies (Bond & Dykstra, 1967). The researchers concluded their large-scale multisite study of the effectiveness of different reading series with the recommendation that, "Future research might well center on teacher and learning situation characteristics rather than methods and materials" (p. 123). They arrived at this conclusion when multiple studies conducted by multiple researchers across the nation provided no clear evidence of the superiority of any one reading series or any particular approach to teaching reading. In other words, nothing worked everywhere and everything worked somewhere.

Likewise, a decade later, the independent evaluators of the Follow Through Project (House, Glass, McLean, & Walker, 1978), another large-scale evaluation of different early education programs, indicated that none of the intervention curricula, including Direct Instruction, produced consistently superior results. None consistently outperformed early education classes that were not using a special intervention program. The evaluators' terse conclusion, "If the concentrated effort of highly competent and well-funded sponsors with a few sites cannot produce uniform results from locality to locality, it seems doubtful that any model program could" (p. 154), summarized one consistent finding in educational research: Programs don't teach, teachers do.

Thus, similar findings (Pogrow, 2000; Venezky, 1998) concerning the inconsistency of the politically popular Success For All program should surprise no one. Nor should we be surprised to observe that districts across the country are dropping Direct Instruction and Success For All programs, even while other districts are adding them. Nor should we be surprised that many districts are looking to replace one basal reading series with another. Everyone is hoping for the magic potion, the quick fix to the reading ills of the school, the district, the state.

PROVEN PROGRAM ADOPTION AS AN ADMISSION OF LIMITED LEADERSHIP CAPACITY

Expert teachers produce readers regardless of the reading series they are mandated to use (Pressley, Allington, Wharton-McDonald, Collins-Block, & Morrow, 2001). Expert teachers alter and modify reading programs to better meet the needs of their students. Expert teachers simply ignore mandates and go about teaching all their students to read. But it is the absence of expertise—let's call it naivete—that leads teachers and administrators to hope upon hope that a new reading series or new intervention program will solve all their woes. It is a sad day when school-district administrators flaunt their limited expertise about effective teaching—their naivete—and publicly announce the purchase of a "proven program." I would think most school administrators would be more than a bit embarrassed to admit they have so little capacity for educational problem solving that they are buying someone else's idea of what might work. It is an even sadder day when a teachers' union (in this case, the American Federation of Teachers) flaunts its naivete by demanding that "proven programs" be implemented in the schools where their members work.

The notion of "proven programs" is simply so wrongheaded that it is hard to believe that it has such widespread currency in the current debates on reforming reading instruction. Can you imagine a "proven" emergency room program? One that provides the emergency room physician with a script to follow? A "one size fits all" script, identical for every patient from the one with appendicitis to the one with an arrow lodged in the forehead? A script that ignores the expertise of the physician? That ignores that available diagnostic evidence on the medical condition?

> But it is the absence of expertise—let's call it naivete—that leads teachers and administrators to hope upon hope that a new reading series or new intervention program will solve all their woes.

Good teaching may actually be more complicated than emergency room medicine is, if only because of the sheer number of students (patients) that need near-constant attention and the general lack of support staff to help attend to those students' needs.

The key question that needs to be asked more often is this: Which would you prefer for your child or grandchild—an expert and engaging teacher who has a mediocre reading program available, or a mediocre teacher with a "proven" reading program? The ideal might seem to be an expert and engaging teacher with a "proven" reading program. But no proven programs make mediocre teachers expert and engaging. The expert and engaging teacher doesn't really need the proven program. In fact, if provided with that program, the expert teacher will reject it or tailor it until it no longer is recognizable.

It isn't that expert primary grade teachers don't use commercial reading programs; they do (Pressley, Allington, et al., 2001). But they dip into those programs selectively rather than using them as designed. They supplement the programs, perhaps because no reading series has ever contained enough reading

"The biggest impediment to substantive [change]...has been the [federal] push for schools to adopt comprehensive schoolwide reform models. Having a vendor take over the curriculum and staff development for a school and provide a one-size-fits-all model is much simpler than struggling to implement improvement principles.

The rhetoric claiming that the effectiveness of the schoolwide reform model has been proven is belied by the fact that during the past decade—when this approach predominated—the achievement gap widened for the first time in decades.

Why would anyone think that a one-size-fits-all schoolwide reform model would work effectively for such a complex process as teaching—especially in schools dealing with an increasingly diverse student body? True leadership occurs when a school or district gets it own act together instead of looking for an outside savior to take control of its basic professional functions and provide a quick fix. A quick fix does not exist."

Source: Pogrow, S. (2002). Avoiding comprehensive school reform models. *Educational Leadership, 58,* 82–83.

material to develop proficient readers. The reading series do offer stories or book excerpts as reading material, and they offer a lesson structure that may make sense for some kids on some days. But the series too often fill up reading lesson time with lots of mindless activity, typically an incoherent array of lower-order tasks and assignments. The criticisms of reading series as a primary reading curriculum go back the full hundred years of debate on improving American reading instruction and enhancing reading achievement.

So why now, one might ask, are "one size fits all" reading series being touted as the next best fix? Why is it that federal and state agencies are now so interested in whether a reading series is based on "scientific research"?

THE 10 PERCENT FALLACY

There is gossip about, gossip that suggests that mandating a "proven program" is necessary because the research says most teachers are not well prepared to teach children to read. For instance, United States Senator Thad Cochrane (1997) stated that

The National Institutes of Child Health and Human Development (NICHD) findings underscore the need to do a better job of training teachers, as researchers found fewer than 10 percent of teachers actually know how to teach reading to children who don't learn to read automatically. I am surprised that the Education Department hasn't looked into this study and found a way to effectively get the information to teachers, schools, parents, and, most importantly, teacher colleges. (P. S6002)

Representative Bill Goodling (1998), chairman of the United States House of Representatives Education and Workforce Committee, repeats this statistic

Fewer than 10 percent of teachers have been taught to teach reading. (p. 1)

This incantation was picked up and disseminated by the popular press. *USA Today* (May 17, 2000) editorialized on the topic, noting that

The effect of teacher colleges' recalcitrance is dramatic: Only about 10 percent of the nation's elementary teachers have the skills to teach phonics effectively, estimate researchers at the National Institutes of Health.

But where do these politicians and the press get such information? What evidence is available to support their assertions?

Actually, tracking down the source of the assertions was relatively easy. The first report I found was offered by Heritage Foundation writer Tyce Palmaffy (1997). In an interview with NICHD bureaucrat G. Reid Lyon, Lyon cites his survey on teachers' perceived adequacy of their preparation (Lyon, Vaasen, & Toomey, 1989). Later Lyon (1997) himself testified before the House Workforce and Education Committee that

Unfortunately, several recent studies and surveys of teacher knowledge about reading development and difficulties indicate that many teachers are under prepared to teach reading. . . . In reading education, teachers are frequently presented with a "one size fits all" philosophy that emphasizes either a "whole language" or "phonics" orientation to instruction. No doubt, this parochial type of preparation places many children at continued risk for reading failure. (p. 9)

But is this what Lyon's 1989 study found (Lyon, Vassen, & Toomey, 1989)? This survey of approximately four hundred teachers reported that most education students had not observed their professors demonstrating "methods of reading instruction tailored to children's differing needs." But given the structure of teacher education, it is hardly surprising that few students had observed their professors demonstrating instructional strategies with children. On the other hand, only 22 percent of regular education and 12 percent of special education teachers responded "no" to a survey question that asked whether their undergraduate teacher education had "adequately prepared me to meet the educational needs of a diverse student population" (78 percent and 88 percent, respectively, of the two groups reported that their preparation had generally prepared them to meet this challenge). Nothing in the study, however, suggests that 90 percent of teachers don't "know how to teach reading to the children who don't learn automatically," as Senator Cochrane suggested. Nothing in the study indicates that teacher education provides a "one size fits all" philosophy, as Lyon testified.

There seems no other "scientific" evidence to support either the 10 percent assertion or the "one size fits all" assertion. For this study to be accepted as reliable evidence of either assertion requires ignoring self-reported teacher satisfaction data from the study (the vast majority felt they had been well prepared) while accepting as fact the responses to a series of unsupported hypothetical characteristics of effective teacher preparation programs.

It is easier for me to understand how a writer from the conservative Heritage Foundation or a conservative politician might misinterpret the study than to understand how the Learning First Alliance (LFA) could do the same. The LFA is a consortium of education professional organizations, including the two major teacher unions (but not including any literacy-oriented professional organizations). The LFA (1998) similarly argued that preservice teacher education is often "discrepant with the research on effective methods" (p. 62), but cited no studies to support this assertion. It couldn't—there are no such studies, only "estimates," as *USA Today* noted, offered by bureaucrats from the NICHD.

ROCKET SCIENCE AND RESEARCH ON TEACHING TEACHERS TO TEACH READING

Both the AFT (1999) and NICHD project director Louisa Moats (1997; 2000) make the same assertion about the shortcomings of teacher education and call for restructuring teacher education through mandated course content and teacher testing. But there are no scientific studies that support the assertion that teacher preparation is "nonscientific" or that it offers a "one size fits all" approach to teaching children to read.

So what evidence was offered to support such claims? The AFT offers none. In her testimony before the House Workforce and Education Committee (1997), and in her paper for the conservative Fordham Foundation (2000), Moats provides a good example of the unreliable evidence that seems to rule when it comes to bashing teachers and teacher education.

In both cases, Moats reported on the survey studies she had conducted in a paper first published (Moats, 1994) in *Annals of Dyslexia* (a later and adapted version was published in *American Educator*, the magazine of the American Federation of Teachers). Let's take a closer look at Moats' "research" (since the National Reading Panel didn't include it in its review of research on teacher preparation).

The data in this report come from eighty-nine surveys given at the beginning of "a number of classes" in a course titled Reading, Spelling, and Phonology. As science goes, this is already off to a shaky start because you can't assume that teachers who choose to take a course of this nature represent a random population. They might be from that minority of teachers who feel that their teacher preparation has not prepared them well to teach reading, or who have been mandated to use a multisensory phonics approach and felt they needed more expertise in phonology and the development of phonological skills. They cannot be said to reflect the expertise (or lack of it) of any representative body of teachers. Thus, Moats' study is unscientific from the get-go.

Interestingly, Moats notes that "about 10 percent" of the teachers who completed the course were unable to develop phonemic awareness during it. She suggests that teacher candidates be screened for phonological awareness before taking coursework and that they be "counseled" about the professional implications of their difficulties. It seems that it never occurred to Moats that someone might similarly counsel her about the effectiveness of the course design or the reliability of the testing she did for phonological awareness development. I have not been able to find a single study that indicates that a teacher's phonological awareness is related to teaching effectiveness. It could be true, of course, but there is no scientific evidence that suggests it is.

Continuing on, Moats reports that this survey "revealed insufficiently developed concepts about language and pervasive conceptual weaknesses in the very skills that are needed for direct, language focused reading instruction" (p. 91). But she provides no evidence that teachers who had "sufficiently developed" skills taught differently or were more successful in developing children's reading, writing, or spelling proficiencies. She argues that, while many of these teachers had developed adequate linguistic awareness to become personally literate, that linguistic awareness was not sufficient to allow them to teach reading and spelling "elements" explicitly to children. But she provides no evidence that supports that assertion. She also asserts that "lower-level language mastery" is as essential for teachers as anatomy is for physicians. That is an impressive claim, so impressive that the AFT used it as a basis for its suggested redesign of teacher education. But there is no scientific evidence to support the claim. None. Reporting on what seem to be the same survey data with the addition of responses from another class of teachers, Moats and Lyon (1996) repeat virtually the same assertions. And still no scientific evidence is offered in support of these claims. None. Nada. Ideology trumps evidence.

Finally, Moats, writing originally under the sponsorship of the International Dyslexia Association (1997), continued this line of argument in calling for a restructuring of teacher education programs. A later version of this report, *Teaching Reading Is Rocket Science*, was circulated to its member colleges by the National

"When, for example, the federal government adopts a policy urging reading programs to be based on 'reliable, replicable research' and accompanies that legislation with a declaration that testimony before the adopting committee indicates that there have been 'scientific breakthroughs' in our knowledge that support direct phonics instruction, the result is a powerful legitimization of phonics-based instruction, quite independent of the extent to which this body of research is complete, accurate, or unchallenged." (p. 331–332)

From: Boyd, W. L., & Mitchell, D. E. (2001). The politics of the reading wars. In T. Loveless (Ed.), *The great curriculum debate*. (pp. 299–342). Washington, DC: Brookings.

Commission on Accreditation of Teacher Education (NCATE) and was widely disseminated by the AFT (1999). All in all, it was an impressive public relations feat. It was even more impressive as a fraud perpetuated on the profession.

My calling this report fraudulent may seem harsh, but I will repeat myself: There was no reliable evidence to support either the implicit assertions or the explicit recommendations on the importance of teacher expertise in phonology, morphology, and so on. No reliable evidence supporting the assertion that 90 percent of teachers are incapable of teaching children to read. No reliable evidence that teacher education favors a narrow and unscientific approach to teaching reading. No reliable evidence that the recommended restructuring would improve reading instruction (or student reading achievement). None. Instead, the reports offered individual ideological interpretation of largely anecdotal information, unreliable "evidence" by anyone's standards. Once again, ideology trumps evidence.

And yet the AFT, the LFA, and NCATE all bit on Moats' recommendations. Moats may be onto something important that is missing from teacher preparation. I doubt it myself, but I hope that before anyone seriously considers making dramatic changes to teacher preparation, someone will produce reliable evidence to support Moats' assertions and recommendations. It wouldn't take a rocket scientist to conduct such a study. But in order to get reliable, unbiased evidence, the study should be conducted independently of Drs. Moats and Lyon, the AFT, the LFA, and NCATE.

Columnist William Raspberry (2000) wrote that educators, and especially professors of education, ignore research and promote fads in the teaching of reading:

> *[Doug] Carnine [the direct-instruction guru] says it's because the other programs are supported by what amounts to a closed circle of true believers—educators and educationists—for whom evidence is less important than faith.*

Was Raspberry talking about Moats? About Lyons? About Senator Cochrane? About the AFT? The LFA? Unfortunately, no. But to accept that 90 percent of America's elementary teachers "don't know how to teach children who don't learn automatically" requires a reliance on faith, not evidence. To assert that a lack of knowledge of phonology is at the root of teachers' inadequacies also requires a huge leap of faith—again, no evidence links such knowledge with effective teaching (even effective teaching of dyslexics, which was Moats' original topic).

WHO BENEFITS FROM BASHING TEACHERS AND TEACHER EDUCATION?

What purpose is served by bashing elementary teachers' ability to teach reading? Or by bashing teacher preparation efforts? I see several possibilities. For one, if teacher preparation is so bad, maybe we should hire teachers without regard to whether they have earned teaching credentials. Columnist Thomas Sowell (2000) wrote

> *Studies show no correlation between education courses and teaching success. Many private schools don't require such courses, and some don't even want to hire people who have been through such drivel. . . . So long as education courses drive away intelligent people, more money will just mean **more expensive** incompetents in the schools. [Emphasis added] (p. A16)*

There you have it: Credentialed teachers cost more! Of course, there is a substantial body of research contradicting Sowell's assertions about the impact of teacher education coursework, but then, he is a columnist, not a researcher, so how would he know?

Where does Sowell get his information? He writes,

A recent book—A Conspiracy of Ignorance *by Martin Gross [2000]—says [teachers are drawn from] the bottom third, but in any case, we are talking about having our children taught by the dregs of the college-educated population.*

Former secretary of education Bill Bennett (1998) also cited the Gross "study" in a *Washington Post* column about teacher capacity as a primary problem in reforming schools.

But Gerald Bracey (2002) notes that the key "study" Gross cites—one purported to show that teachers ranked in the bottom third of their high school class—does not exist. Gross says the study he's referring to was completed by the Pennsylvania Department of Education, but that department conducted no such study. Pennsylvania education officials note that gathering data on high school students' grades and ranks and then linking that to college degree earning patterns would pose enormous difficulties. In fact, the evidence is actually quite different. But Gross said he had "heard about" the study in a campaign speech given by the governor of Pennsylvania. The governor couldn't recall mentioning such a study.

On the other hand, Bruschi and Coley (1999) reported that

On average, teachers perform as well as other college-educated adults. . . . In prose literacy teachers score higher, on average, than managers and administrators . . . they perform at a similar level with lawyers, electrical engineers, accountants and auditors, financial managers, physicians. . . . There are large differences in earnings between teachers and other managerial and professional workers. Teachers rank near the bottom of the list [in earnings]. (p. 3)

The only area in which teachers were deficient compared to other similarly competent and qualified adults was earnings.

As far as the relationship between teaching credentials and student outcomes, Johnston (1999), Darling-Hammond (1996, 1999), Ferguson (1991), Ferguson and Ladd (1996), Fuller (1999), NCTAF (1997), Pearson (2001), and Wenglinsky (2000) all provide powerful quantitative evidence of the positive impact that teacher education and quality professional development have on teaching quality and student achievement.

Darling-Hammond (1999) noted that the quality of a state's teaching force (measured in various ways) is a powerful predictor of student achievement levels, much more powerful than other factors, including student demographic characteristics and measures of school resources. Overall, teacher quality accounted for 40 to 60 percent of the variance in NAEP achievement for fourth- and eighth-grade reading and math. Likewise, Ferguson (1991) noted that in Texas the effect of teachers' academic qualifications and certification was such that "the large disparities between black and white students were almost entirely accounted for by differences in the qualifications of their teachers" (p. 8).

So much for ideological rantings about teachers' lack of intellectual quality and the impotence of teacher education. But how many politicians read Sowell's or Bennett's syndicated columns and how many read Bracey's book? How successful has this "teacher stupidification" campaign been in convincing the public, the press, and the politicians that expert teachers do not much matter in the quest to improve America's schools?

Is it any wonder that there is much political interest in alternative certification programs (e.g., Troops to Teachers, Teach For America) but little support for investing in improving teacher preparation or professional development programs? Is it any wonder that various interest groups keep insisting that anyone with a college degree should be allowed to try out teaching? But if America's elementary schools are filled with inexpert teachers, whether they're credentialed or uncredentialed, how will we ensure that our children will routinely receive high-quality reading instruction?

SCRIPTED CURRICULUM MATERIALS: "ONE SIZE FITS ALL" IS NOT A SOLUTION

One solution that's being touted as the "quick fix" for America's reading "problems" is the wider use of scripted curriculum materials, materials that have been "teacher-proofed." Sigfried Engleman, the advertising executive–turned–curriculum developer, asserted on the television show *20/20* that teachers need not—and indeed could not—"reinvent the wheel," but should instead rely on "proven" lesson scripts such as those provided by his direct-instruction materials. Thus the perceived problems of limited teacher intellectual quality and inexpert teacher preparation can be "solved" by using scripted instructional materials. If that were true, we wouldn't have to worry about hiring people who graduated from college, much less people who completed a professional preparation program. Gosh, maybe even paraprofessionals with no college degree could teach reading. Think how much money that would save!

The problem with that argument is, a veritable trove of scientific research tells us that effective teaching is not standardized and cannot be scripted (Allington & Johnston, 2001; Berliner, 1986; Haberman, 1995; Knapp, 1995; Ladson-Billings, 1994; Mendro, Bembry, & Jordan, 1998; Pressley, Allington, Wharton-McDonald, et al., 2001; Ruddell, 1995; Spencer & Spencer, 1993; Taylor, Pearson, Clark, & Walpole, 1999). Studies of effective teachers quite consistently portray the nature of effective teaching as complex and based essentially on appropriate moment-by-moment instructional decision making. Effective teachers do not offer the "one size fits all" lessons that Lyon (1997) decried, but if scripted curriculum materials are faithfully implemented, that is the only sort of lesson that will be offered.

> Effective teachers do not offer the "one size fits all" lessons that Lyon (1997) decried, but if scripted curriculum materials are faithfully implemented, that is the only sort of lesson that will be offered.

The available evidence suggests that more-effective teachers are better prepared and more likely to be credentialed than less-effective teachers are. As the National Commission on Teaching and America's Future (1997) noted,

> *What teachers know and understand about content and students shapes how judiciously they select from texts and other materials and how effectively they present material in class. Their skill in assessing their students' progress also depends upon how deeply*

they understand learning, and how well they can interpret stu-
dents' discussions and written work. No other intervention can
make the difference that a knowledgeable, skillful teacher can make
in the learning process. (p. 8)

And,

Investments in teacher development produced far greater student
achievement gains than [other] investments . . . spending on
teacher education swamped other variables as the most productive
investment for schools. (p. 9)

But investments in teacher development, both preservice and
inservice, seem to be a less commonly used avenue for improving reading instruction than buying new phonics workbooks (or
a new reading series) is.

In the end, it is the less-expert teacher who relies most
heavily on packaged curriculum products. Doyle (1986) argued
that when teachers are inexpert they tend to create "dumbed
down" curricula that rely on seatwork and low-level tasks, because it takes expertise to develop and orchestrate complex academic tasks. Inexpert teachers are less successful than expert
teachers at teaching children to read even when packaged curriculum products are available. Schools have only two sources for
expertise: Buy it or create it.

Schools might look to hire only the most expert teachers, but
there is little incentive for expert teachers to work in the least
successful schools. It is these schools that are most likely to latch
onto the highly structured reading programs and to exert pressure on teachers to use those programs just as the developer
mandates. In those schools, being an expert or acting upon one's
expertise is a potential liability.

McNeil (2000) demonstrated this dilemma in her study of
mandated instruction in Houston:

They tried to teacher-proof the curriculum with a checklist for
teaching behaviors and the student minimum competence skills
tests. By doing so, they have made schools exceedingly comfort-
able for mediocre teachers who like to teach routine lessons

according to a standard sequence and format, who like working as de-skilled laborers not having to think about their work. They made being a Texas public school teacher extremely uncomfortable for those who know their subjects well, who teach in ways that engage their students, who want their teaching to reflect their own continued learning. (p. 187)

The expert teachers McNeil looked at found teaching more and more stressful as they had to teach against the grain of the mandates to act on their expertise. As one teacher told McNeil, "I am tired of having to lie to do my work" (p. 189).

Schools could work to create expert teachers, but it requires expertise to foster expertise in others. The short supply of such expertise is signaled when a school hops onto the proven-program bandwagon. It requires time and commitment to foster expertise. Far too many schools (and school districts) either have failed to buy (that is, hire) teachers with the expertise needed to offer effective reading lessons, or are ignoring the expertise of their instructional staff. Few school districts (or state education agencies) seem to have a plan for creating expert teachers. In other words, while most school districts have a long-term plan, and a funding stream, for replacing or rehabilitating the roofs of school buildings, almost none has a plan, or the funding, for developing teacher expertise through professional development activities (Allington & Cunningham, 2002).

Most of the heavily promoted packaged reading programs promise a quick and relatively inexpensive solution. "Buy our stuff and your scores will rise next year" is the sales pitch. And for "only a few dollars per kid," too! But reliable scientific evidence demonstrates that investing in developing teacher expertise produces greater student improvement (Darling-Hammond, 1999; Ferguson, 1991) than similar investments in curriculum packages or testing programs do. The evidence on the effectiveness of proven programs is at best mixed (Pogrow, 2002; Sacks, 2002), but funding to buy these programs is now codified into federal law even in the face of evidence of the ineffectiveness of these approaches.

WHY SHOULD WE CARE ABOUT THE TEACHER STUPIDIFICATION CAMPAIGN?

What seems to be under way is an attempt to portray teaching as a blue-collar job: No special skills are needed. Heck, even intellectual capacity doesn't really matter! Teacher education is portrayed as unnecessary—and even damaging. Reading instruction can only be effective when teachers are required to use "proven programs" and follow scripted lesson plans. Reading professionals are not to be trusted. These arguments appear in public testimony, popular media, and trade publications. Why has this campaign gotten this far?

Because, as Reutzel, Hollingsworth, and Cox (1996) report, the information sources that legislators consult most frequently are newspaper articles (85 percent of legislators), national magazine

At the 2002 Research Awards session of the International Reading Association convention in San Francisco, David Pearson, Dean of the College of Education at the University of California at Berkeley, noted that California policy makers and educational leaders find themselves in a terrible bind. With some 40,000 uncertified teachers working in California schools, primarily in high-poverty schools, the dilemma is whether to provide these teachers with a highly scripted and regimented curriculum or to allow them to teach based on some personal recollection of what teachers do.

Neither option is a good one. The reality is that California policy makers have been unwilling to make teaching attractive enough to entice certified teachers to actually teach in California schools. Darling-Hammond (2001) reports that California has 1.3 million certified teachers and only 300,000 teaching positions. In other words, there are roughly 1 million certified teachers living in California who are unwilling to fill 40,000 positions now occupied by uncertified personnel.

The core problem policy makers should address is this: How to make teaching an attractive professional career option. But addressing that problem will likely cost some real money and will also require policy makers provide teachers with professional autonomy on curricular and instructional issues.

articles (80 percent), and radio and TV broadcasts (79 percent). The legislators studied considered information provided to them by legislative research teams and through expert testimony to be sufficient for decision making. But who decides who gets to testify at a legislative hearing? Who gets quoted in a news article?

Lieberman (2000) studied these issues and found that private think tank and corporate personnel are the folks who get quoted and invited to testify. The Enron fiasco illustrates just how much political access big money can buy outside the bright lights of hearing rooms or the media sideshow. Lieberman notes that a primary reason for such exposure is that it is the think tanks and corporations that write most of the press releases that news media rely upon as sources to fill their papers and magazines. She relates that news consultants tell journalists to use these press releases and from one to three sources—and take no more than an hour on a story. In other words, consultants suggest that it's reasonable for a journalist to be expected to produce forty or so stories every week. If you have just an hour to write a news story, a press release is a wonderful thing to have in your hands, especially if that press release also lists the telephone numbers of sources that you can quote to make your story "unique" or "authoritative."

Lieberman (2000) illustrates just how some groups have learned to reduce their messages to sound bites, catchy phrases, to fit this new journalism. She also illustrates the sheer tenacity of these groups' political advocacy. Imagine if the reading profession had someone who, like major industry groups, could write and fax three hundred separate press releases to major news media every weekday for a year! That is precisely what the "think tanks" do.

Duffy and Hoffman (1999) suggest that "Current policy mandates ignore research that tells us improved reading is linked to teachers who use methods thoughtfully, not methods alone. As a result, these policies will fail" (p. 15). Or will they? Yes, they will likely fail to improve reading achievement, but will that failure then be touted as failure of the "faddish" teachers to follow the "proven" scripts and structured lesson plans?

Current policy development seems headed in the direction of less and less professional autonomy paired with more and more accountability—the worst case scenario. No one feels particularly responsible when they simply do what they are told. There is no professional accountability without professional autonomy.

Who would benefit from a teacher-stupidification consensus? The most obvious potential beneficiaries are those who provide educational products or services for profit. Three segments of the for-profit education industry seem most likely to benefit: test and textbook publishers (or at least those who offer "proven programs"), for-profit education providers (Edison, Advantage, eK-12, Dreamcatchers, Sylvan, etc.), and companies that provide teacher training (Skylight, Compass, e-learning, Sylvan, Canter, etc.).

The test and textbook publishers, by and large the same corporations, would benefit from mandates to buy new curriculum materials and to test every child every year. The textbook mandates will, of course, be wrapped in language that requires these products be based on "scientific" research. My hunch is that Texas and California will not be required to dump all those unscientific decodable texts they just made publishers offer, because the mandates aren't really about improved curriculum materials as much as they are about asserting external authority and ideological control over the educational process. In many cases, mandates illustrate that ideology trumps evidence in the political arena.

> Who would benefit from a teacher-stupidification consensus? The most obvious potential beneficiaries are those who provide educational products or services for profit.

The for-profit schools might actually turn a profit, though none has thus far, if they could reduce the number of certified teachers they employ. Personnel costs typically represent 80 percent or more of the cost of educating children. Imagine the savings if you could just go to Kelly Services and hire a clerk to deliver scripted instructional packages! Even better, if you could deliver that scripted instruction over the Web and simply hire low-wage security guards to ensure that the children didn't wander off. These non-teachers are not likely to get uppity and challenge the mandates. But then, not many teachers are resisting openly, either (though the number who resist in more subtle ways seems substantial).

If the public can be convinced that a college degree is not really needed, and especially that teacher education is not just unnecessary but actually damaging to the development of good teachers, there might be a role for for-profit teacher-training ventures. We have already arrived at the point where a for-profit agency has become the nation's largest supplier of teacher certification and where professional development is being contracted to corporate providers (Wasson, 2002). But with just a bit more effort, we may be able to convince more politicians, just as Florida governor Jeb Bush seems to have been convinced, that for-profit corporations are better able than colleges and universities to provide professional development, if only because they seem more interested in adhering to ideologically mandated content than do many college and university professors. This is an especially useful characteristic when state mandates ignore reliable research evidence. Politicians and policy makers seem to see for-profit entities as being more amenable than college professors to following ideological mandates (Shaker & Heilman, 2002). Professors might actually care about what the research says, but corporations worry more about earnings flow.

> Politicians and policy makers seem to see for-profit entities as being more amenable than college professors to following ideological mandates (Shaker & Heilman, 2002).

As I've argued in several recent papers, regardless of the politicians' spin, there is no clear link between reading research and policy making (Allington, 1999; Allington & Woodside-Jiron, 1998, 1999). Instead, the link seems to be between policy making and public opinion polls. Public opinion can be shaped, and there is an ongoing effort to convince the public and policy makers that good teachers and good teacher preparation don't really matter very much. The success of this campaign will depend on whether the profession can counteract the distortions and misrepresentations of research that abound in the policy environment and the media.

CONCLUSION

Shulman (1983) offers the "nightmares" that policy makers and teachers have about schooling and teaching. Policy makers see inept adults who teach only what and who they want; teachers who prefer fads and frills to the hard work of developing basic skills; teachers whose low expectations lead them to ignore the potential of certain groups of children and whose limited expertise in content results in misteaching. Teachers see besieged professionals attempting to work responsibly and effectively under impossible conditions, including mindless, often conflicting, and ever-shifting mandates and directives issued by policy makers who are pursuing a particular political agenda. The policy maker's nightmare scenario suggests a need to better control the largely incompetent, willful, and flighty teacher. In the teacher's nightmare, that is just what has happened, and effective teaching has been made literally impossible because of mindless and ever-shifting mandates and directives (Hunter, 1998).

Recent educational policy making has eroded the autonomy and the level of individual professional responsibility that teachers must have in order to teach well and to respond appropriately to individual instructional needs. In most schools children come and go to not-so-special special programs, inexpert paraprofessionals must be accommodated, subjects must fit into preordained schedules, while new methods and materials for teaching more rigorously and inflexibly are mandated and audit trail records are kept for accountability.

In such circumstances it is difficult for teachers—as it would be for any professional—to accept much individual professional responsibility for student outcomes. When you are told what to teach, how to teach, and when to teach, it is unlikely that you will see bad results as anything other than the responsibility of the system that mandated the instructional plan. When the struggling readers in your room move from program to program throughout the school day, spending only small blocks of time in your classroom, it is unlikely that the failure of those children to develop into proficient readers will be seen as anything other than a failure of the system. Sufficient autonomy is absolutely essential for teachers to accept individual professional responsibility for student outcomes—autonomy in making decisions about how, what, and when children will be taught. If someone else tells you to follow their plan, any failure becomes a failure of their plan, not of yours.

Professionals must be accountable, but as Cunningham (2001) points out, there are no mal-outcomes lawsuits in other professions, just malpractice cases. One cannot sue a doctor, dentist, or lawyer over outcomes. But malpractice can be considered when there is evidence that a professional ignored best practices, as defined by the profession. The truly sorry situation in education is that many of the mandates that have been issued—intensive phonics, decodable texts, grade retention for low-achieving students, proven programs—fail to conform with the reliable research evidence that's available. When teachers follow such mandates, they engage in what in other professions would be considered malpractice.

Perhaps changes are coming. Consider, for instance, the recent announcement that the California Teachers Association was seeking legislation that would allow it to negotiate curriculum and textbook issues. The union president, Wayne Johnson, notes that

> *Because we can bargain only over wages, hours, and working conditions, we are being held accountable in a system over which we have absolutely no control. As a teacher I have no control over curriculum, no control over textbooks, no control over supplies, materials I use. It's all just handed to me. I'm told what to teach. I'm told how to teach. If that doesn't work, I am held accountable. It's an unfair system. (Weintraub, 2002, p. 2)*

If reading instruction is to improve, teachers must feel responsible for student outcomes. Any reform plan that strips teachers of their professional autonomy in instructional decision making lessens the likelihood that teachers will accept professional responsibility for the failure of their instruction to produce positive results. Any plan that reduces teacher autonomy undermines teachers' reflection about the instruction they offer and its effectiveness. Scripted instructional programs demand adherence to the script, not reflection on how a script might be modified and improved.

U.S. schooling cannot be successful without autonomous, expert teachers. Policy makers here might learn from Finland, top-ranked internationally for student reading performance. As Ann-Sofie Selin, a Finnish educational authority, recently explained,

> *I want to highlight three things [about the Finnish system]: teacher education, freedom of curriculum, and no mandatory testing. Every teacher in Finland has a five-year-long university education and a master's degree. As an active teacher she has the freedom to develop curriculum to a great extent. And we have no standardized testing whatsoever in Finland during the nine-year basic school.* (Reading Today, *February, 2002, p. 6*)

In other words, none of the core ingredients in current American education reform drive the process in the world's most successful educational system.

In this chapter I've attempted to provide some perspective on several policy-making efforts. I hope that this short review illustrates my concerns about the use of "evidence" to support educational policy making. What we have, unfortunately, is a record of, at best, the manufacturing of evidence, to borrow Berliner and Biddle's (1996) phrase. There is *no* reliable scientific evidence to support assertions that

- American reading achievement has declined
- 40 percent of fourth graders cannot read independently
- almost half of adults are functionally illiterate
- most teachers are unprepared to teach reading
- teachers need substantial knowledge of phonology
- teacher education is useless at best and damaging at worst
- current reading education uses a "one size fits all" approach
- teachers have limited intellectual capacity and low initiative

- so-called proven programs reliably raise reading achievement
- scripted curricula provide a route to effective instruction

At best we can believe that these assertions are based on a very limited understanding of the available research—on naivete. At worst, these assertions represent the manufacturing of evidence that's based in ideological boosterism.

The NRC and NRP Reports and Their Context

In 1998, the National Research Council, whose members are drawn from the membership of the National Academy of Sciences, the National Academy of Engineering, and the Institute of Medicine, released the report of its Committee on the Prevention of Reading Difficulties in Young Children (Snow, Burns, & Griffin, 1998).

This report, *Preventing Reading Difficulties in Young Children* (PRD), while vigorously criticized (Gee, 1999), was an attempt to understand "what the research says" about beginning reading. As David Pearson (1999) pointed out, this report is just one of a series of modern reports on American reading instruction and what should be done to improve it. Pearson notes that the First-Grade Studies (Bond & Dykstra, 1967), Chall's *Learning to Read: The Great Debate* (1967/1987), the National Academy of Education's *Becoming a Nation of Readers* (Anderson, Hiebert, Scott, & Wilkinson, 1985), and Adams' (1990) congressionally mandated review of the research on beginning reading were part of a family tree of national reports on reading instruction. Each report attempted to summarize the research on beginning reading instruction, and each suggested that a greater emphasis on creating reading instructional settings and experiences that better reflected what "the research said" would lead to enhanced student outcomes.

These reports can be viewed as a sort of yin and yang dance around the role that explicit phonics instruction might play in early reading instruction. When the First-Grade Studies report, a large-scale comparison of different curricular approaches to teaching reading, concluded that the teacher mattered more than the curriculum materials, Chall followed in 1967 with an analysis that came down clearly in favor of code-emphasis (phonics) programs in beginning reading instruction. Likewise, when *Becoming a Nation of Readers* (BNR) recommended something short of explicit phonics instruction, Chall updated her book (1987) and Congress funded Marilyn Adams' (1990) review of research on phonics in beginning reading. Both Chall and Adams proposed an initial code-emphasis (phonics) approach, but both also warned of the dangers of a too narrowly defined beginning reading curriculum. Both authors provided a fairly nuanced view of how beginning reading instruction might be crafted.

A decade passed and again there were calls for a new review of the research on beginning reading. Proponents of new research argued that new research would provide new insights into teaching beginning reading, and that the old research was being ignored by teachers and curriculum developers. It was never clear to me just what new insights this new research brought to the table. There was a fuss about phoneme awareness, of course, but the role phoneme awareness plays in learning to read had been long acknowledged by reading researchers (e.g., Adams, 1990; Clay, 1985; Juel, 1988). In fact, instructional activities fostering the growth of phoneme awareness and segmentation, such as "sound stretching," had become common practice in many primary classrooms and teachers were using analyses of children's early writing to map phonological development. It now seems odd that so much political mileage has been reaped from assertions about U.S. reading achievement and reading instruction that were simply untrue.

Nonetheless, the NRC was tapped to review the research on reading difficulties and propose a research-based action plan for addressing that issue. But even before the committee released its PRD report, legislative activity created a National Reading Panel to supplement the council's work. Catherine Snow (2001) has offered her perspective, as chair of the PRD committee, on why that legislation went forward. She notes that G. Reid Lyon of the NICHD said that the PRD report, as a consensus document, was too ambiguous. Duane Alexander, director of NICHD, said the PRD did not identify what research was trustworthy. According to Snow,

> *The direct instruction advocates anticipated inadequately strong recommendations concerning the importance of the alphabetic principle in instruction. These worries may have strengthened calls for the establishment, in a time period overlapping with the final meetings of the committee, of a federally mandated panel designed to review rigorously the research base on the effectiveness of different instructional techniques. (p. 240)*

In other words, the NRC committee did not actually endorse explicit, systematic phonics as the "scientifically based" plan. So it was time to try another tactic. This time the researchers would be named by government agencies, not by the National Academy of Science.

Two years later, the National Reading Panel (2000), established by Congress, released its report *Teaching children to read: An evidence-based assessment of the scientific research literature on reading and its implications for reading instruction.* This report is now being widely cited (and distorted) in the quest to reshape beginning reading instruction, the quest to craft a national reading instructional methodology.

This volume begins with professional responses to the NRP report and its associated publications. The responses vary in their nature and tone. Each was selected for inclusion in this volume because it stimulated new questions, concerns, and reactions as I read it. Thus, the selection process was a somewhat personal response task. Following the responses to the NRP are papers that examine the bases and effects of recent policy on teaching reading. A *New York Times* (January 9, 2002) headline shouted, *Education Bill Urges New Emphasis on Phonics,* and the article described the "systematic, explicit instruction" that is now mandated.

I close this book by discussing the possibility that this whole misguided venture needs to be rethought. I argue that the No Child Left Behind Act (PL 107-110) is nothing like a new education reform plan. Instead, the law simply expands a thirty-year-old federal accountability mandate, which before targeted only high-poverty schools receiving federal Title 1 funds, to middle-class children. And I argue that what is needed is not more federalized testing and curriculum control, but almost the very opposite—an increase in local control and teacher autonomy, autonomy where professionals take responsibility for providing effective and always-improving literacy instruction through close and expert on-going assessments of children's literacy development.

References

Adams, M. J. (1990). *Beginning to read: Thinking and learning about print*. Cambridge, MA: MIT Press.

Allington, R. L. (1999). Crafting state educational policy: The slippery role of educational research and researchers. *Journal of Literacy Research, 31,* 457–482.

———. (2001). *What really matters for struggling readers: Designing research-based programs*. Boston: Allyn & Bacon.

Allington, R. L., & Cunningham, P. M. (2002). *Schools that work: Where all children read and write* (2nd ed.). Boston: Allyn & Bacon.

Allington, R. L., & Johnston, P. (2001). Characteristics of exemplary fourth grade instruction. In C. Roller (Ed.), *Research on effective teaching*. Newark, DE: International Reading Association.

Allington, R. L., & McGill-Franzen, A. M. (2001). *The impact of summer loss on the reading achievement gap*. Paper submitted for publication.

Allington, R. L., & Woodside-Jiron, H. (1998). Decodable texts in beginning reading: Are mandates based on research? *ERS Spectrum, 16*(2, Spring), 3–11.

———. (1999). The politics of literacy teaching: How "research" shaped educational policy. *Educational Researcher, 28*(8), 4–13.

American Federation of Teachers. (1999). *Teaching reading is rocket science: What expert teachers of reading should know and be able to do*. New York: Author.

Anderson, R. C., Hiebert, E. H., Scott, J. A., & Wilkinson, I. A. G. (1985). *Becoming a nation of readers: The report of the Commission on Reading*. Champaign, IL: Center for the Study of Reading.

Baron, D. (2002, February 1). Anyone accept the good news on literacy? *Chronicle of Higher Education,* p. B10.

Bennett, W. J., Fair, W., Finn, C. E., Flake, F., Marshall, W., & Ravitch, D. (1998). A nation still at risk. *Policy Review, 90* (July–August), 2–9.

Berliner, D. C. (1986). In pursuit of the expert pedagogue. *Educational Researcher, 15,* 5–13.

Berliner, D. C., & Biddle, B. J. (1996). *The manufactured crisis: Myths, fraud, and the attack on America's public schools*. White Plains, NY: Longman.

Bond, G. L., & Dykstra, R. (1967). The cooperative research program in first-grade reading instruction. *Reading Research Quarterly, 2*(4), 5–142.

Bracey, G. W. (1997). *Setting the record straight: Responses to misconceptions about public education in the United States.* Alexandria, VA: Association for Supervision and Curriculum Development.

Bracey, G. W. (2002). *The war against America's public schools: Privatizing schools, commercializing education.* Boston: Allyn & Bacon.

Bruschi, B. A., & Coley, R. J. (1999). *How teachers compare: The prose, document, and quantitative skills of America's teachers.* Princeton, NJ: Educational Testing Service, Policy Information Center.

Chall, J. S. (1967/1987). *Learning to read: The great debate* (Updated ed.). New York: McGraw-Hill.

Clay, M. M. (1985). *The early detection of reading difficulties: A diagnostic survey with recovery procedures* (3rd ed.). Exeter, NH: Heinemann.

Cochrane, T. (June 19, 1997). S. 939. A bill to establish a National Panel on Early Reading Research and Effective Reading Instruction. *Congressional Record - Senate,* S6002-S6003.

Coles, G. (1998). *Reading lessons: The debate over literacy.* New York: Hill & Wang.

Cunningham, J. W. (2001). The National Reading Panel report. *Reading Research Quarterly, 30*(3), 326–335.

Darling-Hammond, L. (1996). The right to learn and the advancement of teaching: Research, policy, and practice for democratic education. *Educational Researcher, 25,* 517.

Darling-Hammond, L. (1999). *Teacher quality and student achievement: A review of state policy evidence.* Seattle: Center for Teaching Policy, University of Washington.

Donahue, P. L., Voelkl, K. E., Campbell, J., & Mazzeo, J. (1999). *NAEP Reading 1998: Reading report card for the nation and the states.* Washington, DC: U.S. Department of Education, Office of Educational Research and Improvement.

Doyle, W. (1986). Content representations in teachers' definitions of academic work. *Journal of Curriculum Studies, 18,* 365–379.

Duffy, G. G., & Hoffman, J. V. (1999). In pursuit of an illusion: The search for a perfect method. *Reading Teacher, 53*(1), 10–16.

Elley, W. B. (1992). *How in the world do students read? IEA study of reading literacy.* The Hague, Netherlands: International Association for the Evaluation of Educational Achievement.

Entwisle, D. R., Alexander, K. L., & Olson, L. S. (1997). *Children, schools, and inequality.* Boulder, CO: Westview Press.

Ferguson, R. F. (1991). Paying for public education: New evidence on how and why money matters. *Harvard Journal on Legislation, 28,* 465–491.

Ferguson, R. F., & Ladd, H. (1996). How and why money matters: An analysis of Alabama schools. In H. Ladd (Ed.), *Holding schools accountable.* Washington, DC: Brookings Institution.

Fuller, E. J. (1999). *Does teacher certification matter? A comparison of TAAS performance in 1997 between schools with high and low percentages of certified teachers.* Austin, TX: University of Texas, Charles Dana Center.

Gee, J. P. (1999). Reading and the new literacy studies: Reframing the National Academy of Sciences report on reading. *Journal of Literacy Research, 31,* 355–374.

Goodling, B. (1998). Statement of Chairman Bill Goodling (R-PA) on the passage of the Reading Excellence Act in the Senate. Washington, DC.

Gross, M. (2000). *A conspiracy of ignorance.* New York: Harper Trade.

Haberman, M. (1995). *Star teachers of children of poverty.* West Lafayette, IN: Kappa Delta Pi.

House, E. R., Glass, G. V., McLean, L., & Walker, D. (1978). No simple answers: Critique of the Follow Through evaluations. *Harvard Educational Review, 48,* 128–160.

Hunter, H. (1998). *Making change: Three educators join the battle for better schools.* Portsmouth, NH: Heinemann.

International Dyslexia Association (1997). *Informed instruction for reading success: Foundation for teacher perparation.* Baltimore: Author.

Johnston, R. C. (1999, March 12). Texas study links teacher certification, student success. *Education Week,* pp. 19–20.

Juel, C. (1988). Learning to read and write: A longitudinal study of 54 children from first through fourth grade. *Journal of Educational Psychology, 80,* 437–447.

Kibby, M. W. (1995). *Student literacy: Myths and realities.* Bloomington, IN: Phi Delta Kappa Educational Foundation.

Knapp, M. S. (1995). *Teaching for meaning in high-poverty classrooms.* New York: Teachers College Press.

Kozol, J. (1991). *Savage inequalities: Children in America's schools.* New York: Crown.

Ladson-Billings, G. (1994). *The Dreamkeepers: Successful teachers of African-American children.* San Francisco: Jossey-Bass.

Learning First Alliance (1998). Every child reading. *American Educator, 22*(Spring/Summer), 52–60.

Lieberman, T. (2000). *Slanting the story: The forces that shape the news.* New York: The New Press.

Lyon, G. R. (1997). Statement of G. Reid Lyon, Ph.D., before the Committee on Education and the Workforce, U.S. House of Representatives. National Institute of Child Health and Human Development, National Institutes of Health: Bethesda, MD.

Lyon, G. R., Vaasen, M., & Toomey, F. (1989). Teachers' perceptions of their undergraduate and graduate preparation. *Teacher Education and Special Education, 12*(4), 164–169.

McNeil, L. M. (2000). *Contradictions of school reform: Educational costs of standardized testing.* New York: Routledge.

Mendro, R., Bembry, K., & Jordan, H. (1998). *Policy implications of long-term teacher effects on student achievement.* Paper presented at the American Educational Research Association, San Diego, CA.

Moats, L. C. (1994). The missing foundation of teacher education: Knowledge of the structure of spoken and written language. *Annals of Dyslexia, 44,* 81–102.

Moats, L. C. (1997). Statement of Louisa C. Moats to the U.S. House of Representatives Committee of Education and the Workforce Hearing on Teachers: *The key to helping America read.* Washington, DC.

Moats, L. C. (2000). *Whole language lives on: The illusion of "balanced" reading instruction.* New York: Thomas Fordham Foundation.

Moats, L. C., & Lyon, G. R. (1996). Wanted: Teachers with knowledge of language. *Topics in Language Disorders, 16,* 73–86.

National Center for Educational Statistics (2001). *Outcomes of learning: Results from the 2000 program for International Student Assessment of 15 year olds.* Washington, DC: U.S. Department of Education. (http://nces.ed.gov/sueveys/pisa).

National Commission on Teaching and America's Future (1997). *Doing what matters most: Investing in quality teaching.* New York: Author.

National Reading Panel (2000). *Teaching children to read: An evidence-based assessment of the scientific research literature on reading and its implications for reading instruction.* (http://www.nationalreadingpanel.org).

Neuman, S., & Celano, D. (2001). Access to print in low-income and middle-income communities. *Reading Research Quarterly, 36,* 1–26.

Palmaffy, T. (1997). See Dick flunk. *Policy Review* (Nov.–Dec. 1997).

Pearson, P. D. (1999). A historically based review of Preventing Reading Difficulties in Young Children. *Reading Research Quarterly, 34*(2), 231–246.

Pearson, P. D. (2001). Learning to teach reading: The status of the knowledge base. In C. Roller (Ed.), *Learning to teach reading: Setting the research agenda* (pp. 4–19). Newark, DE: International Reading Association.

Pellegrino, J. W., Jones, L., & Mitchell, K. (1999). *Grading the nation's report card.* Washington, DC: National Academy Press.

Pogrow, S. (2000). Success For All does not produce success for students. *Phi Delta Kappan, 82*(1), 67–80.

Pogrow, S. (2002). Avoiding comprehensive school reform models. *Educational Leadership, 58,* 82–83.

Pressley, M., Allington, R. L., Wharton-MacDonald, R., Collins-Block, C., & Morrow, L. (2001). *Learning to read: Lessons from exemplary first-grade classrooms.* New York: Guilford.

Pressley, M., Wharton-McDonald, R., Allington, R. L., Block, C. C., Morrow, L., Tracey, D., Baker, K., Brooks, G., Cronin, J., Nelson, E., & Woo, D. (2001). The nature of effective first-grade literacy instruction. *Scientific Studies in Reading, 5,* 35–58.

Raspberry, W. (2000, May 12). They never learn. *Washington Post,* p. A47.

Reutzel, R. R., Hollingsworth, P. M., & Cox, S. A. V. (1996). Issues in reading instruction: U.S. state legislators' perceptions and knowledge. *Reading Research and Instruction, 35*(4), 343–364.

Ruddell, R. B. (1995). Those influential teachers: Meaning negotiators and motivation builders. *Reading Teacher, 48*(6), 454–463.

Sacks, J. L. (2002, January 30). Experts debate effect of whole-school reform. *Education Week,* p. 6.

Shaker, P., & Heilman, E. (2002). Advocacy vs. authority: Silencing the education professorate. *AACTE Policy Perspectives, 3*(1), 1–6.

Shannon, P. (1989). *Broken promises: Reading instruction in twentieth century America.* Granby, MA: Bergin & Garvey.

Shannon, P. (1998). *Reading poverty.* Portsmouth, NH: Heinemann.

Shulman, L. S. (1983). Autonomy and obligation: The remote control of teaching. In L. Shulman & G. Sykes (Eds.), *Handbook of teaching and policy* (pp. 484–504). New York: Longman.

Snow, C. E. (2001). Preventing reading difficulties in young children: Precursors and fallout. In T. Loveless (Ed.), *The great curriculum debate* (pp. 229–246). Washington, DC: Brookings.

Snow, C. E., Burns, M. S., & Griffin, P. (1998). *Preventing reading difficulties in young children: A report of the National Research Council.* Washington, DC: National Academy Press.

Sowell, T. (2000, June 20). A reply to teachers. *Tampa Tribune,* p. A16.

Spencer, L. M., & Spencer, S. M. (1993). *Competence at work: Models for superior performance.* New York: John Wiley & Sons.

Sweet, R. W. (1997). Don't read, don't tell: Clinton's phony war on illiteracy. *Policy Review* (May/June), 38–42.

Taylor, B., Pearson, P. D., Clark, K. F., & Walpole, S. (1999). Effective schools/Accomplished teachers. *Reading Teacher, 53*(2), 156–159.

Venezky, R. L. (1998). An alternate perspective on Success For All. In K. K. Wong (Ed.), *Advances in educational policy* (Vol. 4, pp. 145–165). Greenwich, CT: JAI Press.

Wasson, D. (2002, March 2). Publishers agree to train teachers on phonic method. *Tampa Tribune.* http://www.tampatribune.com/MGA9XF8WAYC.html

Weintraub, D. (2002, February 5). Teachers union seeking power over school policy. *Sacramento Bee*, pp. A1, 8.

Wenglinsky, H. (2000). *How teaching matters: Bringing the classroom back into discussions of teacher quality.* Princeton, NJ: Educational Testing Service and the Milken Family Foundation.

Williams, P. L., Reese, C. M., Campbell, J. R., Mazzeo, J., & Phillips, G. W. (1995). *1994 NAEP Reading: A first look.* Washington, DC: Office of Educational Research and Improvement, U.S. Department of Education.

PART I

Unreliable Evidence:
Responses to the National
Reading Panel Report

2 ∎ The National Reading Panel Report [A Review]

James W. Cunningham
University of North Carolina
at Chapel Hill

Jim Cunningham usually writes about the impact of epistomo-logical orientations and their effects on how we view research and the world. That theme runs through his review of the National Reading Panel (NRP) report, but his constructive critique goes well beyond the report's epistomological framing. He points out that "All research is persuasive to those who already agree with it." His key evaluative question is whether a knowledgeable and fair-minded skeptic would find the NRP report convincing, but he also raises the specter of the report as a signaling of the politiciza-tion of reading research.

Jim recently coauthored a study of the validity of pseudo-words as measures of decoding (Cunningham et al., 1999). This wonderfully crafted experimental study found that real words, usually low-frequency real words, provide more reliable estimates of children's decoding proficiency. This may seem a small tech-nical issue, but, like the issue of decodable texts, the question of whether pseudoword reading is a valid measure is central to how one interprets the NRP's findings on phonics. The conclusion

Jim and his colleagues reached was that pseudoword pronuncia-
tion measures something, but what it measures is task specific
and not strongly related to reading proficiency.

Cunningham, J. W., et al. 1999. Assessing decoding from an onset-
   rime perspective. *Journal of Literacy Research, 31,* 391–414.

At the behest of the United States Congress in 1997, the Director of the National Institute of Child Health and Human Development (NICHD) and the U.S. Secretary of Education selected 14 persons to serve as a National Reading Panel (NRP). Most Panel members were reading researchers in various fields. All but two members held a doctorate. The Panel was charged to review and assess the research on teaching reading, with implications for both classroom practice and further research.

The report of the National Reading Panel was issued in two volumes. The first volume (00–4769) is a succinct summary of how the Panel came to be, the topics it chose to investigate, its procedures and methods, and its findings. The second volume (00–4754) contains the same introductory and methodological information, but presents at great length the work of each of the topical subgroups within the Panel. It is the second volume that one must read to fully understand the findings and recommendations for classroom practice and future research.

In this review, I refer to both volumes collectively as the *NRP Report*. Citations of the first volume contain only page numbers (e.g., p. 4); citations of the second volume contain a section number followed by page numbers because the second volume's pagination starts with 1 in each section (e.g., p. 3:13 means section 3, page 13 of the second volume). Some statements appear verbatim in both volumes.

The NRP's Philosophy of Science

The *NRP Report* should be seen as a manifesto for a particular philosophy of science as much as a summary of particular research findings. Marks of the manifesto are not subtle and, indeed, begin on the cover. The subtitle of both volumes of the report asserts that the Panel has provided us with "an evidence-based assessment of the *scientific* research literature" (covers, emphasis added). The Methodological Overview of the first volume begins with the sentence, "In what may be its most important action, the Panel then developed and adopted a set of *rigorous* research methodological standards" (p. 5, emphasis added). In their Reflections, the Panel claims that its goal had been to contribute "to a better *scientific* understanding of reading development and reading instruction" (p. 21, emphasis added). Upon looking back at its completed work, it assures us that "the evidence ultimately evaluated by the Panel met well-established *objective scientific* standards" (p. 21, emphasis added).

> What are we to make of a report that so boldly lays claim to what science, rigor, and objectivity are in reading research, and first denigrates, then ignores, the preponderance of research literature in our field?

The Report makes it clear that the methodological standards adopted by the Panel did not arise from the research literature on reading, but rather were imposed upon it. Panel members tell us that they developed their criteria "*a priori*," (p. 27; p. 1:5) and that "Unfortunately, only a small fraction of the total reading research literature met the Panel's standards for use in the topic analyses" (p. 27; p. 1:5).

What are we to make of a report that so boldly lays claim to what science, rigor, and objectivity are in reading research, and first denigrates, then ignores, the preponderance of research literature in our field? Even though the NRP's philosophy of science is implied, its consequences are not discussed, so making it explicit and discussing it here is important. The Panel members' position about what kind of research is scientific fits within a historical philosophical context. To the extent that their views on science may affect how funding agencies, reviewers for journals and conference programs, and researchers conduct themselves, they have implications for the nature of future research in reading. If used to inform policy, their views on science will affect classroom reading experiences every day.

DEMARCATION

The Panel members' repeated and unapologetic appropriation of the term *scientific* to describe the results of their work places how they characterize their work in the subdomain of philosophy of science concerned with the demarcation problem. Positivism (Comte, 1830/1988) was an attempt to define *science* as knowledge with no vestige of theology or abstraction. Science was to be differentiated, or demarcated, from nonscience by being limited to beliefs that are so empirically supported they are certain or positive.

In the century after Comte's first work, scientific practice demonstrated that science couldn't be limited to what is known with certainty. Therefore, logical positivism (e.g., Carnap, 1934) took as its main task the establishment of criteria for what would constitute rational scientific inquiry, without regard for how scientists actually conduct their research (Garrison, 1996). In other words, the logical positivists sought a solution to the demarcation problem by defining and delimiting scientific logic.

When the approach to demarcation of the logical positivists was also found by scientists to be an inadequate guide, Karl Popper (1959) attempted to differentiate science from pseudoscience in yet another way. He argued that science progresses by submitting its hypotheses and theories to tests with the potential to falsify them, while the hypotheses and theories of pseudoscience cannot be falsified. Unfortunately, the falsification criterion of demarcation had trouble explaining why scientific theories are seldom discarded when one or a few investigations produce anomalous outcomes for them.

How successful have the various attempts been to demarcate science from nonscience or pseudoscience? Not very. In fact, the consensus view in philosophy of science is that all such efforts have failed completely (Gjertsen, 1989; Laudan, 1981). The issue is not that there is no difference between science and other thoughtful or creative endeavors, but rather that no one has yet devised a set of criteria that reliably distinguishes scientific from nonscientific practices. Contrary to the position of logical positivists, scientists and philosophers of science have been unable to reach consensus on what constitutes scientific logic or the scientific method (Laudan, 1983). It seems that science is recognized more by its discoveries than by whether its methods correspond to any formal standards. Generally, it appears that scientists are those who contribute new knowledge to the sciences, even when they employ unusual or unorthodox methods to do so. In fact, the breadth of what is usually considered scientific across the natural sciences, and their relatives in engineering and the professions, makes it probable that any attempt to narrowly define science is doomed to the failure of rejection by practicing scientists themselves (Laudan, 1983).

It is true that there are a few philosophers of science who still maintain that science can and should be demarcated from nonscience. Even these few (e.g., Fuller, 1985; Gieryn, 1983), however, generally advocate using a kind of jury system. They argue that in such a system the practicing researchers in a field have the right to label those among their peers *scientists* as part of a social phenomenon, without using any objective criteria of methodological form that demarcates their work from nonscience.

At times, the demarcation of science from nonscience has even been a political strategy. The philosopher and historian of science Imre Lakatos (1978) has pointed out that the Catholic Church in the 1600s engaged in demarcation to label findings of heliocentricity in astronomy as pseudoscience and then forced Galileo to recant. He also recalled that the Soviet Union in the mid-1900s used demarcation to label Mendelian genetics as pseudoscience and then tortured and executed its practitioners.

The National Reading Panel chose to engage itself in the messy and so far unsuccessful effort to solve the demarcation problem. The members boldly assert that they have differentiated the small amount of scientific, objective, and rigorous reading research from the great quantity of reading research that fails to merit one or more of these lofty labels. It has been more than 30 years since such a claim would not have appeared naive to anyone familiar with philosophy of science.

Moreover, the Panel's criteria can be applied to its own work, raising several difficult questions. Did the Panel conform to its own standards? By its demarcation criteria, is its own work scientific? Did the members of the Panel operate in a scientific, objective, and rigorous manner when they chose their procedures for conducting their review of reading research? Unfortunately, the answer seems obvious. Where are the scientific, objective, and rigorous studies that compare different ways of selecting and reviewing literature to improve practice? Is there experimental or quasi-experimental evidence demonstrating the superiority of the Panel's approach to determining which studies are a better guide to practice? No, members chose their demarcation criteria on logical rather than empirical grounds. Alas, the NRP's demarcation criteria do not pass its own standard: The Panel members' determination of what reading research is scientific is not scientific, as they themselves define it.

VERIFICATIONISM

Ignoring how practicing scientists conduct their research, positivists of various stripes (old, logical, and neo) have privileged one or another brand of verificationism. For example, verifiability-in-principle was the criterion that the logical positivists employed to demarcate science from nonscience (Ayer, 1946; Carnap, 1934). To them, the meaning of any statement was the method of its verification. That is, any statement, however tentative, that could not be empirically verified was neither right nor wrong, but meaningless. Had scientists listened to the logical positivists—fortunately, most did not—they would have stopped searching for the truth of any hypothesis they did not then know how to verify. While the criterion of verifiability-in-principle was eventually abandoned by almost everyone, a broader and more nuanced neoverificationism still has a few adherents among philosophers today, principally Michael Dummett (1976, 1991).

Verificationism is always concerned with the meaning of statements rather than the nature of reality. It interposes a theory of knowledge and a theory of language between scientists and the objects of their investigation. Positivists want their a priori views of science and of scientific logic and language to dictate what can be known.

The National Reading Panel clearly holds a verificationist philosophy of science. It states that "To sustain a claim of effectiveness [for any instructional practice], the Panel felt it necessary

that there be experimental or quasiexperimental studies of sufficient size or number, and scope...and that these studies be of
moderate to high quality" (p. 1:7). Notice that the emphasis is not
on effectiveness, but rather on *claims* of effectiveness. The true
nature of reading or reading instruction is less important to the
Panel than the need to "sustain [read "verify"] a claim" (p. 1:7)
about it.

The Panel's positivism is strongly held. Because statements
about reading development and instruction apparently have scientific meaning only to the extent that they are empirically and
experimentally verifiable, even a review of the experimental research is "subjective" (p. 5) unless the findings of those experiments can be combined in "a formal statistical meta-analysis" (p.
5). In other words, the Panel holds both a verificationism about
reading research and a metaverificationism about reviewing reading research.

The Panel's verifiable-by-experiment criterion is applied
quite consistently throughout its examination of reading research.
The language of the Report betrays no tentativeness about the
Panel's criterion. When the Panel appears tentative, a careful
reading reveals that this tentativeness is certainly not about the
criterion:

> *It should be made clear that these findings do not negate the posi-
> tive influence that independent reading may have on reading
> fluency. . . . Rather, there are simply no sufficient data from
> well-designed studies capable of testing questions of causation to
> substantiate causal claims. (p. 13)*

In other words, when its criterion for verification (data it considers sufficient from studies it considers well designed) is lacking,
no claim can be verified.

A CRITIQUE OF THE NRP'S PHILOSOPHY OF SCIENCE

Most researchers, at least in the natural sciences, are scientific
realists rather than positivists (Marsonet, 1995; Weinberg, 1992).
Scientific realists are empiricists who build theoretical models,
attempt to represent ever deeper layers of previously hidden

reality, and seek full and satisfying explanations in order to achieve a clear and comprehensive understanding of cause-and-effect relationships (Cunningham & Fitzgerald, 1996). Scientific realists conduct experiments when experiments are called for, but they never confuse their methods with the reality their methods are used to discover.

Like all positivism, the Panel's work reveals a desire for certainty and a willingness to engage in reductionism to achieve it. All positivists have been antirealists (Cunningham & Fitzgerald, 1996), apparently because they are uncomfortable with the wide and never-closing gap between our knowledge and our questions

> Practicing scientists of reading should be embarrassed by the simplistic, old-fashioned, and generally discredited verificationism of the National Reading Panel.

(Searle, 1995). Their strategy has been to increase their comfort by reducing the questions one is permitted to ask, and reducing the ways one is permitted to answer them.

Practicing scientists of reading should be embarrassed by the simplistic, old-fashioned, and generally discredited verificationism of the National Reading Panel. In its assertions about the relationship between causal claims and the need for experimental evidence, the Panel has unwittingly allied itself with the research arm of the U.S. tobacco industry, the Tobacco Institute, which has long argued that the Surgeon General or anyone else has no right to claim that smoking causes cancer because the relationship is merely correlational (Giere, 1997).

The efforts of the NRP to formally demarcate science in reading from pseudoscience may actually be dangerous. While the members of the Panel I know personally are unquestionably well intentioned, one can be forgiven for being less certain about the Congress that requested the Report. I fear the philosophy of science that begins and permeates the *NRP Report* may have a chilling effect on the funding, publication, and influence of all reading research that fails to follow the positivist methodological standards it prescribes for our field.

The NRP's Doctrine of Research Design

The *NRP Report* should also be seen as a declaration of a particular doctrine of research design. By largely limiting itself to the examination of experimental and quasiexperimental studies of reading, the NRP echoes the raging battle between experimentalists and correlationists in the social sciences of the 1950s and early 1960s. Its repeated view is that "correlations tell us nothing about the direction or sequence of a relationship" (p. 3:10). In fact, the Methodological Overview of the *NRP Report* reads almost as if there had been an open copy of Campbell and Stanley's (1963) work in front of each of the Panel members as they developed their methodological standards.

In 1956, Lee Cronbach (1957) addressed an audience at the meeting of the American Psychological Association (APA). Unlike the NRP, Cronbach was willing in the title of his talk ("The Two Disciplines of Scientific Psychology") to refer to some of both experimental and correlational research as scientific. In his presentation, Cronbach famously called for a crossbreeding of experimental psychological research methods with those correlational methods used to investigate individual differences in psychology. This new genre of research came to be known as the study or science of Aptitude by Treatment Interactions (ATIs).

Eighteen years later, Cronbach returned to APA (1975) to discuss the state of the then-thriving subdiscipline of ATI research. Surely his comments were not what his audience had expected. After praising what ATI research, especially in instruction, had contributed, he stated that such research was no longer sufficient because "Interactions are not confined to the first order; the dimensions of the situation and of the person enter into complex interactions" (Cronbach, 1975, p. 116). Stepping back to evaluate the previous 30 years of research in psychology, Cronbach said that, "Taking stock today, I think most of us judge theoretical progress to have been disappointing" (p. 116). In this evaluation of research, including ATI studies, he especially noted the limitations of the "two-group experiment" (p. 116).

With courageous candor, Cronbach related how he and his coauthor, Richard Snow, had "been thwarted by the inconsistent findings from roughly similar inquiries" (Cronbach, 1975, p. 119) in their attempts to generalize from results of ATI studies on instruction. From this experience, he came to realize that untested interactions, especially of a higher order, can always be envisioned for any study. Then, in comments anyone today should find eerily prophetic, Cronbach questioned the eagerness of some social scientists of the time "to establish rigorous generalizations about social policy by conducting experiments in the field" (p. 122).

Cronbach (1975) did not conclude his remarks by opposing scientific psychology or calling for an end to experimentation. On the contrary, he expected both to continue and prosper. What he did call for was the end to simplistic and reductionist reporting of scientific research. If he were to make the same talk today, surely he would castigate the reporting of nothing but effect sizes with the same fervor he expressed then against the reporting of "nothing save F ratios" (p. 124). What he endorsed instead was "the scientific observation of human behavior" (p. 124) with an emphasis on descriptions. In opposition to purely numerical products of research, he cited Meehl (1957) to agree with him that "we [social scientists] have to use our heads" (p. 126).

Whether either of them were present to hear, or later read, Cronbach's (1975) remarks, Jay Samuels and David Pearson worked to establish a similar spirit of broadened and balanced inquiry in our field during their editorship of *Reading Research Quarterly* from 1979–1985. Early on, they expressed an appreciation for the strengths and limitations of both experiments and naturalistic observation and called for the recognition of "the symbiotic relationship between paradigms" (Pearson & Samuels, 1980, p. 430). Later in his tenure as coeditor, Samuels (1984) echoed Cronbach's concern with complex interactions that make it impossible to expect experimental science to find simple, all-embracing laws that generalize. He then discussed the implications for reading instruction of overlooking such interactions:

> *Many of our educational pundits appear to believe there are universal approaches to instruction and development of curricular materials which will work for all children under all conditions.*

They seem to ignore differences in intelligence and home background conditions. Depending on these variables as well as the degree of motivation and prior knowledge brought to the task of learning to read, it is highly likely that some approaches to instruction should be better for some children and different approaches should work better for other children. (Samuels, 1984, p. 391)

In light of this historical background, the experimentalism of the NRP reminds me of Rip Van Winkle. It is almost as if the Panel fell mysteriously asleep 20 years ago and awoke just in time to do what the Congress and the NICHD convened them to do.

EQUATING READING EDUCATION WITH INTERVENTIONS

The NRP maintains that "The evidence-based methodological standards adopted by the Panel are essentially those normally used in research studies of the efficacy of interventions in psychological and medical research" and states its belief "that the efficacy of materials and methodologies used in the teaching of reading and in the prevention or treatment of reading disabilities should be tested no less rigorously" (p. 27; p. 1:5).

This argument is based on a metaphor of reading instruction being like the curing of psychological and physical diseases. The Panel's unquestioned assumption of this metaphor has the regrettable effect of reducing schooling in general, and reading education in particular, to a series of low- or noninteracting interventions. What if healthy human development is a better metaphor for schooling and the teaching of reading, pre-K through Grade 5 and beyond, than is the metaphor of treatments for specific mental or medical ailments? This metaphor would not negate the need for intervention research when particular treatments for specific reading disabilities or particular short-term learning outcomes are tested, but it would certainly broaden the research base for "the teaching of reading and in prevention . . . of reading disabilities" (p. 27; p. 1:5) beyond that considered scientific, objective, and rigorous by the Panel.

The NRP's findings relative to the value of systematic phonics instruction and attempts to increase independent reading illustrate the limitations of experimentalism as a doctrine of research design and treating ailments as a metaphor for reading education. To see the inadequacy, consider two possible claims one could make about reading instruction:

1. Systematic phonics instruction in first grade is a cause of better reading ability by fifth grade and beyond.
2. Increased independent reading in the elementary grades is a cause of better reading ability by fifth grade and beyond.

It is difficult to see anything unreasonable about either of these claims or anything unscientific about wanting to evaluate them.

Because of its doctrinaire experimentalism, however, the Panel chose to evaluate all allegations about the effectiveness of systematic phonics instruction and attempts to increase independent reading in ways that cannot serve to shed much light on important claims like the two stated above. First, the Panel limited the duration of the effect of instruction to the length of time between the official onset of the intervention and the final data collection in each particular study. Such studies of the effects of smoking would be far less threatening to the tobacco companies than the devastating studies of longer term effects have been. Indeed, it may be the long-term and complex nature of reading development, and indeed of all schooling, that makes the NRP's experimentalism most questionable.

Second, the Panel members forced themselves to attempt to select one or a few dependent variables that would permit them to conduct a meta-analysis or, at least, a "subjective qualitative analysis" (p. 5). So they tried to measure the short-term value of systematic phonics instruction using a reading comprehension dependent measure. Equally oddly, they tried to evaluate the short-term value of increased independent reading using a fluency dependent measure. Surely, these are examples of trying to pound square pegs into round holes because someone decided a priori that it would be easier to compare only round holes with one another.

What research designs would be more appropriate if healthy development were a better metaphor for learning to read than treating a range and sequence of diseases? They would be designs

that test aspects of sophisticated theories of reading development. Wouldn't it have made much more sense for the Panel to attempt to test one or more theories of reading development that endeavor to come to grips with the long-term and interactive nature of schooling? Why not, for example, identify a theory or model of reading or of reading development that includes a complex causal network?
I have argued, for example, that decoding by phonics has only small direct causal value for silent reading comprehension, but that it has important indirect causal value (Cunningham, 1993). That is, decoding by phonics contributes directly to the acquisition of automatic word recognition, which, in turn, has direct causal value for silent reading comprehension. This aspect of my model has much research to support it (e.g., Share, 1995), but it is difficult to imagine an experiment or quasi-experiment that would last long enough to conclusively test this indirect yet still causal relationship. Even if such an experimental study has been or could be done, it is a real stretch of the imagination to expect enough of them to make a meta-analysis possible. Yet do we want to ignore, or leave untested, theories that posit long-term, indirect causal relationships between decoding by phonics and ultimate reading comprehension ability, or between world knowledge, wide independent reading, and ultimate attitudes toward reading, self, and school?

> When the Panel equated reading education with a series of interventions, it made a fatal error our field cannot afford to accept.

When the Panel equated reading education with a series of interventions, it made a fatal error our field cannot afford to accept. It seems especially ironic that it made this error in the name of an organization given to the study of health and human development.

A CRITIQUE OF THE NRP'S DOCTRINE OF RESEARCH DESIGN

I contend that education, including the teaching of reading, is more like fostering healthy human development, building a successful business, maintaining an effective military, and providing good parenting than it is like administering medical or psychological interventions. American business and the American military are each the envy of the world, yet imagine how little of their cumulative wisdom and common practice is supported by the kind of research the NRP would insist upon for investigating claims about reading instruction. For instance, what would happen if parents began to feel doubts about any practice that does not have enough experimental support to conduct a meta-analysis?

Get intelligent people together as a committee and sometimes they collectively act with less common sense than any individual among them has. The experimentalism held so unwaveringly by the NRP violates all common wisdom. Such a doctrine will not do in reading education and must not go unchallenged.

The NRP's Findings and Determinations

The members of the Panel divided themselves into five subgroups, with several members serving on more than one. These subgroups each examined the experimental and quasi-experimental research on the five main topics they had chosen: alphabetics, fluency, comprehension, teacher education and reading instruction, and computer technology and reading instruction. In this section, I will briefly review the findings and determinations of the five subgroups. Before doing so, however, it is important to consider whether such a review is even necessary after critiquing the Panel's philosophy of science and doctrine of research design that guided all five subgroups in their work.

If the Panel's philosophy of science and doctrine of research design are seriously flawed, as I have argued, does that mean its findings are inevitably also flawed? Positivists and other anti-realists would think so, because they hold that reality is always determined by the methods and language employed to examine and interpret it. Scientific realists do not concur. We agree that a misunderstanding of science or a limited approach to research design will inevitably lead to some mistaken or limited findings, but not all findings will necessarily be mistaken or limited. In the case of the *NRP Report*, it may be that some or even all the findings of the Panel happen to be what would have been found had members approached their job differently. Therefore, I conclude that the findings of the Panel still need to be evaluated on their likelihood to conform to reality given a broader view of epistemology, a more versatile set of research tools, and a different metaphor of reading education.

Other questions also require an analysis of the Panel's results and interpretations. What is the relationship between the Panel's approach and its findings? How consistently did Panel members apply their own standards when they conducted their selection, analysis, and interpretation of literature on reading instruction and development? These questions can be answered only by a review of the actual findings and determinations of the subgroups.

Alphabetics

The word *alphabetics* is utilized by the Panel to group and label research on the topics of phonemic awareness (PA) and phonics instruction. The two topics are dealt with separately, with little explicit discussion of the relationship between them.

Phonemic awareness. The PA training that the Panel finds most effective is 5 to 18 hours of explicit and systematic, small-group instruction with one or two tasks of manipulating phonemes with letters, given to preschool and kindergarten children. Because the recommended instruction is "with letters" (p. 8; p. 2:4), the Panel's finding is tantamount to endorsing systematic phonics instruction in preschool and kindergarten (Yopp & Yopp, 2000). How should we, as a field, react to such a recommendation?

It does seem to me that, at the present time, the burden of proof (Giere, 1997) is on those who would have us do nothing instructional to foster the development of children's phonemic awareness. I believe we now have enough evidence that phonemic awareness is a necessary component of learning to identify words and that it is lacking in enough learners so we, as a field, must not leave its acquisition to chance. Had the Panel stopped there, I would endorse the finding wholeheartedly.

I also contend, however, that the burden of proof at this time is on those who would standardize PA training when so many questions about it remain unanswered. The chief question is the one that the Panel largely ignored throughout its entire work, even including its calls for future research: What are the long-term effects on silent reading comprehension ability, the reading habit, and attitudes toward reading, self, and school of its recommended changes in early reading instruction? Specific to PA training, would the future results in fifth grade and beyond justify the revolution in preschool and kindergarten education that implementing the Panel's PA findings would entail? When the first finding of the report is based primarily on short-term dependent measures of words in isolation that are not scientifically linked in a causal chain to appropriate long-term measures, the onus is on the Panel.

Another important question regarding PA training is one that the Panel also generally ignored throughout its work: What quality of instruction did the control group receive? Because of the Panel's verificationist philosophy of science, members were likely to be satisfied when they found enough well-designed experimental and quasiexperimental studies to generate a meta-analysis. They sometimes sugarcoat their findings and determinations with cautions, but by their own standards these cautions are not scientific. Their often mechanistic approach to selection, analysis, and interpretation of studies did not readily allow them to consult their professional judgment of what children actually need and when they need it, so their findings usually contain the implicit assumption that more and earlier are better. When such thinking rules, it can be all right if the control groups in many of the experiments received no instruction at all, mere placebos, or alternative treatments not developed by career reading educators committed to teaching phonemic awareness in a developmentally appropriate manner that recognizes the complex demands of the reading curriculum to come.

I contend that the burden of proof is with the Panel to show that research-based practices such as shared reading of books that play with sounds, writing with invented spelling, and teaching onsets using a variety of activities (key actions, students' names, and key foods or beverages) do not help most children develop the necessary phonemic awareness they need. Until this happens, the Panel's rush to standardization of how and when to best develop the essentials of phonemic awareness should be ignored or opposed.

Phonics instruction. The Alphabetics subgroup of the Panel makes three major distinctions among phonics instructional programs. First, it distinguishes explicit and systematic programs from programs providing nonsystematic phonics or no phonics at all. Second, it classifies explicit and systematic phonics programs into three categories: (a) synthetic, (b) larger unit, and (c) miscellaneous. Third, it looks at whether phonics is more effective when taught one-on-one, in small groups, or to the whole class.

> The Panel's findings on phonics are also susceptible to the objection I raised earlier, that the studies to date really do not tell us that it matters—by fifth grade and beyond on the most important variables—how students were taught phonics in kindergarten and first grade.

The principal findings of the meta-analyses are that explicit and systematic phonics is superior to nonsystematic or no phonics, but that there is no significant difference in effectiveness among the three kinds of systematic phonics instruction. The subgroup also found no significant difference in effectiveness among tutoring, small-group, or whole-class phonics instruction.

The Panel's findings, based on a meta-analysis of 66 comparisons from 38 experimental and quasi-experimental studies published since 1970, are consistent with the much broader body of literature on beginning reading instruction and the reading process. Surely, by now, the preponderance of logic and evidence is against those who contend that it is all right to provide young school children with reading instruction containing little or no phonics, with any phonics included being taught unsystematically. The *NRP Report* does nothing to change this.

What the Panel's findings may do, however, is move the burden of proof within the competition among advocates of different kinds of systematic phonics instruction. Historically, systematic phonics instruction has meant *synthetic* phonics instruction to many advocates. Recently, systematic phonics instruction in some states has come to mean *synthetic phonics instruction with at least 75 or 80% decodable text.* The onus has long been on those of us who believe that newer methods of systematic phonics instruction can be equally if not more effective than traditional synthetic programs over the long run. The *NRP Report* on phonics instruction may shift the burden of proof from advocates of these newer phonics methods to those who would impose synthetic phonics with high levels of decodable text on whole districts and states of children, because the advocates of such an imposition have always claimed that the research finds synthetic phonics to be superior to all other kinds. Will the *NRP Report* contribute to a shift of the burden of proof to those political activists who insist that synthetic phonics is best? Forgive me for not being overly optimistic, because the lack of scientific research supporting the link between retention in grade or grammar instruction hasn't kept these from being widely imposed on many public school children in the U.S. during the recent reforms.

The Panel's findings on phonics are also susceptible to the objection I raised earlier, that the studies to date really do not tell us that it matters—by fifth grade and beyond on the most important variables—how students were taught phonics in kindergarten and first grade. As an advocate of a type of systematic phonics instruction, I find this embarrassing for our field. Still, it was the responsibility of the Panel, and is the responsibility of us who read their report, to work to change that situation. Would that the Panel had taken the opportunity to instruct NICHD, Congress, and the nation on their responsibility to fund the kind of research that can eventually help us determine the long-term, multivariate, cause-and-effect chains that comprise healthy reading development. Sadly, the methods advocated by the Panel will almost certainly have the opposite effect—the funding and publication of more short-term, univariate, and single-cause studies.

Critique of the findings on alphabetics. I sense a hidden tension in this section of the Report between implicit or even subconscious views of the relationship linking phonemic awareness and phonics instruction. One view holds that phonemic awareness is prerequisite to learning phonics well; the other view holds that phonemic awareness is best taught when combined with systematic phonics instruction. The members of the subgroup resolve this tension by trying to have it both ways. They implicitly take the first or prerequisite view when they encourage the explicit and systematic teaching of phonemic awareness in preschool and kindergarten. They implicitly take the second or combined view when they advocate that phonemic awareness instruction be done with letters. A more straightforward approach would have been for them to acknowledge that two views exist and take one side or the other or admit that taking a side is currently premature.

FLUENCY

The Panel's discussion of reading fluency reveals another intriguing mix of opposing views underlying a report that feigns unanimity. One view is manifest in a summary of the theoretical relationship between automaticity and fluency that brings to bear eye movement research and a logical analysis of the reading task to include the roles of punctuation clues, grouping words into syntactic units, assigning emphasis to certain words, and pause behavior. Those in the subgroup who hold this view seem to see fluency as a construct and process underlying both oral and silent reading.

The other view is present in the identification of fluency with oral reading in both definition—"speed and accuracy of oral reading" (p. 3:28)—and measurement. "All [fluency] assessment procedures require oral reading of text" (p. 3:9). Those in the subgroup who hold this view seem to see fluency as a behavior and product of fluency instruction.

Because members of the Fluency subgroup were unaware of this tension in their midst or were unable to resolve it, they include independent silent reading as a treatment whose effectiveness should be measured with an oral reading dependent measure. No wonder they couldn't find a single study that evaluated interventions to encourage more independent silent reading with an oral reading fluency test. At that point, they should have realized that perhaps they had put the research on independent silent reading in the wrong subgroup.

Guided oral reading. The Fluency subgroup finds that guided oral reading, especially repeated reading, leads to improved oral reading fluency. With welcome candor, members admit they could locate no multiyear studies on this issue. Still, because professional wisdom and the literature the Panel ignored also support the claim that guided oral reading and repeated reading increase fluency, this finding of the Panel seems likely to hold up over time in the real world.

Independent silent reading. Beyond the questionable decision assigning this topic to the Fluency subgroup, the Panel's analysis of the research on independent silent reading manifests an appalling misunderstanding of even the narrow kind of research being endorsed by the NRP.

Although members claim that their methods are those used to study "the efficacy of interventions in psychological and medical research" (p. 27; p. 1:5), they misrepresent much psychological and medical research. No intervention to treat clinical depression is tested on patients who aren't depressed. No drug to treat kidney infections is tested on patients who don't have kidney disease. Moreover, treatments in psychological or medical research are ordinarily not administered even to patients having the targeted problems if they also have other problems that could prevent the intervention from working. For example, a treatment for heart disease probably won't be tested on patients who have heart disease combined with a serious lung ailment.

Yet, throughout its work, the NRP routinely selected and analyzed studies that tested the efficacy of a treatment in reading without ensuring that the participants needed what the treatment was designed to teach or that their other abilities made them likely candidates to benefit from the treatment. If the Panel was going to go the experimental and quasi-experimental route, it should have established criteria excluding any intervention study that did not screen participants to select those for whom the treatment would be appropriate and likely to work if effective.

Specific to this finding, if reading research should really be like psychological and medical intervention research, interventions designed to encourage students to increase their independent silent reading should only be tested using participants who have the ability and opportunity outside of school to read independently but who do not regularly do so.

COMPREHENSION

This section of the *NRP Report* demonstrates the need and value of going beyond a critique of the methods the Panel adopted to look at the findings themselves. Members of the Comprehension subgroup found few studies that met the NRP criteria and did not perform any meta-analyses, but they chose to summarize the research they examined and make instructional recommendations anyway.

Vocabulary instruction. Because the 50 studies that were selected tested 21 different methods of teaching vocabulary, the Comprehension subgroup felt it should not perform a meta-analysis. Apparently, there was no consensus among members on a few distinctive features that some—but not all—methods shared. As a result, their instructional recommendations for vocabulary tend to be more balanced and less standardized than those of other subgroups.

Text comprehension instruction. Again, the subgroup found too few studies that met NRP criteria and too many different instructional methods to conduct a meta-analysis. Still, the subgroup found that seven of 16 types of text comprehension instruction have some support of effectiveness. Taking a balanced and practical, rather than verificationist tack, members recommend a combination of these and other types.

A critique of the findings on comprehension. This section of the Report is more like past major reviews of research on teaching reading comprehension (e.g., Pearson & Fielding, 1991; Tierney & Cunningham, 1984) than it is like other sections of the report. To me, at least, this section is more interesting and potentially valuable than the others, precisely because the Comprehension subgroup chose not to adhere too closely to the Panel's a priori methodological standards.

There is a definite downside, however, to the Panel's willingness to make instructional recommendations for comprehension based on looser criteria than it was willing to follow in the alphabetics and fluency sections. For example, members are willing to endorse text comprehension instruction but not interventions to increase independent silent reading, even though neither type of instruction met their original specifications for classroom implementation. Doesn't this reveal a bias toward explicit instruction rather than just a scientific finding of its superiority? Doesn't this suggest that the Panel thinks word identification and oral reading are more important and, therefore, more deserving of scientific, objective, and rigorous research standards than comprehension and independent silent reading?

> [M]embers are willing to endorse text comprehension instruction but not interventions to increase independent silent reading, even though neither type of instruction met their original specifications for classroom implementation. Doesn't this reveal a bias toward explicit instruction rather than just a scientific finding of its superiority?

TEACHER EDUCATION AND READING INSTRUCTION

The Panel located 32 studies of the effects of teacher preservice or inservice education that met the general methodological standards, but again these studies represented too large a range of treatments to combine into a meta-analysis. The subgroup then added the additional criterion that "both teacher and student outcomes must be reported" (p. 17). The 11 studies with preservice teachers as participants all failed to meet this additional standard. Only about half of the 21 studies with inservice teachers met it. As a set, these studies of teacher inservice education indicated that professional development does increase student achievement, at least in the short-to-medium term.

In this section of the Report, the Panel's standard that preservice and inservice education be ultimately evaluated based on student outcomes is unfortunate. It certainly fits with the current political climate but ignores much that we know about professionalism. The members of no other profession are held accountable for client outcomes. No doctor, dentist, lawyer, or clinical psychologist is liable to be sued successfully or even professionally censured based on outcomes. (There is malpractice, but no such thing as a maloutcome suit.) Rather, these other professionals are held accountable for conforming to established best practices in their respective fields (Cunningham, 1999).

The purpose of research on teacher education is—or should be—to test theoretical models of how teachers gain and maintain professional competence and what conditions permit them to display that competence. To make every study on teacher education another experiment on teaching phonemic awareness, phonics, fluency, and so on is to place a burden on it that it cannot and should not bear. The research on teacher education should tell us how to promote professional practice.

COMPUTER TECHNOLOGY AND READING INSTRUCTION

Again, the Panel located relatively few studies that met the NRP criteria and not enough of any kind to conduct a meta-analysis. Because all the studies reported positive results, the subgroup concluded that, "It is clear that some students can benefit from the use of computer technology in reading instruction" (p. 6:2). The subgroup also expressed some cautions. Let us hope the readers of the report do not conclude that anything taught on a computer will work.

A CRITIQUE OF THE NRP'S FINDINGS AND DETERMINATIONS

Most readers of the *NRP Report* will probably find themselves agreeing with at least one of the findings. Perhaps a majority of readers will agree with a majority of the findings. However, the test of quality for scientific research is whether knowledgeable and fair-minded *skeptics* find it persuasive. All research is persuasive to those who already agree with it. No research is persuasive to the person with a closed mind on the subject. The best science has the power to change the thinking of those who previously disagreed with its conclusions but who are fair-minded enough to admit they were wrong once the case has been made. Who is a fair-minded skeptic? Anyone who can point to several important issues in the past on which she or he has changed her or his mind because of research results.

The test of the scientific quality of the NRP's findings will be whether very many knowledgeable people who previously thought differently change their minds to agree with the Panel that preschool and kindergarten children should receive explicit and systematic phonemic awareness instruction with letters, or that efforts to increase independent silent reading are probably not effective in helping children acquire automaticity in reading.

> I predict that the knowledgeable and fair-minded skeptics who change their minds based on the NRP's findings will be few and far between.

How likely is that to happen? I predict that the knowledgeable and fair-minded skeptics who change their minds based on the NRP's findings will be few and far between. Too much professional and historical knowledge about teaching reading is ignored, too little common sense is brought to bear, and too little reading research is considered worthy of consultation.

The Context of the NRP Report

What if there had been no National Reading Panel, but the identical manifesto for a positivist philosophy of science in reading, the identical doctrine of experimentalism in reading research design, and the identical findings had been published in a series of articles in various major journals? I, for one, would have had the same substantive comments to make, but I would be much less fearful than I am now about what could come of it all. The U.S. Congress, the NICHD (an influential agency of the federal government), and the Secretary of Education convened the Panel and shaped its goals and operation. Does this mean the National Reading Panel was a bold attempt by powerful political forces to gain control of reading research? That will depend on whether persuasion or enforcement was the goal, and only time will tell.

References

Ayer, A.J. (1946). *Language, truth and logic* (2nd ed.). London: V. Gollancz.

Campbell, D.T., & Stanley, J.C. (1963). *Experimental and quasi-experimental designs for research.* Chicago: Rand McNally.

Carnap, R. (1934). *The unity of science* (M. Black, Trans.). London: Kegan Paul, Trench, Trubner & Co.

Comte, A. (1988). *Introduction to positive philosophy* (P. Descours, H.G. Jones, & F. Ferré, Trans., F. Ferré, Ed.). Indianapolis, IN: Hackett. (Original work published 1830)

Cronbach, L.J. (1957). The two disciplines of scientific psychology. *American Psychologist, 12,* 671–684.

Cronbach, L.J. (1975). Beyond the two disciplines of scientific psychology. *American Psychologist, 30,* 116–127.

Cunningham, J.W. (1993). Whole-to-part reading diagnosis. *Reading and Writing Quarterly, 9,* 31–49.

Cunningham, J.W. (1999). How we can achieve best practices in literacy instruction? In L.B. Gambrell, L.M. Morrow, S.B. Neuman, & M. Pressley (Eds.), *Best practices in literacy instruction* (pp. 34–45). New York: Guilford.

Cunningham, J.W., & Fitzgerald, J. (1996). Epistemology and reading. *Reading Research Quarterly, 31,* 36–60.

Dummett, M. (1976). What is a theory of meaning? (II). In G. Evans & J. McDowell (Eds.), *Truth and meaning: Essays in semantics* (pp. 67–137). New York: Oxford University Press.

Dummett, M. (1991). *The logical basis of metaphysics.* Cambridge, MA: Harvard University Press.

Fuller, S. (1985). The demarcation of science: A problem whose demise has been greatly exaggerated. *Pacific Philosophical Quarterly, 66,* 329–341.

Garrison, J.W. (1996). Science, philosophy of. In J.J. Chambliss (Ed.), *Philosophy of education: An encyclopedia* (pp. 590–592). New York: Garland.

Giere, R.N. (1997). *Understanding scientific reasoning* (4th ed.). Orlando, FL: Harcourt Brace College.

Gieryn, T.F. (1983). Boundary work and the demarcation of science from non-science: Strains and interests in professional ideologies of scientists. *American Sociological Review, 48,* 781–795.

Gjertsen, D. (1989). *Science and philosophy: Past and present.* New York: Penguin.

Lakatos, I. (1978). *The methodology of scientific research programmes* (Philosophical Papers, Vol. 1, J. Worrall & G. Currie, Eds.). New York: Cambridge University Press.

Laudan, L. (1981). A problem-solving approach to scientific progress. In I. Hacking (Ed.), *Scientific revolutions* (pp. 144–155). New York: Oxford University Press.

Laudan, L. (1983). The demise of the demarcation problem. In R. S. Cohen & L. Laudan (Eds.), *Physics, philosophy and psychoanalysis: Essays in honor of Adolf Grunbaum* (pp. 111–127). Boston: D. Reidel.

Marsonet, M. (1995). *Science, reality, and language.* Albany, NY: State University of New York Press.

Meehl, P.E. (1957). When shall we use our heads instead of the formula? *Journal of Counseling Psychology, 4,* 268–273.

Pearson, P.D., & Fielding, L. (1991). Comprehension instruction. In R. Barr, M.L. Kamil, P.B. Mosenthal, & P.D. Pearson (Eds.), *Handbook of reading research* (Vol. 2, pp. 815–860). White Plains, NY: Longman.

Pearson, P.D., & Samuels, S.J. (1980). Editorial. *Reading Research Quarterly, 15,* 429–430.

Popper, K.R. (1959). *The logic of scientific discovery.* London: Hutchinson.

Samuels, S.J. (1984). Editorial. *Reading Research Quarterly, 19,* 390–392.

Searle, J.R. (1995). *The construction of social reality.* New York: The Free Press.

Share, D.L. (1995). Phonological recoding and self-teaching: *Sine qua non* of reading acquisition. *Cognition, 55,* 151–218.

Tierney, R.J., & Cunningham, J.W. (1984). Research on teaching reading comprehension. In P.D. Pearson, R. Barr, M.L. Kamil, & P. Mosenthal (Eds.), *Handbook of reading research* (Vol. 1, pp. 609–655). White Plains, NY: Longman.

Weinberg, S. (1992). *Dreams of a final theory.* New York: Pantheon.

Yopp, H.K., & Yopp, R.H. (2000). Supporting phonemic awareness development in the classroom. *The Reading Teacher, 54,* 130–43.

3 ■ Why the National Reading Panel's Recommendations Are Not Enough

Michael Pressley, Sara Dolezal,
Alysia D. Roehrig, and
Katherine Hilden
with the Notre Dame
Reading Research Seminar*

Mike Pressley and I worked together for several years as co-directors of the exemplary first-grade teacher project of the National Research Center for English Learning and Achievement (Pressley, Allington, et al., 2001). We coauthored a paper contrasting the breadth and diversity of the reading research funded by the U.S. Office of Education's Office of Educational Research and Improvement to the narrow focus of the studies funded by the National Institute of Child Health and Human Development (NICHD) (Pressley & Allington, 1999).

In December 2001, Mike gave the Oscar Causey Award address at the National Reading Conference in San Antonio. He opened that address by noting, "I find it puzzling that scientists

---

*The Notre Dame Reading Research Seminar consists of undergraduate students Sarah Benton, Stephanie Collins, Antonio DeSapio, Annie Moses, Katie Solic, and Erin Wibbens.

as good as the ones on the [National Reading] Panel could have convinced themselves to take these conceptually and method-ologically narrow approaches. The conceptual narrowness and the showcasing only of effects replicated many times over dooms the NRP report to obscurity, in my view. I would be surprised if the document is still being cited a decade from now" (Pressley, 2001, p. 1).

Mike went on to set out what he viewed as the particularly important limitations of the NRP report. (He expands on these in a soon to be published paper [Pressley, in press]). At the time, Mike was the editor of the most influential educational research journal, the Journal of Educational Psychology. *He has a substantial reputation for being an empirical and scientific researcher (the reason he received the Causey Award, as well as several others that recognize the importance of his research), and he is also one of the coauthors of the Open Court reading program. Thus, Mike's words at the conference carried particular weight.*

I asked Mike if he would write a reflection on the responses he got to his critique of the NPA report. He got his research group at Notre Dame together and in a remarkably short time provided this paper.

Michael Pressley has publicly expressed reservations about the National Reading Panel's 2000 report, raising concerns about both its methodological narrowness (Pressley, 2001) and conceptual narrowness (Pressley, in press). As a group, we stand with those original conclusions, with most of us joining the standing ovation given to Pressley when he delivered his address at the National Reading Conference in San Antonio in December 2001—an ovation that reflected that he had captured the frustration about the NRP felt by many.

In the three months since that address was delivered, much has happened. Pressley has been touring the country talking about literacy research, particularly comprehension instruction, focusing on the new directions being identified by cutting-edge researchers (Block & Pressley, 2002; Pressley, 2002a). Comprehension instruction researchers believe that comprehension should be the primary goal of elementary reading instruction—that reading is about understanding, not just recognizing the words.

Audiences have responded with enthusiasm to Pressley's summaries of the recent work on comprehension instruction, and many listeners have said that they find his presentation refreshing given the barrage of pressure to focus on word level skills alone—on the alphabetics that were so emphasized in the National Reading Panel's report.

Supporters of the panel could respond that comprehension was certainly included in the report. Well, yes; but somehow in discussion after discussion about the report and its implications for instruction in the United States, alphabetics has been emphasized to the exclusion of almost everything else. In March 2002, Pressley attended a meeting in Washington D.C. that was sponsored by the Secretary of Education and intended to brief the states about how to secure Reading First and Early Learning First funds. The message was clear: The proposals that succeeded would be the ones for getting scientifically defensible instruction into schools. But speaker after speaker had something to say about phonemic awareness and phonics, with only the occasional mention of comprehension. Videos shown to the audience were of children learning to sound out words, rather than of children learning how to grapple with complex meanings in text.

One perspective that was offered during this meeting was that schools should buy reading programs that include scientifically validated instruction. As the author of one of the favored programs, Pressley might have taken heart, except that the sense conveyed during the meeting was that the program he co-authored was nothing more than instruction in phonemic awareness and phonics. Although this program balances alphabetic skills instruction and holistic literary experiences, little mention was made of the idea that it is important for primary-grade reading to include holistic experiences, such as reading and discussing excellent literature and writing. Small wonder that many in the audience seemed to feel that they could encourage schools simply to add more alphabetics to their instruction in order to be eligible for the federal government's Early Learning First and Reading First funds.

Just this morning, Pressley met with some Hawaii school officials. They have carefully assessed their students, and they know that most of their middle-grades elementary students can recognize the words that fourth and fifth graders should be expected to recognize. They also know that their students' comprehension is not what they would like it to be. They presented Pressley with very credible data that they have many "difference poor readers"—a 1960s term for readers who can decode the words in a text but fail to understand what they read (Wiener & Cromer, 1967). What was bugging these teachers was that they were receiving input from powerful people who were asserting that the NRP had concluded that what students with low standardized reading scores need is direct phonics instruction—that low scores on standardized reading tests are due to word recognition deficiencies. Educators who have worked hard to assess their children's deficiencies are in a better position to make instructional decisions than those who have only read a summary of a federal report that focused on alphabetics. Even well-meaning readers of the NRP report are likely to advocate instruction that is mismatched to the needs of the children they intend to help.

Since delivering his address to the National Reading Conference, Pressley has been confronted by well-informed educators who have concerns about the National Reading Panel's conclusions—conclusions that are being used to leverage curriculum decision making in directions that do not seem appropriate for many of the students they are teaching. In his interactions with these educators, Pressley has emphasized the need to balance skills instruction and holistic reading and writing (e.g., Pressley, 2002a), and that message is well received. The message is consistent with the very best primary-grades instruction (Pressley, Allington, et al., 2001), instruction that results in high student engagement and achievement. Effective primary teachers are exceptionally skilled at matching their teaching to the needs of individual students, and they successfully balance curriculum and instruction. They continuously monitor their students in order to provide them with instruction and experiences that are appropriately challenging to each learner and that keep each child moving upward. Effective primary classrooms are massively motivating. In them, you can see teachers doing something to motivate students every single moment of the school day, with these teachers using more than forty different well-validated motivational mechanisms each day (Bogner, Raphael, & Pressley, 2002). The classroom management is so good that it is impossible even to discern a teacher's discipline plan. The Pressley group has visited the classrooms of some effective teachers who do not have a single disciplinary event in the course of a year. These teachers often prevent disciplinary events from occurring by redirecting students quietly and quickly, with a minimum of disruption.

Excellent primary classrooms are inspiring. They are also complicated. We have yet to see an excellent classroom where all of the children were being taken through an overwhelmingly alphabetics-driven curriculum. Yes, alphabetics is covered, especially for the students who need it in excellent primary classrooms. But excellent teachers understand subtleties in the NRP report that the extreme advocates of phonics and skills instruction seem to miss: A skill like phonemic awareness does not require much instruction to develop. The NRP found that during the kindergarten year, eighteen hours total of phonemic awareness instruction—just thirty minutes a week, six minutes a day—provided maximum advantage. Systematic phonics instruction is useful. The National Reading Panel reported that the most intense phonics interventions are no more effective than programs that take much less time. What Pressley et al. (2001) observed was that effective teachers were providing as much skills instruction as individual students needed,

> Excellent primary classrooms are inspiring. They are also complicated. We have yet to see an excellent classroom where all of the children were being taken through an overwhelmingly alphabetics-driven curriculum.

with some getting a lot and others much less. Despite some federal officials' insinuations to the contrary, the reading program Pressley coauthors balances skills instruction, literature experiences, and writing, rather than being just a phonemic awareness program in kindergarten or a phonics program in grade one. Instruction that is carefully thought out by experienced teachers and curriculum developers who are fully informed about the research is not as extreme as the instruction that's being advocated by those who see the NRP report as a guide for beginning reading instruction.

While Pressley has been touring the country talking to educator groups, his graduate students have been hard at work on an important next step in the campaign for balanced, effective beginning literacy instruction. They have been reviewing the literature to identify the many elements of instruction that can boost reading achievement during the primary years, favoring the same kind of evidence that the National Reading Panel favored—validation in true experiments. Of course, some will immediately react that the panel members did not set out to catalog every instructional element that can increase reading achievement; rather, they decided in advance to favor only the elements that they felt were most likely to be important. That would have been all right if those who present the panel's conclusions to others would remind their listeners and readers of that decision, but they do not. Instead, they act as if the only interventions that are scientifically validated are the ones covered in the NRP report. And that is simply not true.

We are currently preparing a book-length summary of the interventions that have at least some validation in improving primary-level reading achievement. We could not possibly do justice here to what we have found. What we offer to conclude this chapter is a preview of what we will be reporting in our book. We hope this preview will whet your appetite not just for our forthcoming book, but for a broad exploration of the elements that should be included in primary-grades reading instruction. Such elements deserve a place in the work of any teacher who is determined to provide primary-grades literacy instruction that is scientifically informed.

Scientific Findings the NRP Did Not Report

We were taken back by the NRP's neglect of the preschool years. Waiting for children to arrive at the kindergarten classroom door before worrying about their literacy development is contrary to the scientific data. Indeed, given what we know, it is absolutely indefensible that the NRP ignored interventions that can affect children's literacy development during the preschool years.

The richer the language a preschooler experiences, the richer the child's language development, including in ways that are critical to later reading achievement (see, for example, Scarborough, 2001). From an intervention perspective, it has been known since Whitehurst's seminal work (Whitehurst et al., 1994) that parents and others can learn to interact with their children over books in ways that stimulate language development. A more encompassing intervention is high quality preschool, which certainly has a positive impact on literacy-related language competencies (Barnett, 2001). High quality day care also has positive effects on preschoolers' language and cognitive development (National Institute of Child Health and Human Development Early Child Care Research Network, 2000), and is associated with later reading achievement (Peisner-Feinberg et al., 2001). *Sesame Street* has been positively affecting the literacy development of preschoolers for more than three decades (Rice et al., 1990). That there is a correlation between poverty and literacy underachievement is well established. Huston et al. (2001) carried out an important true experiment demonstrating that by reducing poverty through wage and other subsidies when children are preschoolers, it is possible to positively affect their later academic achievement. In

> The richer the language a preschooler experiences, the richer the child's language development, including in ways that are critical to later reading achievement.

short, there is a great deal of evidence that it is possible to intervene during the preschool years to promote literacy achievement.

An even greater variety of interventions affect literacy achievement during the elementary years. Just attending school makes a difference (Ceci, 1991; Crone & Whitehurst, 1999). Attending a school that takes improving student literacy very seriously is even better, with the effective schools research making clear that some schools are more effective than other schools serving similar student populations. The more effective schools have principals who prioritize academic achievement, focusing their resources on basic literacy and numeracy to the exclusion of all else, and project to both teachers and students their high expectations for achievement in the school to be impressive—and their belief that every student can achieve (see Firestone, 1991; Hoffman, 1991; Taylor, Pearson, Clark, & Walpole, 2000).

As the authors of this chapter note, there are non-educational interventions that have demonstrated positive effects on reading achievement that rarely are featured in educational policy discussions. Some of these studies are "scientific" in that they used random assignment and replicable intervention designs. One example is the two-year experimental test of an employment-based anti-poverty program with three primary components: a) wage supports to raise family income above the poverty threshold, b) subsidies for child care, and c) health insurance. The average participating family received approximately $1200 per month in such support. The 379 parents randomly selected to participate were overwhelmingly female (90 percent), half of whom had not completed high school and half who had three or more children. Nine out of ten of these parents earned less than $10,000 in the year preceding the beginning of the study.

Over the course of a two-year period parents in the experimental program could tap any of the three sources of financial supports as needed. The primary educational impacts of this experiment were observed on boys in the project. Program boys had academic achievement significantly higher than control boys (ES=.33), better social behavior (ES=.50), higher expectations for educational attainment (ES=.57), and were less likely to have been retained in grade or identified as a pupil with a disability. While positive academic achievement effects were observed for girls in the program, that effect was smaller (ES=.12). Few other differences between program and control girls were observed.

Given the greater vulnerability of boys, especially poor boys, to early reading difficulties and school failure, one wonders why experimental interventions such as this one are not being widely supported in the political arena. The observed effects were as large or larger than the observed effects for systematic phonics interventions and larger than the effects observed in most schoolwide systemic reform efforts. Why is giving poor families direct financial support less attractive than giving that support to educational bureaucracies and for-profit educational concerns?

From: Huston, A. C., Duncan, G. J., Granger, R., Bos, J., McLoyd, V., Mistry, R., Crosby, D., Gibson, C., Magnuson, K., Romich, J., & Ventura, A. (2001). Work-based antipoverty programs for parents can enhance the school performance and social behavior of children. *Child Development*, 72(1), 318–336.

At the classroom level, there is much that primary-grades teachers can do to improve literacy achievement. For example, during the process-product era of research (the 1960s and 1970s), many teacher behaviors were identified as being associated with increased literacy achievement in the primary grades (e.g., efficient transitions, practice opportunities for individual students, ordered turn-taking, minimizing call outs, sustained feedback, and moderate but specific use of praise): When teachers change their teaching in the direction of these behaviors, reading achievement improves (Anderson, Evertson, & Brophy, 1979).

School districts can make decisions about classroom organization that will positively affect literacy achievement. For example, they can reduce class size (Finn & Achilles, 1990). Experiencing several years of small classes has a greater impact on a child's long-term achievement than having just one year in a small class does (Finn et al., 2001). Indeed, being in small classes from kindergarten through grade three confers almost a full year of achievement advantage by the time a child has reached eighth grade.

Teachers can make decisions about classroom organization that affect achievement. They can decide to use cooperative learning procedures (Johnson & Johnson, 1975). They can set up their classrooms so that there is lots of peer tutoring (Arreaga-Mayer, Terry, & Greenwood, 1998; Fantuzzo & Ginsburg-Block, 1998; Fuchs, Fuchs, Mathes, & Simmons, 1997). They can ensure children are given lots of opportunities to read; for example, by providing books that they can read and reread at school and at home (Koskinen, et al., 2000). They can provide opportunities to read books. Reading children's literature improves children's attitudes toward reading (Morrow, O'Connor, & Smith, 1990) as it also teaches them the structures of stories (Dahl and Freppon, 1995) and expository writing (Duke and Kays, 1998). When children read literature, their vocabularies increase (Elley, 1998; Robbins and Ehri, 1994; Rosenhouse et al., 1997). Despite the unwillingness of the National Reading Panel to conclude that sustained silent reading affects reading achievement positively, there are at least a few interpretable studies that are consistent with this conclusion (Yoon and Won, 2001).

Technology is giving us new kinds of books, including talking books, that seem to improve sight-word and vocabulary development (McKenna & Watkins, 1994, 1995, 1996). The old technology of television can also play a role in literacy development during the elementary years. For example, the Public Broadcasting System's *Reading Between the Lions* aims to develop emergent literacy skills (concepts of print, phonemic awareness, letter-sound correspondences) as well as beginning word skills (e.g., sight-word recognition and vocabulary). The effects of this program are most pronounced for kindergarten children, especially those with reasonably developed emergent literacy skills (Linebarger, Kosanic, & Doku, in press). Slightly older children benefited from *The Electric Company*, a Public Broadcasting System production intended to stimulate a variety of primary-grades literacy skills (Ball & Bogatz, 1970). There is also high-quality informational television, such as that provided by the Discovery Channel, which also has a positive impact on literacy (Koolstra, van der Voort, & van der Kamp, 1997; Wright et al., 2001).

Primary-grades children who are experiencing reading difficulties benefit from tutoring, whether it is Reading Recovery instruction done by a highly trained teacher (Shanahan & Barr, 1995) or a less expensive approach, such as Early Steps (Morris, Tyner, & Perney, 2000; Santa & Høien, 1999). A very important finding in recent years is that even volunteer tutors, such as college students, can have a positive impact on the reading

> In reading the National Reading Panel's report and listening to the speakers at the Secretary of Education's meeting, Pressley found it striking that the government pays so little attention to writing as part of the literacy mix . . .

achievement of primary students (Fitzgerald, 2001). Effective tutoring typically includes explicit teaching of word-recognition skills, but it usually includes more than that.

In reading the National Reading Panel's report and listening to the speakers at the Secretary of Education's meeting, Pressley found it striking that the government pays so little attention to writing as part of the literacy mix: Writing is always prominent in the literacy instruction of effective primary-grades teachers. It should be, for it does affect literacy. For example, composing opportunities improve children's spelling (Graham, 2000). One of the most important educational research discoveries of the past quarter-century is that teaching students to plan, draft, and revise profoundly improves their writing, with many wrinkles about how to do so effectively having been identified (e.g., Englert, et al., 1991; Harris & Graham, 1996). No summary of scientifically-validated literacy instruction is complete without discussion of the work on composing.

To sum up, based on the work of our group and colleagues (e.g., Pressley, Allington, et al., 2001), we know that excellent primary-level instruction is complex. In light of our observations, it is difficult to accept the assertions of some that all U.S. primary schoolers require in order to become good readers is large doses of alphabetics. As working scientists, we have been aware for a very long time of a number of interventions that increase primary-grades reading achievement. We are now systematically organizing what we know and preparing a book on scientifically-validated instruction that improves literacy achievement in the primary grades. There is a great need for wider dissemination of such knowledge, for just as we have observed many primary-grades classrooms that are excellent, we have observed many that are not engaging and do not produce student literacy achievement as impressive as that of the exemplary classrooms showcased in our work (Pressley, Allington, et al., 2001). The United States cannot afford the narrow-mindedness of those who believe that the National Reading Panel's report should be a guide to primary-grades literacy instructional reform. Yes, the components the panel identified as validated should be included in primary-grades reading instruction, but there is much, much more that could and should be in the mix.

References

Anderson, L. M., Evertson, C. M., & Brophy, J. E. (1979). An experimental study of effective teaching in first-grade reading. *Elementary School Journal, 79,* 193–223.

Arreaga-Mayer, C., Terry, B. J., & Greenwood, C. R. (1998). Classwide peer tutoring. In K. Topping & S. Ehly (Eds.), *Peer-assisted learning*. Mahwah, NJ: Erlbaum.

Ball, S., & Bogatz, G. A. (1970). *The first year of "Sesame Street": An evaluation*. Princeton, NJ: Educational Testing Service.

Barnett , W. S. (2001). Preschool education for economically disadvantaged children: Effects on reading achievement and related outcomes. In S. B. Neuman & D. K. Dickinson (Eds.), *Handbook of early literacy research* (pp. 421–443). New York: Guilford.

Block, C. C., & Pressley, M. (Eds.). (2002). *Comprehension instruction*. New York: Guilford.

Bogner, K., Raphael, L. M., & Pressley, M. (2002). How grade-1 teachers motivate literate activity by their students. *Scientific Studies of Reading, 6*, 135–165.

Ceci, S. J. (1991). How much does schooling influence general intelligence and its cognitive components? A reassessment of the evidence. *Developmental Psychology, 27*, 703–722.

Crone, D. A., & Whitehurst, G. J. (1999). Age and schooling effects on emergent literacy and early reading skills. *Journal of Educational Psychology, 91*, 604–614.

Dahl, K. L., & Freppon, P. A. (1995). A comparison of inner-city children's interpretations of reading and writing instruction in the early grades in skills-based and whole language classrooms. *Reading Research Quarterly, 30*, 50–74.

Duke, N. K., & Kays, J. (1998). Can I say 'once upon a time'?: Kindergarten children developing knowledge of information book language. *Early Childhood Research Quarterly, 13* (2), 295–318.

Elley, W. B. (1996). Lifting literacy levels in developing countries: Some implications from an IEA study. In V. Greaney (Ed.), *Promoting reading in developing countries* (pp. 39–63). Newark, DE: International Reading Association.

Englert, C. S., Raphael, T. E., Anderson, L. M., Anthony, H. M., & Stevens, D. D. (1991). Making strategies and self-talk visible: Writing instruction in regular and special education classrooms. *American Educational Research Journal, 28*, 337–372.

Fantuzzo, J., & Ginsburg-Block, M. (1998). Reciprocal peer tutoring: Developing and testing effective peer collaborations for elementary school students. In K. Topping & S. Ehly (Eds.), *Peer-assisted learning*. Mahwah, NJ: Erlbaum.

Finn, J. D., & Achilles, C. M. (1990). Answers and questions about class size: A statewide experiment. *American Educational Research Journal, 27*, 557–577.

Finn, J., Gerber, S., Achilles, C., & Boyd-Zaharias, J. (2001). The enduring effects of small classes. *Teachers College Record, 103,* 145–183.

Firestone, W. A. (1991). Educators, researchers, and the effective schools movement. In J. R. Bliss, W. A. Firestone, & C. E. Richards (Eds.), *Rethinking effective schools research and practice* (pp. 12–27). Englewood Cliffs, NJ: Prentice-Hall.

Fitzgerald, J. (2001). Can minimally trained college student volunteers help young at-risk children to read better? *Reading Research Quarterly, 36,* 28–47.

Fuchs, D., Fuchs, L. S., Mathes, P. G., & Simmons, D. C. (1997). Peer-assisted learning strategies: Making classrooms more responsive to diversity. *American Educational Research Journal, 34,* 174–206.

Graham, S. (2000). Should the natural learning approach replace spelling instruction? *Journal of Educational Psychology, 92,* 235–247.

Harris, K. R., & Graham, S. (1996). *Making the writing process work: Strategies for composition and self-regulation.* Cambridge, MA: Brookline Books.

Hoffman, J. V. (1991). Teacher and school effects in learning to read. In R. Barr, M. L. Kamil, P. B. Mosenthal, & P. D. Pearson (Eds.), *Handbook of reading research, Vol. 2* (pp. 911–950). New York: Longman.

Huston, A. C., Duncan, G. J., Granger, R., Bos, J., McLoyd, V., Mistry, R., Crosby, D., Gibson, C., Magnuson, K., Romich, J., & Ventura, A. (2001). Work-based antipoverty programs for parents can enhance the school performance and social behavior of children. *Child Development, 72,* 318–336.

Johnson, D. W., & Johnson, R. T. (1975). *Learning together and alone.* Englewood Cliffs, NJ: Prentice-Hall.

Koolstra, C. M., van der Voort, T. H. A., & van der Kamp, L. J. T. (1997). Television's impact on children's reading comprehension and decoding skills: A 3-year panel study. *Reading Research Quarterly, 32,* 128–152.

Koskinen, P. S., Blum, I. H., Bisson, S. A., Phillips, S. M., Creamer, T. S., & Baker, T. K. (2000). Book access, shared reading, and audio models: The effects of supporting the literacy learning of linguistically diverse students in school and at home. *Journal of Educational Psychology, 92,* 23–36.

Linebarger, D. L., Kosanic, A., & Doku, N. S. (in press). Effects of viewing the television program *Between the Lions* on the emergent literacy skills of young children. *Journal of Educational Psychology.*

McKenna, M. C., & Watkins, J. H. (1994, December). *Computer-mediated books for beginning readers.* Paper presented at the meeting of the National Reading Conference, San Diego, CA.

McKenna, M. C., & Watkins, J. H. (1995, November). *Effects of computer-mediated books on the development of beginning readers.* Paper presented at the meeting of the National Reading Conference, New Orleans, LA.

McKenna, M. C., & Watkins, J .H. (1996, December). *The effects of computer-mediated trade books on sight word acquisition and the development of phonics ability.* Paper presented at the meeting of the National Reading Conference, Charleston, SC.

Morris, D., Tyner, B., & Perney, J. (2000). Early steps: Replicating the effects of a first-grade reading intervention program. *Journal of Educational Psychology, 92,* 681–693.

Morrow, L. M., O'Connor, E. M., & Smith, J. K. (1990). Effects of a story reading program on the literacy development of at-risk kindergarten children. *Journal of Reading Behavior, 22,* 255–275.

National Institute of Child Health and Human Development Early Child Care Research Network (2000). The relation of child care to cognitive and language development. *Child Development, 71,* 960–980.

National Reading Panel (2000). *Teaching children to read: An evidence-based assessment of the scientific research literature on reading and its implications for reading instruction: Reports of the subgroups.* Washington, DC: National Institute of Child Health and Human Development.

Peisner-Feinberg, E. S., Burchinal, M. R., Clifford, R. M., Culkin, M. L., Howes, C., Kagan, S. L., & Yazejian, N. (2001). The relation of preschool child-care quality to children's cognitive and social developmental trajectories through second grade. *Child Development, 72,* 1534–1553.

Pressley, M. (in press). Effective beginning reading instruction: A paper commissioned by the National Reading Conference. *Journal of Literacy Research.*

Pressley, M. (2001, December). *What I have learned up until now about research methods in reading education.* Presented at the 50th annual meeting of the National Reading Conference, San Antonio.

Pressley, M. (2002a). Comprehension strategies instruction: A turn-of-the-century status report. In M. Pressley & C. C. Block (Eds.), *Comprehension instruction* (pp. 11–27). New York: Guilford.

Pressley, M. (2002b). *Reading instruction that works: The case for balanced teaching* (2nd ed.). New York: Guilford.

Pressley, M., Allington, R., Wharton-McDonald, R., Block, C. C., & Morrow, L. M. (2001). *Learning to read: Lessons from exemplary first grade classrooms.* New York: Guilford.

Rice, M. L., Huston, A. C., Truglio, R., & Wright, L. C. (1990). Words from "Sesame Street": Learning vocabulary while viewing. *Developmental Psychology, 26,* 421–428.

Robbins, C., & Ehri, L. C. (1994). Reading storybooks to kindergartners helps them learn new vocabulary words. *Journal of Educational Psychology, 86,* 54–64.

Rosengren, K. E., & Windahl, S. (1989). *Media matter: TV use in childhood and adolescence.* Norwood, NJ: Ablex.

Rosenhouse, J., Feitelson, D., Kita, B., & Goldstein, Z. (1997). Interactive reading aloud to Israeli first graders: Its contribution to literacy development. *Reading Research Quarterly, 32,* 168–183.

Santa, C. M., & Høien, T. (1999). The assessment of Early Steps: A program for early intervention of reading problems. *Reading Research Quarterly, 34,* 54–79.

Scarborough, H. S. (2001). Connecting early language and literacy to later reading (dis)abilities: Evidence, theory, and practice. In S. B. Neuman & D. K. Dickinson (Eds.), *Handbook of early literacy research* (pp. 97–110). New York: Guilford.

Shanahan, T., & Barr, R. (1995). Reading Recovery: An independent evaluation of the effects of an early instructional intervention for at-risk learners. *Reading Research Quarterly, 30,* 958–996.

Taylor, B. M., Pearson, P. D., Clark, K., Walpole, S. (2000). Effective schools and accomplished teachers: Lessons from primary-grade reading instruction in low-income schools. *Elementary School Journal, 101,* 121–165.

Whitehurst, G. J., Arnold, D. H., Epstein, J. N., Angell, A. L., Smith, M., & Fischel, J. E. (1994). A picture book reading intervention in day care and home for children from low-income families. *Developmental Psychology, 30,* 679–689.

Wiener, M., & Cromer, W. (1967). Reading and reading difficulty: A conceptual analysis. *Harvard Educational Review, 37,* 620–643.

Wright, J. C., Huston, A. C., Murphy, K. C., St. Peters, M., Piñon, M., Scantlin, R., & Kotler, J. (2001). Yager, S. Johnson, D. W., & Johnson, R. T. (1985). Oral discussion, group-to-individual transfer, and achievement in cooperative learning groups. *Journal of Educational Psychology, 77*(1), 60–66.

Yoon, J-C., & Won, J-S. (2001, December). *Three decades of sustained silent reading: A meta-review of its effects on reading attitude and reading comprehension.* Presented at the 51st annual meeting of the National Reading Conference, San Antonio, TX.

4 ■ Beyond the Smoke and Mirrors: A Critique of the National Reading Panel Report on Phonics

Elaine M. Garan
California State University, Fresno

Elaine Garan brought to my attention the discrepancies between the original NRP report and the Summary. Like a good skeptic, I accepted her challenge and went to the pages she cited just to make sure her reporting was accurate. It is.

For many of the reasons outlined by Jim Cunningham (Chapter 2) and Mike Pressley (Chapter 3), I hadn't actually read the Summary. It sat undisturbed on a shelf in my office. Having read the full report (500-plus pages), I thought that the NRP had been sufficiently circumspect in its conclusions given the narrow methodological and conceptual box that the members had created for themselves. I was resigned to the fact that, given the restrictions the panel placed on itself, there was little else it could have found. However, because of those restrictions, I found the report of little use in thinking about real children in real classrooms. Anyone who has spent any time in primary classrooms knows that using an add-on, external expert intervention model to research how to teach reading is an enormously flawed approach that disregards the complexities of classroom life and learning. I was perturbed that the NRP report was seen by policy makers as having something important to say (Allington, 2001).

But Elaine's exposé rocked me. I guess I should have expected that ideology would trump evidence, given the findings of Anne McGill-Franzen's and my four years of studying reading policy in Texas and California (Allington, 1999; McGill-Franzen, 2000). But for some reason, it hadn't occurred to me that it would be this easy to politicize both the NRP and the U.S. Department of Education. It's one thing when profiteers and ideologues (sometimes one and the same) distort the research to fit their agendas, but it is something quite different when the distortion carries the imprimatur of the federal government.

Elaine has written a slender but powerful book, Resisting Reading Mandates *(Heinemann 2002), that extends the findings she reports in this paper. Every reading professional in the country should have a copy—and every one of them should be mad as hell at the ideological sleight of hand that she documents.*

When it was released in April 1999, the report of the National Reading Panel (NRP) on the research on phonics instruction splashed down in the midst of a wave of controversy. In the ensuing philosophical turmoil, I reread with interest the "Editor's Page" in the March 1989 issue of the *Kappan.* At that time, many readers vehemently objected to the publication of "Debunking the Great Phonics Myth," Marie Carbo's critique of the research base for Jeanne Chall's *Learning to Read: The Great Debate.* I found it fascinating that the respondents tended to react to Carbo's challenge in ways that were in line with their basic philosophies rather than to critique the merits of her analysis. For many readers, the central issue was whether they agreed or disagreed with Chall's findings, rather than whether or not those findings were based on sound research protocols.

Indeed, some readers believed that it was inappropriate for Carbo to challenge Chall's research at all. They viewed the critique as a personal attack on Chall herself, and chastised the *Kappan* for publishing the article. Editor Pauline Gough responded, "It is entirely proper—indeed, essential—for a profession to examine its knowledge base at periodic intervals. *Without prejudice. . . .* We expect physicians to thoughtfully examine their knowledge base—not to rely on intuition—and then to modify their practices accordingly. Should we expect less from educators? . . . Knowledge advances through just such thoughtful give-and-take."[1]

I remind readers of this advice at the outset. Please try to set aside your own beliefs and "thoughtfully and without prejudice" critique with me the research summarized in the NRP's subgroup report on phonics. My purpose here is not to engage in the never-ending debate over whether code-first (i.e., phonics) or meaning-first instruction works best in teaching reading, the perennial issue that bubbles at the white-hot center of the interminable Reading Wars. Nor do I wish to take sides in the ancillary debate over the relative merits or demerits of quantitative versus qualitative methods of research. Rather, I request simply that we approach our mission as responsible professionals and ask only, "Is the NRP report on phonics based on sound research?" The following critique answers this question.

Background of the National Reading Panel

In 1997 Congress asked the director of the National Institute of Child Health and Human Development (NICHD) to appoint a panel to conduct a comprehensive investigation of research in the field of reading. The NRP was charged with compiling a report assessing "the status of research-based knowledge, including the effectiveness of various approaches to teaching children to read," and, if appropriate, with designing "a strategy for rapidly disseminating this information to facilitate effective instruction in the schools." In its 13 April 2000 press release, NRP members and Duane Alexander, the director of NICHD, hailed the NRP report as a landmark contribution to education that "clearly articulates the most comprehensive review of existing reading research to be undertaken in American education." Donald Langenberg, chair of the panel, states that the NRP "was committed to identifying the most reliable research so it can be put into practice in all classrooms in America."

The NRP report certainly seems destined to have considerable clout. Backed by Congress and the NICHD, it has an unprecedented potential for affecting reading instruction in the U.S. Before the recommendations of the NRP report are put into practice in classrooms, it is vital, then, that we carefully examine its analysis from a research perspective and resist the temptation to react to the findings alone.

The Organization of the Report

Whenever research is presented, the citations must be clear and the references identified. However, readers of the NRP report will find the cross-checking of information at best confusing because the NRP published at least two different versions of the report, without distinguishing between the various editions. The original, posted on the NRP website in April 2000, did not include a complete table of contents. Not listed was the "minority report" by panel member Joanne Yatvin, which was originally included at the end of the nearly 600-page document. Then, without indicating that any changes had been made in the document, the panel at some later date posted a second version of the NRP report in which the text was altered and in which Yatvin's minority report was listed in the table of contents. Therefore, it is difficult for readers using different versions of the NRP report to check the information. (In this article, I will cite page numbers from the version currently posted on the Web.)

To further the confusion, the NRP report exists in three separate "formats," all of which have the title *Report of the National Reading Panel: Teaching Children to Read: An Evidence-Based Assessment of the Scientific Research Literature on Reading and Its Implications for Reading Instruction.* I have distinguished between the three formats (not to be confused with the different *versions*) as follows: 1) *Summary* indicates a 34-page overview, which appears when you go to the NRP website, <www.nichd.nih.gov/publications/nrp/smallbook.htm>; 2) *Reports of the Subgroups* refers to the nearly 600-page document that contains the data, discussion, tables, and appendices and can be downloaded as a PDF file from the same site; and 3) NRP video refers to a publicity video distributed by NICHD that promotes the research without any mention of the limitations of the panel's analysis.

Yet more confusion results from the fact that the panel incorrectly listed the studies used in the meta-analysis. Appendix A of the Phonics Subgroup Report,[2] titled "Studies Included in the Meta-analysis" (*Reports of the Subgroups,* p. 2:145), includes a total of 49 studies. However, the discussion section and Appendix G of the Phonics Subgroup Report list only 38 studies. Such unfortunate inaccuracy is at odds with the panel's claims of scientific rigor and makes it difficult to see how "anyone can check the veracity of any claim."[3] (Both Appendix A and Appendix G can be found at <www.nichd.nih.gov/publications/nrp/smallbook.htm>.)

Methodology Employed

Before examining the quality of the panel's analysis, let me present a brief overview of the process of selecting studies and of the methodology used to evaluate them. The process began with a series of questions concerning phonics instruction that the panel selected as being relevant; next the panel set criteria for inclusion.[4] The NRP *Summary* states:

> *In what may be its most important action, the Panel then developed a set of rigorous research methodological standards. . . . This screening process identified a final set of experimental or quasi-experimental research studies that were then subjected to detailed analysis. The evidence-based methodological standards adopted by the Panel are essentially those normally used in research studies of the efficacy of interventions in psychological and medical research. These include behaviorally based interventions, medications, or medical procedures proposed for use in the fostering of robust health and psychological development and the prevention or treatment of disease.* (Summary, *p. 8*)

In addition to requiring experimental or quasi-experimental control groups, other basic selection criteria were established. Each study had to "measure reading as an outcome" and include descriptions of participants, interventions, study methods, and outcome measures in sufficient detail to "contribute to the validity of any conclusions drawn" (*Summary*, p. 28). From the "potentially relevant" list of 75 studies, 37 were eliminated. The *Summary* continues, "Unfortunately, only a small fraction of the total reading research literature [38 studies] met the Panel's standards for use in the topic analysis." Nevertheless, the NRP conducted a meta-analysis on the unfortunately small number they eventually selected. As most readers know, a meta-analysis compares results across many research studies, all of which must assess a common outcome or dependent variable. Therefore, the greater the number of studies, the more reliable the results of the meta-analysis. The NRP's claim to a comprehensive, scientific review of reading research on phonics—based on a mere 38 studies for a meta-analysis—makes the reliability of its conclusions questionable from the outset.

The NRP determined that the studies it did include had to address the impact of phonics instruction on one or more of six isolated reading skills. The panel did not include reading comprehension or the application of phonics skills in authentic literacy events as necessary criteria in establishing what it termed a "general literacy" outcome. The discrete, isolated subcategories that the panel considered as representing "growth in reading" were:

- *Decoding*. This subcategory assessed the reading of words with regular spelling patterns in isolation—for example, "cat," "fat," "mat."
- *Pseudowords*. This subcategory assessed children's ability to "read" pseudowords with regular spelling patterns—for example, "dat," "wat," "gat."
- *Word identification*. This subcategory assessed children's ability to read words in isolation; some consisted of regular spelling patterns, while others did not.
- *Spelling*. This subcategory assessed children's ability to spell words. With children in kindergarten and first grade, invented spelling was accepted—for example, "fet" for "feet" and "kr" for "car"; for older children (grades 2 through 6), only conventional spelling was accepted.

- *Oral reading.* No description of oral reading was provided.
- *Comprehension.* For younger children, this usually involved "extremely short (usually one sentence) 'passages.'" Often the assessments used favored "phonetically regular words" (*Reports of the Subgroups,* p. 2:115). For older children, the assessments usually involved passages from standardized tests or were developed by the researchers for training purposes.
- *General reading/general literacy.* The effect sizes (the size of impact of a treatment) for all the subcategories above were combined for each of the 38 studies to produce a measure of what was termed "general literacy."[5] The general literacy effect size for each study was averaged across all the studies and groups. Although a study could assess six subcategories, most looked at no more than two or three. Some studies tested only one subcategory. Few studies tested for all six, and the majority of the comparisons (76%) focused on single words or pseudowords, rather than on comprehension. According to Appendix G of the Phonics Subgroup Report (*Reports of the Subgroups,* p. 2:169 through p. 2:175), only two of the individual studies (numbers 55 and 72) actually assessed or used a term such as "general literacy" or "reading growth" as an outcome measure. Thus "general literacy" was not assessed in 36 of the 38 studies but was a term assigned by the NRP that could—and sometimes did—refer to a single outcome, such as "word identification" (study number 52). The averaged, overall effect size of these "general literacy" outcomes across the treatments was determined by the NRP to represent "reading growth."

> [T]he majority of the comparisons (76%) focused on single words or pseudowords, rather than on comprehension.

It is important to note that the means across the studies were inconsistent in two ways: 1) in the number of discrete skills (subcategories the studies assessed) and 2) in the types of skills those comparisons represented. In other words, the "general literacy" effect size from a study that looked at one or two outcomes (e.g., "decoding" or "word identification") influenced the overall effect size as much as a study that assessed more subcategories. Therefore, an outcome assessing only isolated skills had as much of an impact on the overall effect size as a study that also tested for "comprehension." I will discuss the implications of this decision below. (See Table 1 of this article for the overall results of the NRP's meta-analysis and for effect sizes for the individual subcategories.)

The effect sizes for each subcategory, as well as the general effect size, were measured in standard deviation units. The mean for each of the subcategories in each study was calculated and expressed as 0. Thus an effect size of 0 indicates that there was no difference between the results for the treatment and control groups. An effect size of 1.0 indicates that the treatment group mean was one standard deviation higher than the control group mean. The NRP decided that an effect size of .20 is small, an effect size of .50 is moderate, and an effect size of .80 is large. For a more detailed description of the statistical procedures the NRP used, see the section "Coding the Data" in the *Summary* (pp. 30–33).

A Critique of the Research

Let us now examine the quality of the research in terms of whether: 1) the research base was appropriate for a meta-analysis, 2) the findings were generalizable based on the studies' student populations and sampling sizes, 3) the results were reliable, 4) the NRP's research was valid (that is, the research methodology examined what the NRP determined was important), and 5) the NRP accurately represented the data in its conclusions.

APPROPRIATENESS OF THE RESEARCH BASE

Meta-analysis, a term coined in 1976 by Gene Glass, is an approach that makes it possible to summarize the results of individual experiments across a large number of studies. While a

TABLE 1.
Results of the National Reading Panel's Analysis of Phonics Instruction

	Effect Sizes for the Subcategories						
	Decoding Words with regular spelling patterns only	Pseudoword Reading nonwords with regular spelling patterns only	Word Identification Some words irregularly spelled	Spelling	Oral Reading	Comprehension	General Reading Effect size of all categories
At-risk kindergarten and first-grade students	.98 high	.67 moderate	.45 small	.67 moderate Accepted invented spellings	.23 small Based on two K and four first-grade studies	.51 moderate Based on one K and 10 first-grade studies	.56 (K) and .54 (first grade) moderate
Grades 2–6, disabled and low-achieving readers*	.49 small to moderate	.52 moderate	.33 small	Not significant	.24 small	Not significant	Not significant

*The database may have included too few studies of low-achieving readers (eight) to draw firm conslusions.

meta-analysis does not require that the same instrument be used in each of the studies, it does require that the studies involved assess the same conceptual outcome or dependent variable.[6]

The NRP's meta-analysis fails to meet both of these basic criteria. First, the panel included only 38 studies, a number that even it calls "unfortunately" limited (*Summary*, p. 8). Furthermore, after its rigorous screening process and after it had already analyzed the data, the NRP concluded, "There may [have been] too few studies of low-achieving readers in the database (only eight) to draw firm conclusions," and the results may not "even [be] reliable" (*Reports of the Subgroups*, pp. 2:117, 2:94). Those studies that the NRP dismissed as being of questionable reliability were also those that produced nonsignificant results for "spelling," for "comprehension," and for the "general reading" outcomes for low-achieving readers in grades 2 through 6. Here, we can conclude, based on the panel's own determination, that only 30 studies in the meta-analysis maintained even the *possibility* of reliable, generalizable results. I'll examine the reliability of the eight dismissed studies, as well as of the other 30, when I consider reliability below.

The NRP's research fails to meet the requirement that the studies' outcomes—the dependent variables across studies—be conceptually consistent. As noted previously, most of the studies (76%) assessed isolated skills, while only 24% required that children apply their skills to actual text. Proficiency in isolated skills and the authentic application of those skills (comprehension) are *not* conceptually consistent outcomes. For example, sounding out the word *ilk* and understanding its meaning are separate concepts.

In fact, the NRP's own meta-analysis clearly establishes that it is possible for children to perform phonics tasks in isolation and yet not apply those skills to authentic literacy events, such as comprehension or spelling. That is, with the exception of a weak, statistically significant effect size of .24 for "oral reading," the NRP's analysis shows that systematic phonics resulted in significant outcomes *only* on those subcategories assessing phonetically regular words or words tested in isolation for grades 2 through 6. Phonics had no statistically significant impact on tasks requiring authentic application. "Spelling" and "comprehension" outcomes for these children were not statistically significant (effect sizes of .09 and .12 respectively). In fact, in referring to the "older children" (those in grades 2 through 6), the NRP states, "Phonics instruction appears to contribute only weakly, *if at all*, in helping . . . apply these skills to read text and to spell words" (*Reports of the Subgroups*, p. 2:116, emphasis added). This discrepancy firmly establishes the conceptual dissimilarity between proficiency in isolated skills and in those required for the more complex processes needed for comprehension. In fact, the NRP alludes to the conceptual inconsistency in the following statements: "The imbalance favoring single words is not surprising given that the focus of phonics instruction is on improving children's ability to read and spell words" (*Reports of the Subgroups*, p. 2:92) and "the purpose of this practice [phonics instruction] is centered on word recognition rather than on comprehending and thinking about the meaning of what is being read. This may be another reason why effect sizes on text comprehension were smaller than effect sizes on word reading" (*Reports of the Subgroups*, p. 2:123).

In summary, then, the NRP report fails to meet the criteria for a sound meta-analysis for two reasons: 1) the small number of studies seriously compromises the reliability of the results, and 2) the dependent variables of the meta-analysis are conceptually inconsistent.

GENERALIZABILITY OF RESULTS

Let me now turn our attention to the generalizability of the reported results to student populations and classroom environments throughout the nation. I will also examine the chronological context during which the studies were conducted.

Student populations. The NRP states that its meta-analysis is based on "studies that examined the effectiveness of phonics programs with three types of problem readers: children in kindergarten or first grade who were at risk for developing reading problems; older . . . disabled readers; [and] low achieving readers" (*Reports of the Subgroups*, p. 2:90). The NRP concludes, many pages later, "There were insufficient data to draw any conclusions about the effects of phonics instruction with normally developing readers above first grade" (*Reports of the Subgroups*, p. 2:116).

Compare the preceding quotation with this one:

Findings . . . regarding the effectiveness of systematic phonics in-struction were derived from studies conducted in many classrooms with typical classroom teachers and typical American or English-speaking students from a variety of backgrounds. . . . Thus the re-sults of the analysis are indicative of what can be accomplished when systematic phonics programs are implemented in today's classrooms. (Reports of the Subgroups, *pp.* 2:96, 2:135)

Thus this meta-analysis began with three groups of problem read-ers, and it ended by generalizing the results to typical children in today's classrooms.

The NRP's analysis included studies with such titles as "Can Dyslexia Be Treated? Treatment-Specific and Generalized Treat-ment Effects in Dyslexic Children's Response to Remediation."[7] Such narrowly focused research does not include "typical" chil-dren, nor can the results be generalized to them. "Typical" U.S. classrooms include normally achieving students, high-achieving students, and students with limited proficiency in English—three major categories of children that the NRP chose to exclude from its analysis. Furthermore, in some states, such as California, chil-dren with limited proficiency in English *are* the "typical" student population. The insufficient data on normally progressing read-ers, coupled with the exclusion of other important student popu-lations, indicate that the NRP phonics results are not generalizable to typical classrooms.

CLASSROOM ENVIRONMENTS AND METHODS USED IN THE STUDIES

Classroom environments and social contexts are important fac-tors influencing instruction. Jeanne Chall and Shirley Feldmann found that there is considerable variation in instruction even in classrooms whose teachers profess to use the same methods.[8] These differences are confounded when we include foreign con-texts, and, of the 38 studies that the NRP analyzed, nine were done in foreign countries (*Reports of the Subgroups*, p. 2:112). Al-though the foreign countries involved in the studies were English speaking, we cannot assume that the social and instructional environments were typical of those in the U.S. and could be generalized to U.S. classrooms.

The majority of the studies (28 of the 38 as indicated in Appendix D of the Phonics Subgroup Report) involved commercial phonics programs as the treatments. The NRP states that "some" of the phonics programs were scripted, thus largely eliminating the role of the teacher. Furthermore, still others required "a sophisticated understanding of spelling, structural linguistics, and word etymology" (*Reports of the Subgroups,* p. 2:135). Again, the use of scripted programs in some instances and the need for teacher training to implement other programs are conditions that do not typify most classrooms.

Time periods. Of the 38 studies analyzed, 10 were conducted more than a decade ago (*Reports of the Subgroups,* Appendix G, p. 2:169 through p. 2:175). This time element is important because in some studies basal readers were used in treatment groups, while in other studies from different eras they were used in control groups. Basal readers, as the NRP notes, have changed over the years and are "presumably more eclectic" than they were in earlier years (*Reports of the Subgroups,* p. 2:124). As the NRP notes, the chronological context of the study affects the validity of the analysis as well as its generalizability. The panel states:

> *Perhaps the reading instruction experienced by students in control groups included more phonics than the reading instruction received by control groups in earlier years. . . . Table 2 identifies the control groups used in studies in the corpus. Whereas some groups were true "no-phonics" controls, other groups received some phonics instruction. It may be that, instead of examining the difference between phonics instruction and no phonics instruction, a substantial number of studies [in the meta-analysis] actually compared more systematic phonics instruction to less phonics instruction.* (Reports of the Subgroups, p. 2:124)

Recall that the NRP staked a claim to rigorous, scientific screening, which suggests that it knew the characteristics of the studies selected for analysis. Now ask why the NRP decided only after analyzing the data that the treatment and control groups might have been inappropriate and that the outcomes were based on conceptually incompatible dependent variables. If this was the case, how did they then generalize the results to "typical" populations in the *Summary* and NRP video?

Here, let me pause to revisit one of the basic issues in research: because everyone in a given population cannot be tested, researchers must select a sample. That sample must be a subset of the larger population to which the results will be generalized. Here is Neil Salkind on the matter of sampling: "Good sampling requires maximizing the degree to which this selected group represents the population. . . . For it is only if the results can be generalized from a sample to a greater population that the results of research have meaning beyond the limited setting in which they were originally obtained."[9] In terms of location, inconsistencies between treatment and control groups, time frames of studies, and especially the narrowness of sampling of student population, the studies in the meta-analysis do not represent a subset of the larger student population and classroom environments to which the NRP generalizes its findings. In light of this background information, consider carefully the panel's conclusions, "Thus, the results of the analysis are indicative of what can be accomplished when explicit, systematic phonics programs are implemented in today's classrooms" (*Summary*, p. 13).

RELIABILITY

Before I discuss the importance of reliability in a study, we should pause to refresh our memories about related statistical terminology. Statistical reliability can be defined as the degree to which the results of a given study are predictable or consistent. Are the findings unique, or are they truly indicative of what we can expect from a given assessment or treatment? That is, does a test measure the same behavior or performance each time it is used, and does it result in similar outcomes? While the term is generally applied to testing instruments, the NRP applies both *reliability* and *validity* (discussed below) to the process and conclusions of its meta-analysis.[10]

Recall that the NRP, after its "rigorous" screening procedures, determined that the outcomes for low-achieving readers were "inconclusive" because there were too few studies (eight) to ensure a reasonable expectation of reliability (*Reports of the Subgroups*, pp. 2:117, 2:94). However, the NRP did not question the reliability of the nine studies involving students with reading disabilities, studies that incidentally produced slightly higher results in "comprehension" and "general reading" outcomes than those for "low-achieving readers." Eight was too few. Nine was just fine.

> Based on only one comparison, the panel concludes that phonics affects the "comprehension" of kindergartners.

Moreover, throughout the report, the panel drew conclusions and generalized from findings drawn from far fewer than eight studies.

- Based on only one comparison, the panel concludes that phonics affects the "comprehension" of kindergartners; the "comprehension" results for first grade are based on six studies and 10 comparisons (*Reports of the Subgroups*, p. 2:115; see also Appendix G, p. 2:169 through p. 2:175).

- Based on only two kindergarten and four first-grade comparisons (two and four studies respectively), the panel concludes that systematic phonics affects the "oral reading" of "younger children" (*Reports of the Subgroups*, p. 2:115; see also Appendix G, p. 2:169 through p. 2:175). Both kindergarten studies had effect sizes that were not significant (.13 and .15). Two of the four "oral reading" effect sizes for first grade were not significant (0 and .03). These non-significant effect sizes were influenced by the two effect sizes in "oral reading" that were significant (8.79 and 2.18). It is not clear whether the panel adjusted these two effect sizes that appear to be large outliers (*Reports of the Subgroups*, Appendix G, p. 2:169 through p. 2:175). Based on so few studies with such uneven results, it is unlikely that the outcome for oral reading is reliable.

The studies analyzed by the NRP are also limited in terms of the numbers of children involved. While it is certainly important to keep in mind that we are dealing with a total of only 38 studies, it is also important to consider that 38% of them included fewer than 40 students. Moreover, two studies involved just 20 children (*Reports of the Subgroups*, Appendix G, p. 2:169 through 2:175). Thus the comprehensive, landmark research of the National Reading Panel involves a limited number of studies of a narrow population involving small numbers of children. And yet these results were generalized to include normal student populations in typical classrooms.

If we ignore the contradictions inherent in the NRP's conclusions as they are reported in the *Summary* and accept the statements in the lengthy *Reports of the Subgroups*, we see that the NRP itself recognized that, in terms of reliability and generalizability, its report is an extremely flawed research effort.

VALIDITY

Let us pause here to revisit the concept of "validity" and its relationship to "reliability." Reliability is a necessary, but not sufficient, condition for validity. That is, to be valid, a measure must first be reliable. In summarizing the analysis of the reliability and generalizability of the NRP report on phonics thus far, note that we have agreed with the panel's conclusions that there are too few studies above first grade and too few studies below first grade from which to draw conclusions. By applying basic principles of research, we have established that the results of the NRP analysis are *not* generalizable to typical student populations and classroom environments. Given these severe limitations, it is hardly necessary to continue. Nevertheless, I will now very briefly address the issue of validity. Do the outcomes of the NRP's meta-analysis actually reflect what they were intended to measure?

The results of the meta-analysis produced a "general literacy" or "general reading" outcome. The NRP's intention in determining a "general literacy" outcome and what it meant by using the term "reading growth" remain unclear. That is, the NRP does not articulate a cogent definition of the reading process in *Teaching Children to Read*. The panel does, however, state that phonics is but a tool, "a means to an end," the ultimate goal of which is to ensure that children "know how to apply this knowledge in their reading and writing" (*Reports of the Subgroups*,

p. 2:96). If this is, indeed, the NRP's philosophy with regard to the role of phonics in instruction, then the report is fatally flawed. Only 24% of the comparisons examined the impact of phonics on reading texts, and this 24% included both oral reading and comprehension. Of course, as any teacher of reading knows, it is possible for a child to "call" words without comprehending them. Therefore, less than the 24% of the total studies actually looked at what the NRP itself declared to be the essential outcome of phonics instruction: comprehension and the meaningful application of phonics skills (*Reports of the Subgroups*, p. 2:111).

The NRP cautions, "Educators must keep the end in mind and ensure that children understand the purpose of learning letter sounds" (*Summary*, p. 14). Ironically, the NRP neglected to take its own advice and focused primarily on studies that had nothing to do with what it declared to be the ultimate goal of phonics instruction.

ACCURACY OF THE DATA REPORTED

At the outset, let us note some important observations about educational research. First, it seldom proves anything. As a rule, educational research raises more questions than it answers, and it is notoriously vulnerable to interpretation both by the researchers and by the audience, all of whom bring their own philosophies to the table. Second, the results of educational research involve a leap of faith of sorts for the reviewers of the findings. In other words, no one was present when the research was conducted except the researchers and the subjects. Therefore, we rely very heavily on the accuracy of the data as they are reported. Thus it is appropriate that we now examine the consistency of the conclusions and accuracy of the data.

In order to understand the discrepancies between the data, the translation of those data into the NRP's findings, and the conclusions drawn by the panel, we must briefly review the organization and distribution of *Teaching Children to Read*. Recall that the report is distributed in three separate formats, each under separate cover. The brief, 34-page reader-friendly *Summary* is available through the NRP's website and was distributed by the hundreds at the International Reading Association Conference in May 2000.

In this *Summary,* the 84 pages of data and discussion in the phonics section of the *Reports of the Subgroups* are condensed to fewer than four pages. A free, user-friendly publicity video is also available from the NRP's website, as are the other sections of the NRP report. Neither the *Summary* nor the video makes reference to any of the limitations of the study. Indeed, in some instances, the conclusions in these short versions directly contradict the data and the NRP's own statements in the *Reports of the Subgroups.*

It is important to distinguish between the various formats of the NRP report because it is reasonable to assume that teachers, parents, and even busy university professors will be more likely to read the *Summary* or perhaps view the video and overlook the actual data as presented in the *Reports of the Subgroups.* Given the status of the members of the panel and given the NRP's a priori claim to scientific, objective analysis, most people—myself included—simply assumed that the data and the conclusions, while they might be subject to interpretation, would at least be accurately reported in all formats. However, I discovered that this was not the case.

It is interesting that while the *Reports of the Subgroups* includes many tables, it doesn't include a clear table illustrating the point of the entire meta-analysis: that is, the results. I found it impossible to track the findings without such a table, and so I constructed my own. Table 1 shows my effort to clarify the results. The following examples show discrepancies between the data and the conclusions as they are presented in the *Reports of the Subgroups* and as they are publicized in the *Summary* and NRP video.

- *Claim.* "The meta-analysis revealed that systematic phonics instruction produces significant benefits for students in kindergarten through sixth grade and for children having difficulty learning to read" (*Summary,* p. 13).
- *Contradiction.* "There were insufficient data to draw any conclusions about the effects of phonics instruction with normally developing readers above first grade" (*Reports of the Subgroups,* p. 2:116). This statement directly contradicts the claim in the *Summary* and on the video that the results apply to the general student population. Furthermore, the

effect sizes for children in grades 2 through 6 were not statistically significant for "spelling" (.09), "comprehension" (.12), or "reading growth" (*Reports of the Subgroups*, p. 2:116).

- *Claim.* "Across all grade levels, systematic phonics instruction improved the ability of good readers to spell. The impact was strongest for kindergartners and decreased in later grades. For poor readers, the impact of phonics instruction was small" (*Summary*, p. 13).

- *Contradiction.* "The effect size [for spelling for children in second through sixth grade] was not statistically different from zero. . . . [Phonics was] not more effective than other forms of instruction in producing growth in spelling" (*Reports of the Subgroups*, p. 2:116). There are no data, at any grade level, indicating that phonics helped children to spell conventionally. The studies for younger children accepted invented spellings, and the results for all children in higher grades showed no significant effect sizes. In addition, there were no results reported anywhere for "good readers"—a population mentioned for the only time in the *Summary*.

- *Claim.* The NRP's results indicate "what can be accomplished when explicit, systematic phonics programs are implemented in today's classrooms" (*Summary*, p. 13).

- *Contradiction.* "There were insufficient data to draw any conclusions about the effects of phonics instruction with normally developing readers above first grade" (*Reports of the Subgroups*, p. 2:116).

> While the results of any research are subject to interpretation, it is hard to reconcile the direct contradictions between the data presented in the *Reports of the Subgroups* and the conclusions stated in the *Summary* with the NRP's claim of scientific rigor and objectivity.

While the results of any research are subject to interpretation, it is hard to reconcile the direct contradictions between the data presented in the *Reports of the Subgroups* and the conclusions stated in the *Summary* with the NRP's claim of scientific rigor and objectivity.

Summary

If *Teaching Children to Read* were a typical research study, published in an education journal and destined to be read only by other researchers, then I could simply end my analysis by saying that the panel's own words have established that the research base in its report on phonics is so flawed that the results do not even matter. However, as we have seen, this study has clout. It has a public relations machine behind it that has already promulgated the results throughout a very wide, very public arena as representing unbiased scientific "truth." Both Congress and the National Institute of Child Health and Human Development are committed to ensuring that the findings of the NRP report affect classroom instruction.

The conclusions of this study as reported in the *Summary* have generated headlines not only in education publications, such as *Education Week* and *Reading Today,* but also in such newspapers as *USA Today,* the *Cleveland Plain Dealer,* and the *Indianapolis Star.* It is, perhaps, too late to mitigate the effects of this widely distributed, widely publicized project. However, I can hope that this analysis will provide a tool for others who will want to delve more deeply into the findings of the NRP report before accepting or rejecting it on the basis of the philosophical hot topics that the research addresses. If our instructional methods are to be dictated by research, then shouldn't that research be sound? Let me close as I began, by reminding readers that "it is entirely proper—indeed, essential—for a profession to examine its knowledge base at periodic intervals. *Without prejudice. . . .* Knowledge advances through just such thoughtful give-and-take."[11]

I hope that you will use this analysis as a starting point; take a long, hard look at the NRP report; and draw your own conclusions—without prejudice—based on the research alone.

1. Pauline B. Gough, "fon'ks wôrz," *Phi Delta Kappan,* March 1989, p. 498.

2. For ease of citation, we will use the title "Phonics Subgroup Report" to refer to Chapter 2, Part II, of the *Reports of the Subgroups.*

3. Timothy Shanahan, "National Reading Panel Report: Work Praised, but Distortion Fears Persist," *Reading Today,* June/July 2000, p. 4.

4. *Reports of the Subgroups,* pp. 2:89 through 2:90. The questions the panel sought to answer through its meta-analysis were:

- Does systematic phonics instruction help children learn to read better than nonsystematic phonics instruction or instruction teaching no phonics?

- Are some types of phonics instruction more effective than others? Are some phonics programs more effective than others?

- Is phonics instruction more effective when students are taught individually, in small groups, or in whole classes?

- Is phonics instruction more effective when it is introduced in kindergarten or first grade to students not yet reading or in later grades after students have begun to read?

- Is phonics instruction beneficial for children who are having difficulty learning to read? Is it effective in preventing reading failure among children who are at risk for developing reading problems in the future? Is it effective in remediating reading difficulties among children who have not made normal progress in learning to read?

- Does phonics instruction improve children's ability to read and comprehend texts as well as their decoding and word-reading skills?

- Does phonics instruction have an impact on children's growth in spelling?

- Is phonics instruction effective with children at different socioeconomic levels?

- Does the type of instruction given to control groups as part of a study to evaluate phonics make a difference?

- If phonics instruction is found to be more effective than less-phonics instruction, were the experiments that showed these effects well designed or poorly designed?

5. In most cases, effect sizes are calculated by subtracting the mean of the comparison group from the mean of the experimental group and dividing this number by the pooled standard deviation. Occasionally, other procedures are used. All calculations reported by the NRP were conducted with DSTAT, a software package for statistical analysis published by Erlbaum.

6. Neil J. Salkind, *Exploring Research* (Upper Saddle Creek, N.J.: McGraw-Hill, 2000), p. 181.

7. See study number 32, Appendix G: Maureen Lovett et al., "Can Dyslexia Be Treated? Treatment-Specific and Generalized Treatment Effects in Dyslexic Children's Response to Remediation," *Brain and Language,* vol. 37, 1989, pp. 90–121.

8. Jeanne Chall and Shirley Feldmann, "First-Grade Reading: An Analysis of the Interactions of Professed Methods, Teacher Implementation, and Child Background," *Reading Teacher,* vol. 19, 1966, pp. 569–75.

9. Salkind, p. 86.

10. "National Reading Panel Releases Report on Research-Based Approaches to Reading Instruction: Expert Panel Offers Its Groundbreaking Findings to Congress and the Nation," press release, 13 April 2000. The term "reliability" is used to refer to the general findings of the NRP report (*Reports of the Subgroups,* p. 2:94). The term "validity" is applied to the conclusions of the meta-analysis (*Summary,* p. 28).

11. Gough, p. 498.

5 ■ More Smoke and Mirrors: A Critique of the National Reading Panel Report on Fluency

Stephen Krashen
University of Southern California,
Los Angeles

Publication of Steve Krashen's article followed Elaine Garan's by a couple of months. Krashen focused on the problems in the fluency section of the NRP report, while Garan had focused on the phonics section. As Jim Cunningham noted in his review of the report, two aspects of the NRP's conclusions stand out:

First, while acknowledging that "literally hundreds of correlational studies" indicate that better readers read more than other readers, the NRP, like the Tobacco Institute, argued that experimental studies were needed to verify the observed effect. But true experimental studies will probably not be done because, given the correlational evidence, parents aren't likely to give informed consent for their children to be assigned to a no-reading control group.

Second, the NRP elected to employ different criteria in determining the adequacy of the available evidence in the areas of of extensive-reading and comprehension-strategy instruction. Although it found the research in both areas lacking, the panel conducted a meta-analysis on the handful of available extensive-reading studies and concluded that that activity had no observed benefit. On the other hand, the panel supported comprehension-strategy instruction even though it declined to conduct a meta-analysis of the handful of available studies in that area.

Steve Krashen points out a number of other problems in the treatment of extensive reading as an instructional activity. He presents overlooked studies, clarifies mistakes made by the panel in describing studies, and reanalyzes the full set of studies in a way that leads to a very different conclusion than the one reported by the NRP.

One of the NRP's ideas that may catch on is that all other educational interventions should be evaluated against having kids "just read." In other words, using more phonics worksheets should be tested against having students spend the same time just reading independently. Teaching comprehension strategies should be tested against having students just read. And so on. As Krashen points out, even in the worst-case studies, just reading usually produced gains on reading achievement tests that equaled or exceeded the gains produced by whatever other activities kids in the control groups were doing.

In her review of the report on phonics by the National Reading Panel (NRP), Elaine Garan concluded that the report involved "a limited number of studies of a narrow population."[1] I will argue that this problem is not limited to the section on phonics: it also applies to the section of the report on fluency. It is only by omitting a large number of relevant studies—and misinterpreting the ones that were included—that the NRP was able to reach the startling conclusion that there is no clear evidence that encouraging children to read more actually improves reading achievement.[2]

Omissions

The selection criteria used by the NRP to choose studies for its report were as follows:

1. The study had to be a research study that appeared to consider the effect of encouraging students to read more on reading achievement.
2. The study had to focus on English reading education, conducted with children (K–12).
3. The study itself had to have appeared in a refereed journal.
4. The study had to have been carried out with English language reading.[3]

The NRP claimed that it could find only 14 studies that met these criteria.[4] Of these, 10 were studies of the impact of sustained silent reading (SSR) programs in which some class time is set aside for free reading with little or no "accountability." Of these 10, three had positive results, with the students who were engaged in free voluntary reading outperforming comparison groups. Another study showed positive results for one condition but not for other conditions, and the rest of the studies showed no difference between groups or no gains. Table 1 summarizes these outcomes.[5]

In other sections of the NRP report, such as the sections on phonics and phonemic awareness, the NRP listed studies that were excluded from its analysis. This was not done for the sec-

---

TABLE 1.
Duration of Treatment and Outcomes of SSR Studies: NRP Set*

Duration	Positive**	No Difference	Negative
Less than seven months	2	8	0
Seven months to one year	2	2	0

*The table shows 14 comparisons derived from a total of 10 studies.
**Students in sustained silent reading programs outperform students in control groups.

TABLE 2.
Duration of Treatment and Outcomes of SSR Studies: Expanded Set

Duration	Positive	No Difference	Negative
Less than seven months	7	13	3
Seven months to one year	9	11	0
More than one year	8	2	0

tion on fluency. We do not know, therefore, which excluded studies were simply missed and which were rejected, nor do we know the specific rationale for their rejection.

In Table 2, I present an "expanded" set of SSR studies in which tests of reading comprehension were used. Many of the studies summarized in Table 2 meet the four criteria of the NRP and were apparently missed. But there were some "violations." A few were done with students slightly older than the age limit imposed by the NRP; in all such cases, the subjects were undergraduate college students. Subjects in some of the studies were students of English as a second language.[6] In several studies, students read in Spanish, not English; in these cases, the students were native speakers of Spanish. Finally, some studies were not published in refereed journals.

Table 2 summarizes the results of these studies. It includes studies included by the NRP as well as those that the NRP did not include.[7]

In the studies in Table 2, SSR students did as well as or better than comparison students in 50 out of 53 comparisons. For longer-term studies (those longer than one year), SSR students were superior in eight of 10 studies, and there was no difference in the other two. Moreover, there are plausible reasons why the results were not even more positive. In one study by Isabel Schon, Kenneth Hopkins, and Carol Vojir, there was no difference between SSR students and comparison groups, but only five of the 11 SSR teachers actually carried out SSR conscientiously.[8] The classes taught by these five achieved significantly better gains.

In a study by Ruth Cline and George Kretke, another study showing no difference, the subjects were junior high school students who were reading two years above grade level and probably had already established a reading habit.[9] Similarly, in Zephaniah Davis' study of eighth-graders, SSR helped medium-level readers but not better readers.[10] SSR appears to be most effective for less mature readers, its aim being to interest them in outside reading. Those who are already dedicated readers will not show dramatic gains. It is doubtful, for example, that readers of this article will show much improvement if they add to their daily schedule an extra 10 minutes of reading.

> It is important to note that the NRP did not include any studies lasting longer than one year.

It is important to note that the NRP did not include any studies lasting longer than one year. A more comprehensive review of the literature indicates that the positive impact of recreational reading increases over time.

Even applying the NRP's stricter criteria, SSR does very well, with readers doing as well as or better than controls in 35 out of 36 comparisons. This suggests that the "violations" do not affect the central issue of whether encouraging recreational reading affects literacy development. Even if one allows only those studies that strictly meet the NRP's criteria, the result still favors recreational reading.

Misinterpreted Studies

In addition to excluding relevant studies, the NRP misinterpreted some of the studies that it did include. The study by Ronald Carver and Robert Liebert should not have been cited as evidence for or against recreational reading, because the students were constrained with respect to what they could read. They were allowed to read books only at or below their level, and the choice of books was limited to 135 titles (the regular library stacks were off limits). There was heavy use of extrinsic motivators, the students had to take multiple-choice tests on the books they read, and reading time was heavily concentrated, with students reading in two-hour blocks.[11] Successful SSR programs allow students to read any books they wish, do not use extrinsic motivators, do not make students accountable for what they read, provide a wide variety of books to choose from, and typically meet for a short time each day over a long period.[12]

The NRP claimed that the advantage shown by Joanne Burley's study[13] was "small." Students in SSR were clearly significantly better in reading comprehension than comparison students in three other conditions, but it was not possible to calculate measures of the size of the effect. It is not clear how the NRP concluded that the difference was small, especially considering the fact that the treatment lasted only six weeks and contained only 14 hours of reading. In a response to a commentary of mine, Shanahan claimed that "the problem here was not with the statistics, but with the design of the study. Each of the four treatments was offered by a different teacher, and students were not randomly assigned to the groups. It is impossible to unambiguously attribute the treatment differences to the methods."[14] This is not accurate. Student assignment was in fact random, and each of the four teachers was randomly assigned to one of the four groups.[15] In addition, the group that did SSR was superior to all three comparison groups, taught by three different teachers.

Not included in my summary of studies in Table 2 is a study that the NRP did include. Janet Langford and Elizabeth Allen used the Slossen Oral Reading Test, which consisted of reading words aloud, which may or may not involve genuine reading comprehension. The difference between the groups was highly significant, and I calculated an effect size of 1.005, which is quite large. Nevertheless, in discussing this study, the NRP concluded that "the gains were so small as to be of questionable educational value."[16]

In another study, students who engaged in SSR made better gains than a comparison group, but the difference was not statistically significant. SSR was significantly better than traditional instruction, however, when readers interacted with one another, that is, when they discussed their reading with one another and shared books. The NRP refers to this group's advantage as "slight,"[17] but it is not clear how the panel arrived at this conclusion. I computed a respectable effect size of .57 for the difference between the peer-interaction group and the comparison group.

The NRP interpreted a study by Sandra Holt and Frances O'Tuel as showing no difference between readers and comparison groups in reading comprehension.[18] This study contained two samples: seventh- and eighth-graders. According to the text of the article, for the total sample, the readers were significantly better on tests of reading comprehension. The text also states that the difference was statistically significant for the seventh-graders but not the eighth-graders, a conclusion that is consistent with mean posttest scores presented in the researchers' Table 1 (pretest means were not presented). In their Table 2, however, the difference for reading comprehension for grade 7 was not statistically significant. The effect size for grade 7 (my calculations), based on posttest means, was a substantial .58. The NRP did not mention this discrepancy. I classified the results of this study as a split decision.

The NRP included a 1991 study and reported that the study found no differences between SSR and skills practice.[19] What the panel did not mention is that the entire treatment lasted only 10 days (not one month, as the NRP reports) and that each of four skills groups did intensive work on specific comprehension skills (locating details, drawing conclusions, finding the main idea, finding the sequence). The researchers found no difference among the five groups on tests of comprehension skills and concluded that "engaging in sustained reading of connected and meaningful text appeared to be just as effective as spending time on the learning and practicing of discrete comprehension skills."[20]

The NRP included a 1991 study and reported that the study found no differences between SSR and skill practice.[19] What the panel did not mention is that the entire treatment lasted only 10 days . . .

Additional Evidence

I should also point out that the case for reading does not rest entirely on studies of sustained silent reading. In "read and test" studies, subjects show clear gains in vocabulary and spelling after a brief exposure to comprehensible text.[21] It is hard to attribute these gains to anything but reading. In addition, there are compelling case histories that cannot be easily explained on the basis of a competing hypothesis—cases such as Richard Wright, who credits reading with providing him with high levels of literacy development: "I wanted to write, and I did not even know the English language. I bought English grammars and found them dull. I felt that I was getting a better sense of the language from novels than from grammars."[22] Or consider Ben Carson, a neurosurgeon who says that his mother's insistence that he read two books (of his own choosing) each week when he was in the fifth grade was a turning point in his life. Carson credits reading with improving his reading comprehension, vocabulary, and spelling, as well as helping him move from the bottom of his class in grade 5 to the top in grade 7.[23] Yes, I know: there was no control group, no tests were given, and the results were not in a refereed journal. But it is hard to imagine any other source for this obvious improvement. And cases like these are not uncommon.

Conclusions

The NRP concluded that "the handful of experimental studies" in which encouraging voluntary reading has been done "raise serious questions" about its efficacy. [24] There are more than a handful of studies. Moreover, the addition of more studies to the analysis provides substantial evidence in support of the effectiveness of recreational reading.

Note that even a finding of "no difference" between free readers and students in traditional programs suggests that free reading is *just as good as* traditional instruction, which confirms that free reading does indeed result in literacy growth, an important theoretical and practical point. Because free reading is so much more pleasant than regular instruction (for both students and teachers) and because it provides students with valuable information and insights, a finding of no difference provides strong evidence in favor of free reading in classrooms.

At worst, the impact of free reading appears to be the same as that of traditional instruction, and it is often better, especially when studies are continued for more than an academic year, a finding that the National Reading Panel has obscured by omitting important studies and by describing others incorrectly. Garan asks that we look beneath the smoke and behind the mirrors of the NRP report on phonics. The same needs to be done with the NRP report on "encouraging fluency."

At worst, the impact of free reading appears to be the same as that of traditional instruction, and it is often better, especially when studies are continued for more than an academic year . . .

1. Elaine Garan, "Beyond the Smoke and Mirrors: A Critique of the National Reading Panel Report on Phonics," *Phi Delta Kappan*, March 2001, p. 505.

2. The report on fluency is one of the *Reports of the Subgroups* that make up the *Report of the National Reading Panel: Teaching Children to Read*. The document is available at <www.nichd.nih.gov/publications/nrp/report.htm>.

3. Ibid., p. 3:23.

4. The NRP report devoted only six pages to recreational reading. In contrast, 66 pages are devoted to phonemic awareness and nearly as many to phonics.

5. The studies included in Table 1 follow. **Duration less than seven months, findings positive**: Joanne Burley, "Short-Term, High-Intensity Reading Practice Methods for Upward Bound Students: An Appraisal," *Negro Educational Review*, vol. 31, 1980, pp. 156–61; and Judith Langford and Elizabeth Allen, "The Effects of U.S.S.R. on Students' Attitudes and Achievements," *Reading Horizons*, vol. 23, 1983, pp. 194–200. **Duration less than seven months, findings of no difference**: Howard Evans and John Towner, "Sustained Silent Reading: Does It Increase Skills?," *Reading Teacher*, vol. 29, 1975, pp. 155–56; Cathy Collins, "Sustained Silent Reading Periods: Effect on Teachers' Behaviors and Students' Achievements," *Elementary School Journal*, vol. 81, 1980, pp. 109–14; Edward Summers and J. V. McClelland, "A Field-Based Evaluation of Sustained Silent Reading (SSR) in Intermediate Grades," *Alberta Journal of Educational Research*, vol. 28, 1982, pp. 110–12 (three groups); D. Ray Reutzel

and Paul M. Hollingsworth, "Reading Comprehension Skills: Testing the Distinctiveness Hypothesis," *Reading Research and Instruction*, vol. 30, 1991, pp. 32–46; Sandra Holt and Frances O'Tuel, "The Effect of Sustained Silent Reading and Writing on Achievement and Attitudes of Seventh- and Eighth-Grade Students Reading Two Years Below Grade Level," *Reading Improvement*, vol. 26, 1989, pp. 290–97; and Ronald Carver and Robert Liebert, "The Effect of Reading Library Books at Different Levels of Difficulty upon Gains in Reading," *Reading Research Quarterly*, vol. 30, 1995, pp. 26–48. **Duration seven months to one year, findings positive**: Zephaniah Davis, "A Comparison of the Effectiveness of Sustained Silent Reading and Directed Reading Activity on Students' Reading Achievement," *High School Journal*, vol. 72, 1988, pp. 46–48; and Gary Manning and Maryann Manning, "What Models of Recreational Reading Make a Difference?," *Reading World*, vol. 23, 1984, pp. 375–80 (peer-interaction condition). **Duration seven months to one year, findings of no difference**: Manning and Manning, op. cit. (pure SSR and student/teacher conference conditions).

6. In a response to a commentary of mine published as a letter in *Education Week* (Stephen Krashen, "Reading Report: One Researcher's 'Errors and Omissions,'" *Education Week*, 10 May 2000, p. 49), Timothy Shanahan, speaking for the NRP, noted that some studies were omitted because "The panel did not attempt to address second-language issues as the report clearly states." See Timothy Shanahan, "Reading Panel: A Member Responds to a Critic," *Education Week*, 31 May 2000, p. 39. The NRP selection criteria do not mention English as a second language. Instead, the report notes only that the studies had to be carried out with "English language reading" (p. 3:23). Excluding second-language learners resulted in ignoring some of the most important studies in the literature, in terms of both theory and practice.

7. Studies included in Table 2 follow. **Duration less than seven months, findings positive**: Anne Wolf and Larry Mikulecky, "Effects of Uninterrupted Sustained Silent Reading and of Reading Skills Instruction on Changes in Secondary School Students' Reading Attitudes and Achievement," in P. David Pearson and Jane Hanson, eds., *27th Yearbook of the National Reading Conference* (Clemson, S.C.: National Reading Conference, 1978), pp. 226–28; Mabel Aranha, "Sustained Silent Reading Goes East," *Reading Teacher*, vol. 39, 1985, pp. 214–17; Ira Gordon and Christine Clark, "An Experiment in Individualized Reading," *Childhood Education*, vol. 38, 1961, pp. 112–13; Holt and O'Tuel, op. cit.; Mary Huser, "Reading and More Reading," *Elementary English*, vol. 44, 1967, pp. 378–85 (grade 6, p. 382); Beniko Mason and Stephen Krashen, "Extensive Reading in English as a Foreign Language," *System*, vol. 25, 1997, pp. 91–102 (study 1); and Burley, op. cit. **Duration less than seven**

months, findings of no difference: Evans and Towner, op. cit.; Collins, op. cit.; Edith Sperzl, "The Effect of Comic Books on Vocabulary Growth and Reading Comprehension," *Elementary English*, vol. 25, 1948, pp. 109–13; Marvin Oliver, "The Effect of High-Intensity Practice on Reading Comprehension," *Reading Improvement*, vol. 10, 1973, pp. 16–18; idem, "The Effect of High-Intensity Practice on Reading Achievement," *Reading Improvement*, vol. 13, 1976, pp. 226–28; Isabel Schon, Kenneth Hopkins, and Carol Vojir, "The Effects of Spanish Reading Emphasis on the English and Spanish Reading Abilities of Hispanic High School Students," *Bilingual Review*, vol. 11, 1984, pp. 33–39 (Tempe group); Harry Sartain, "The Roseville Experiment with Individualized Reading," *Reading Teacher*, vol. 12, 1960, pp. 277–81 ("good reader" group); Summers and McClelland, op. cit. (three groups); Husar, op. cit. (grades 4 and 5); and Holt and O'Tuel, op. cit. (grade 8). **Duration less than seven months, findings negative**: Hoyle Lawson, "Effects of Free Reading on the Reading Achievement of Sixth-Grade Pupils," in J. A. Figuerel, ed., *Forging Ahead in Reading* (Newark, Del.: International Reading Association, 1968), pp. 501–4; Sartain, op. cit. ("slow reader" group); and San Diego County, "A Plan for Research," in Sam Duker, ed., *Individualized Reading: Readings* (Metuchen, N.J.: Scarecrow Press, 1965), pp. 359–63. **Duration seven months to one year, findings positive:** Manning and Manning, op. cit. (peer-interaction condition); Warwick Elley, "Acquiring Literacy in a Second Language: The Effect of Book-Based Programs," *Language Learning*, vol. 41, 1991, pp. 375411 (Singapore, P1 survey); Marion Jenkins, "Self-Selection in Reading," *Reading Teacher*, vol. 11, 1957, pp. 84–90; Lois Bader, Jeannette Veatch, and J. Lloyd Eldridge, "Trade Books or Basal Readers?," *Reading Improvement*, vol. 24, 1987, pp. 62–67; Davis, op. cit. (medium-ability readers); Mason and Krashen, op. cit. (studies 2a, 2b, 3); and Propitas Lituanas, George Jacobs, and Willy Renandya, "A Study of Extensive Reading with Remedial Reading Students," in Y. M. Cheah and S. M. Ng, eds., *Language Instructional Issues in Asian Classrooms* (Newark, Del.: International Reading Association, 1999), pp. 89–104. **Duration seven months to one year, findings of no difference**: Manning and Manning, op. cit. (pure SSR and student/ teacher conference conditions); Schon, Hopkins, and Vojir, op. cit. (Chandler School District); Isabel Schon, Kenneth Hopkins, and Carol Vojir, "The Effects of Special Reading Time in Spanish on the Reading Abilities and Attitudes of Hispanic Junior High School Students," *Journal of Psycholinguistic Research*, vol. 14, 1985, pp. 57–65 (grades 7 and 8); James McDonald, Theodore Harris, and John Mann, "Individual Versus Group Instruction in First-Grade Reading," *Reading Teacher*, vol. 19, 1966, pp. 643–46, 652; Vincent Greaney, "A Comparison of Individualized and Basal Reader Approaches to Reading Instruction," *Irish Journal* *of Education*, vol. 1, 1970, pp.19–29; Floyd Davis and James Lucas, "An Experiment in Individualized Reading," *Reading Teacher*, vol. 24, 1971, pp. 737–43, 747 (grades 7 and 8); Ann Healy, "Changing Children's Attitudes Toward Reading," *Elementary English*, vol. 40, 1963, pp. 255–57, 279; and Davis, op. cit. (high-ability readers). **Duration longer than one year, findings positive:** Warwick Elley and Francis Mangubhai, "The Impact of Reading on Second Language Learning," *Reading Research Quarterly*, vol. 19, 1983, pp. 53–67 (grades 4 and 5); Elley, op. cit. (Singapore, sample of 512 and P3 survey); Miriam Aronow, "A Study of the Effect of Individualized Reading on Children's Reading Test Scores," *Reading Teacher*, vol. 15, 1961, pp. 86–91; Ben Bohnhorst and Sophia Sellars, "Individual Reading Instruction vs. Basal Textbook Instruction: Some Tentative Explorations," *Elementary English*, vol. 36; 1959, pp. 185–90, 202; Frances Cyrog, "Self-Selection in Reading: Report of a Longitudinal Study," in Malcolm Douglas, ed., *Claremont Reading Conference: 26th Yearbook* (Claremont, Calif.: Claremont Graduate; School, 1962), pp. 106–13; and Rodney Johnson, "Individualized and Basal Primary Reading Programs," *Elementary English*, vol. 42, 1965, pp. 902–4, 915. **Duration longer than one year, findings of no difference**: Ruth Cline and George Kretke, "An Evaluation of Long-Term SSR in the Junior High School," *Journal of Reading*, March, 1980, pp. 503–6; and Warwick Elley et al., "The Role of Grammar in a Secondary School Curriculum," *Research in the Teaching of English*, vol. 10, 1976, pp. 5–21.

Shanahan claimed that most of the omitted studies of SSR using native speakers of English were unpublished dissertations (Shanahan, op. cit.). None of the studies listed above are unpublished dissertations. All were published in refereed journals, except for two studies published in the national yearbooks (Lawson; Wolf and Mikulecky), one study from a book published by the International Reading Association (Lituanas, Jacobs, and Renandya), one study from the Claremont Conference Yearbook (Cyrog), and one school district report (San Diego County).

8. Schon, Hopkins, and Vojir, "The Effects of Special Reading Time."

9. Cline and Kretke, op. cit.

10. Davis, op. cit.

11. Carver and Liebert, op. cit.

12. See, for example, Janice Pilgreen, *The SSR Handbook: How to Organize and Maintain a Sustained Silent Reading Program* (Portsmouth, N.H.: Heinemann, 2000).

13. Burley, op. cit.

14. Krashen, op. cit.; and Shanahan, op. cit.

15. Burley, p. 158.

16. *Report of the National Reading Panel*, p. 3:26.

17. Ibid.; the study in question was Manning and Manning, op. cit.

18. Ibid., p. 3:25.

19. Ibid. p. 3:24; the study is Reutzel and Hollingsworth, op. cit.

20. Reutzel and Hollingsworth, p. 41.

21. For a review, see Stephen Krashen, *The Power of Reading* (Englewood, Colo.: Libraries Unlimited, 1993).

22. Richard Wright, *Black Boy* (New York: Harper & Row, 1966), p. 275.

23. Ben Carson, *Gifted Hands* (Grand Rapids, Mich.: Zondervan Books, 1990).

24. *Report of the National Reading Panel*, p. 3:27.

6 ■ Babes in the Woods: The Wanderings of the National Reading Panel

Joanne Yatvin
Portland State University,
Portland, Oregon

As is appropriate when a disagreement has not been resolved, Joanne Yatvin, a member of the National Reading Panel, wrote a minority report. You can find it tucked way back behind the 500-plus pages of the full report. I imagine that few people have read it, although at three pages in length it is the shortest section of the full report.

The minority report concludes, "In the end, the work of the NRP is not of poor quality; it is just unbalanced and, to some extent, irrelevant." I'd venture that Joanne might now modify that statement about quality, but quality must always be judged against the conditions and resources that are available. As Joanne points out in this article, the task presented the NRP was un-doable, and that was its undoing. I take no comfort in the fact that I predicted in an Education Week article that the lack of re-sources and limited time frame would result in a less-than-satisfactory product (Manzo, 1998). I thought then, and continue to think, that any federally funded report that is intended to provide recommendations about educational policy must be free of political influence, adequately funded, and subjected to rigorous peer review prior to public release. Unfortunately, as Joanne points out, the NRP report meets none of those criteria.

Joanne's minority report makes a dark prediction:

> But because of these deficiencies, bad things will happen. Summaries of, and sound bites about, the Panel's findings will be used to make policy decisions at the national, state, and local levels. Topics that were never investigated will be misconstrued as failed practices. Unanswered questions will be assumed to have been answered negatively. Unfortunately, most policymakers and ordinary citizens will not read the full reviews. . . . Ironically, the report that Congress intended to be a boon to the teaching of reading will turn out to be a further detriment.

Joanne asked Congress not to take any actions based on the panel's findings, a request that went unheeded. As Mike Pressley pointed out in his December 6, 2001 address to the National Reading Conference, the NRP and Congress should have listened to the only experienced classroom teacher on the panel—the only person who had spent a career working in schools and classrooms: They should have listened to Joanne Yatvin. Had the NRP listened, it might have advanced the profession toward more expert, more effective teaching of reading. Had Congress listened, it would not have allowed ideology to trump evidence in a national reading campaign.

Manzo, K. K. (1998, February 2). New national reading panel faulted before it's formed. *Education Week* [online] Available: <www.edweek.com/ew/1998/23nichd.h17>

When they heard that I had been appointed to the National Reading Panel (NRP), my friends predicted, "They'll eat you alive." But it was never like that. When we panelists began our journey to discover what "research says about the best methods for teaching children to read," we were all searchers after truth, each knowledgeable and respected in his

or her professional domain and each dedicated to working together toward our joint goal. Along the trail, pressured by isolation, time limits, lack of support, and the political aims of others,
we lost our way—and our integrity.[1]

To begin with, Congress, which had commissioned our journey, was naive to believe that a panel of 15 people, all employed
full time elsewhere and working without a support staff, could
in six months' time sift through a mountain of research studies
and draw from them conclusions about the best ways of teaching reading. And the National Institute of Child Health and
Human Development (NICHD), designated as our guide and pro-
visioner on the journey, was irresponsible both in advising Congress that the task could be done in that way and in selecting the
wrong combination of people to do it.

In late 1997 Congress passed legislation authorizing the
"Director of the National Institute of Child Health and Human
Development (NICHD), in consultation with the Secretary of
Education," to select the members of the panel from more than
300 nominations by individuals and organizations involved in
reading education. The bill specified that the panel was to be
made up of "15 individuals, who are not officers or employees
of the Federal Government and include leading scientists in reading research, representatives of colleges of education, reading
teachers, education administrators, and parents."

NICHD stretched that definition to its limits by appointing
12 university professors. Eight of them were reading researchers,
two were administrators without backgrounds in reading or
teacher education, one was a teacher educator, and one was a
medical doctor. Other categories were represented by one parent,
one elementary school principal, and one middle school language
arts teacher.[2] There was no reading teacher in the sense I believe
Congress intended. When, shortly after the initial panel meeting,
one of the university researchers resigned, I suggested that it
made sense to replace him with a primary-level teacher of reading. A month later, at our second meeting, the panel chair announced that, "after considerable discussion, we concluded that
at this stage in the game we might just as well not replace him."[3]
The panel was not told who the "we" were. And since the work
of the panel had scarcely begun, the explanation offered was

scarcely credible. Why wouldn't NICHD officials want someone on the panel who actually taught young children how to read?

The appointment of the medical doctor was also troubling. Although, technically, she was a reading researcher who worked in the controversial area of brain activity in reading, she had no knowledge or experience in reading instruction. What really made her an inappropriate choice, however, was her close professional association with NICHD. In a videotape later produced under the direction of NICHD, this doctor appears five times, hailing the breakthrough accomplishments of the panel, while other members who were far more involved in the panel's research appear once or not at all.

At the first meeting of the panel in April 1998, another troubling fact about NICHD's appointments became apparent. All the scientist members held the same general view of the reading process. With no powerful voices from other philosophical camps on the panel, it was easy for this majority to believe that theirs was the only legitimate view.

Without debate, the panel accepted as the basis for its investigations a model composed of a three-part hierarchy: decoding, fluency, and comprehension. Theoretically, the components of the model are both discrete and sequential. This skills model posits that learners begin to read by separating out the individual sounds of language and matching them to written letters and combinations of letters. Learners then move on to decoding words and stringing them together into sentences. Since most words in grade-appropriate texts are already in learners' spoken vocabularies, understanding emerges from correct pronunciation. For sentences to be understood, rapid, conversational verbalization is required; this is called fluency. The understanding of texts was seen to depend on building a larger vocabulary and using strategies to uncover ideas and the structures that bind them together in written discourse. Despite minor differences of opinion that surfaced in discussion from time to time, this hierarchy-of-skills model was always the official view of the panel.

For scientists to take such a quick and unequivocal stand was disturbing, since there are two other models of reading that currently claim legitimacy, each with numerous adherents. In one of them, a holistic or constructivist view, readers must do many things at once, right from the beginning. They identify words by visual memory, match sound to letters, pull word meanings from context, understand sentences as complex structures, figure out how the whole system of written language works, obtain information about content, and predict both the words and the content to come. Of course, the texts young learners attempt to read are short and simple in the beginning and grow more challenging as their facility grows.

The other dominant model among conservative thinkers and in the public mind is a simple decoding model. It posits that learners begin in the same way as in the skills model—by separating oral language into sounds and matching those sounds to written letters. With increasing mastery of this one skill, learners can read anything. Understanding the meaning of what one reads and acquiring new words and ideas are seen as separate from learning to read. These processes are facilitated by the teaching of school subject matter, by life experiences, and by reading more advanced material.

The decision to use only one model for all its investigations was critical in sending the NRP down a particular path in its journey. It excluded any lines of research that were not part of this model, among them how children's knowledge of oral language, literature and its conventions, and the world apart from print affects their ability to learn to read. It also excluded any investigation of the interdependence between reading and writing and of the effects of the types, quality, or amounts of material children read.[4] Contrary to interpretations made by many politicians, members of the press, and ordinary citizens, the NRP report does not—and cannot—repudiate instructional practices that make use of any of these components because the research studies on them were never examined.

Despite the choice of a single research path, a large number and a wide range of topics were proposed and discussed by panel members at our second meeting in July 1998. Several of those topics were in fact outside the boundaries of the accepted skills model—such as writing and literature—but the panel members were then in an optimistic frame of mind, thinking that those topics could be worked into the narrow structure we had decided upon. At that time, we were roaming free.

By October of that year, as the reality of the limits of our time and energy and the vastness of the body of research on reading were beginning to sink in, the panel created a list of 32 relevant topics and voted to investigate 13 of them, including oral language, home influences, print awareness, instructional materials, and assessment instruments. This occasion, incidentally, was the only time that the panel took a formal vote on anything. Our usual manner of making decisions was to talk an issue to death until the chair decided that one position was more solid than others. From my perspective, it appeared that he was more favorably disposed toward the contributions of the scientists than those of other panel members. I began to realize who was leading this expedition.

> [T]he panel created a list of 32 relevant topics and voted to investigae 13 of them, including oral language, home influences, print awareness, instructional materials, and assessment instruments.

A second critical decision, urged by NICHD at the first panel meeting and later accepted by the panel and codified in a lengthy and detailed methodology, was that only experimental and quasi-experimental studies would be included in the review of research. NICHD's premise was that a great deal of published research is of poor quality. It exhorted the panel to set higher standards, comparable to those used in medical research. No one discussed the fact that the type of medical research referred to is applied to the treatment of disease or deficiency, not to the processes of normal, healthy development, which is what learning to read is for most children. Moreover, medical research differs in two important ways from educational research: experimental subjects are randomly selected from homogeneous populations, and most treatments are given under a "double-blind" protocol, in which neither the subjects nor the experimenters know who is getting the treatment and who is getting a placebo. Such conditions are impossible to re-create in educational settings.

Two nondecisions by the NRP are also worth mentioning: not to use a compass and not to consult knowledgeable guides.

Despite several discussions about formulating our own definition of reading, we never did so. And despite my repeated requests that subcommittee reports be reviewed by outside practitioners as well as by researchers before the panel accepted them, the panel never said yes or no. In the end, the reports were submitted only to other researchers. With regard to definitions, although reading has been defined often and well in the past, it was important for the NRP to make clear its own use of the term. In the various subcommittee reports, "reading" is used to represent many different kinds of operations, from accurate pronunciation of nonsense words to a thorough understanding of a written text. When a subcommittee report asserts that a particular instructional technique "improves children's reading," the public deserves to know whether the authors mean word calling, speed, smoothness, literal comprehension, or the ability to assimilate a subtle and complex set of ideas.

With regard to review by practitioners, it was also important to get reactions from teachers, who are at the heart of the instructional process. One component of the charge from Congress to the NRP was that it determine "the readiness for application in the classroom of the results of this research." How could a group that included only one classroom teacher make such a determination without consulting a number of teachers?

Once the panel began digging into research studies in the summer of 1998, the members realized that, even with a limited number of topics and strict selection criteria in place, the tasks of analysis and synthesis were overwhelming. Clearly, more time was needed. Late in the fall, as the original deadline approached, NICHD asked for and received a year's extension from Congress. But even that was far from enough time. Three years might have allowed the panel to investigate thoroughly all the topics it had originally identified.

The huge volume of work to be done brought to light another adverse pressure on the panel. Outside of a research librarian who would do electronic searches on request from panel members, NICHD supplied no support staff. Although the organization was willing to pay assistants employed by panel members to screen, analyze, and code the relevant studies, enough hands were simply not available. The only members who had assistants qualified to do such work were the university researchers. And most of their assistants were graduate students, already deeply immersed in their own research projects and reluctant to take on a new line of inquiry that would not benefit them directly.

As time wound down, the effects of insufficient time and support were all too apparent. In October 1999, with a January 31 deadline looming, investigations of many of the priority topics identified by the panel a year earlier had not even begun. One of those topics was phonics, clearly the one of most interest to educational decision makers and to the public. Although the panel felt that such a study should be done, the alphabetics subcommittee, which had not quite finished its review of phonemic awareness, could not take it on at this late date. And so, contrary to the guidelines specified by NICHD at the outset, an outside researcher who had not shared in the panel's journey was commissioned to do the review.

In the end, only 428 studies were included in the NRP subcommittee reports. Thousands of studies were rejected without analysis because their titles, publishing circumstances, or abstracts revealed that they did not meet the panel's criteria. Since the release of the report, outside reading experts have charged that the panel missed many qualified studies. I cannot say if that charge is true, but it certainly seems possible that the shortage of time and support staff could have led to errors of omission.

At the October 1999 meeting, subcommittee chairs summarized their findings before the whole panel for the first time. Although there was general satisfaction with the content of the reports presented, the panel members were worried. There was no time to give the reports careful and critical scrutiny. In fact, even then, not all the reports were in finished, written form. Moreover, individual members were more interested in finishing their own reports than in scrutinizing the work of others. In that respect, we had reached a point where it was "every man for himself."

Panel members were also dismayed to realize that only eight topics had been covered. Somehow, each subcommittee thought— perhaps hoped—that the others were covering more ground. It also became apparent that different subcommittees had used different approaches to their topics. Although the agreed-upon plan had been for all subcommittees to use common procedures for search, selection, analysis, and reporting, this turned out to be impossible for most of the topics. Often there were too few studies, or the studies were too diverse to do the meta-analyses originally intended. Most discussion at that October meeting focused on how to present these facts honestly and clearly to prospective audiences. Ultimately, the panel decided to explain

> Panel members were also dismayed to realize that only eight topics had been covered. Somehow, each subcommittee thought—perhaps hoped—that the others were covering more ground.

its difficulties in the full report in the belief that the various audiences for the report would understand and respect the panel's decisions.

It was at this meeting that I formed the intention of submitting a "minority report." Shortly thereafter, I informed the panel chair in writing and sent a copy to the director of NICHD. I felt that we had done an incomplete, flawed, and narrowly focused job and that our explanations would not make up for it, even if the public read them, which was unlikely, given the fact that they would be buried in a more than 500-page report. Receiving no response to my letter, I drafted a minority report expressing my dissatisfaction with our work and submitted it to the panel. For the most part, the panel members received my report without comment, although the chair and the executive director tried to persuade me that my points could be incorporated into the body of the full report.[5] Right up to the deadline for publication, I was ready to withdraw my report if I could be shown that my concerns were met in some other way.

The NRP's last bad decision was to call its report finished and submit it for publication. Members convinced themselves that, because they had worked hard under adverse conditions, the report was satisfactory. Most of the scientists also seemed to believe that the standards they had set and the methodology they had developed were accomplishments important enough to compensate for the shortcomings in their work. To justify themselves, they added a special section titled "Next Steps" that explained the small number of topics investigated and suggested areas for future investigation. Another special section called "Reflections" was also added to summarize and emphasize the panel's accomplishments. These last-ditch efforts were to no avail. The panel's claim to scientific objectivity and comprehensiveness was lost.

Still, the panel's trials were not over. The situation worsened when the phonics report was not finished by the January 31 deadline. NICHD officials, who wanted it badly, gave that subcommittee more time without informing the other subcommittees of this special dispensation. The phonics report in its completed form was not seen, even by the whole subcommittee, of which I was a member, until February 25, four days before the full report was to go to press. By that time, not even all the small technical errors could be corrected, much less the logical contradictions and imprecise language. Although a few changes were made before time ran out, most of the report was submitted "as is." Thus the phonics report became part of the full report of the NRP uncorrected, undeliberated, and unapproved. For me, that was the last straw, and I informed my fellow panel members that I wanted my minority report to be included.

> [T]he phonics report became part of the full report of the NRP uncorrected, undeliberated, and unapproved. For me, that was the last straw . . .

As I feared, since April 2000, when the report of the National Reading Panel was released, it has been carelessly read and misinterpreted on a grand scale. Many journalists, politicians, and spokespersons for special interests have declared, for example, that 100,000 studies were analyzed by the panel and that we now know all we need to know about teaching reading. Government agencies at all levels are calling for changes in school instruction and teacher education derived from the "science" of the NRP report. NICHD has done its part to misinform the public by disseminating a summary booklet and the aforementioned video, which, in addition to being inaccurate about the actual findings, tout the panel's work in a manner more akin to commercial advertising than to scientific reporting. Neither includes any mention of a minority report.

I said above that the NRP's last bad decision was to publish its findings as if they were complete and definitive. Unfortunately, that has proved to be untrue. Individually, members of the panel have made the decision not to speak out against the misrepresentations and misinterpretations of their work. A few have even jumped on the NICHD bandwagon for reasons I can only imagine. Most have simply remained silent.

Although NICHD will not provide all-expenses-paid trips[6] for panel members who might say anything critical—or even altogether accurate—about the NRP report, those who wish to speak out are not without access to professional and public audiences. Why not write letters to editors, speak at professional conferences, seek meetings with legislators? Perhaps the silent ones have convinced themselves that the NRP report really is all that NICHD claims it to be or that, whatever its flaws, it is doing more good than ill. Unquestionably, it would be difficult for them to admit that the panel lost its bearings and let guides who had other goals lead it in the wrong direction. Or perhaps they have more selfish reasons. As one researcher on the panel told me in private conversation, "I agree with you on many points, but I depend on NICHD for funding my research."

1. I apologize to readers if my chronology of events contains minor errors. During the time I was writing the article, officials at NICHD prevented me from gaining access to the panel's archives, which previously had been open to all panel members and which were reopened briefly after the article was submitted to the *Kappan*.

2. Although I know I was nominated by the executive board of the International Reading Association, I have no idea how my name rose to the top of the list. At the time of my nomination I was a school district superintendent, but before the panel convened, my district merged with a larger one, and I became principal of two schools. I can only speculate that NICHD wanted someone with the title of superintendent and was not aware that my position had changed.

3. *NRP Proceedings*, 24 July 1998.

4. The only exception was an investigation of one aspect of the amount of student reading: nonstructured, nonsupervised, silent reading.

5. The executive director, an independent contractor, was hired by NICHD to guide the technical work of the NRP. His main function at this time was to synthesize the various subcommittee reports into a coherent whole.

6. NICHD has refused to pay any of my expenses for speaking at professional conferences. At one conference where another panel member and I took part in the same presentation, NICHD paid his expenses, but not mine.

7 ■ Can Teachers and Policy Makers Learn to Talk to One Another?

Cathy A. Toll
Illinois State University,
Normal, Illinois

Cathy Toll begins her paper with a quick journey into an area that many educators will find unfamiliar and maybe a bit challenging: discourse analysis. This background is essential to the point she makes about the different views expressed in two reports on what the research says about teaching children to read, the National Reading Panel's April 2000 report and the National Education Association's February 2000 report. Cathy argues that the NRP privileges the scientist and the scientific over teachers' own experience and expertise.

She doesn't say so, but the NRP's narrow view resulted in its wholly ignoring research conducted at the National Reading Research Center that focused on fostering children's engagement in reading. That focus resulted from asking a national sample of classroom teachers about the most difficult issues they faced in teaching reading: motivating students to read and to engage in reading for pleasure, learning, and personal growth. Why didn't the NRP include the NRRC studies in its meta-analyses? It's not that they didn't meet the panel's narrow guidelines for which research "counts"—the center's studies spanned the range of research methodologies, including experimental and quasi-experimental. No, none of the NRRC studies were included because the issue of motivation—of engagement in reading and learning—was of insufficient interest to the panel.

Where teachers see kids who can read but don't, experimental psychologists see problems in phoneme awareness or the level of explicitness of the phonics. Perhaps Cathy shouldn't have been surprised by differences in the language of the two reports: One actually involved teachers and the other ignored them.

Anyone who has been a new teacher in a school knows something about discourses. At every school there are unwritten rules about how to behave and act, such as how one gets supplies, who sits where in the teachers' lounge, how casually one dresses on Fridays, what terms like *Child Study Team* mean. These unwritten rules make up the discourse of that school—the "how to belong here" of a place or a group. A newcomer spends a great deal of energy, consciously and unconsciously, in deciphering these rules and assimilating them as quickly as possible in order to fit in. At the same time, and perhaps what makes this newness tolerable, the newcomer knows many things about fitting in already. For instance, there are discourses of the teaching profession that the new teacher may already know: We consider children to grow in developmental stages, the teacher is expected to be in charge of the classroom, being prepared for each day is valuable, and so on. There are discourses, too, for schools: Spaces in the building are divided into classrooms, a principal is in charge, parents participate but only in limited ways, and so on. And there are discourses about learning: It is incremental, it thrives when the learner is motivated, it requires discipline, and so on.

Perhaps you disagreed as you read the examples above. For instance, maybe you know of a school without a principal, or you believe that learning is natural and doesn't require any special discipline. As you read my statements, then, you may have felt an urge to pick a fight with me, to argue that I was making inaccurate assumptions about the discourses I was describing. This is one of the effects of discourse: One's own discourse seems so natural, so logical, and so right that it becomes difficult to see the acceptability of alternative discourses. This is also one of the dangers of discourse: It creates such a strong sense of what is normal that it often becomes impossible to think that things could be any different.

The definition of discourse that I use here comes from the sociolinguist Gee (1996), who explained that a discourse is

> *a socially accepted association among ways of using language, other symbolic expressions, and "artifacts," of thinking, feeling, believing, valuing, and acting that can be used to identify oneself as a member of a socially meaningful group or "social network," or to signal (that one is playing) a socially meaningful "role."* (p. 131)

I am attracted to this concept because it fits with my experiences—in schools and in life more generally—and because it has helped me make sense of some dilemmas surrounding school change, particularly in relation to literacy instruction. Discourses affect efforts to change schools. The sense of "how things are done around here"—that is, what is normal—is strong in schools, and this discourse makes change especially difficult. From this perspective, change requires a willingness to do things differently in schools, and implicit in that willingness is the requirement that one's existing sense of the way to do things may not be accurate or best. Of course, change does take place in schools, as it does elsewhere, and so we do indeed have the ability to alter our discourses, although this work is often a struggle.

What may make school change even more of a challenge, however, is that there are discourses of school change as well. I am going to give some examples of the discourses of change that I find among teachers as they talk about their literacy instruction, drawn from interviews I have conducted with them, and compare them with the discourses of change that I find among policy makers, drawn from published policy documents. This will give a sense of the competing discourses of change that can be found in education. I'll then discuss how educators might use this information in considering school change.

Teachers' Talk of Change

The discourse of teaching includes beliefs and actions that affect change. Among these are decision making based on engagement with students, concern for children's affect, and controlling one's choices. I will elaborate on each of these.

Decision making based on engagement with students. Teachers frequently express a desire to engage with their students to the extent that the teachers know what students need educationally and can provide it. For instance, Amanda Petrie (all names are pseudonyms) has changed her practice from one in which she tries to "cover the book" to one in which she tries to teach what her students seem to need next. She states that "it's important to really look at children; they're all going through different developmental steps."

Barbara Callahan, a school library specialist, has altered her approach to book selection. Her goal is no longer to have children reading certain kinds of "quality" literature but rather to have them reading at all. She explains that this change began by "just noticing the kids. You have to take the kids where they are."

Concern for children's affect. Teachers' discourses include frequent references to children's affect, and these concerns appear influential upon teachers' reasons for change. For instance, Alice Trimberger, a sixth-grade teacher, is delighted to report that, due to her new literature-based language arts program, "probably at least 8 out of 10 kids will say their favorite subject is language arts." She goes on to describe the "different look in the kids' eyes" that expresses the pleasure they derive from their reading. Alice is focusing on the children's personal, emotional responses to what happens in class.

Similarly, Beth Randall describes her reasons for changing to a new literacy program:

> I want them [her students] to be interested in what they're doing. I
> want them to be involved. . . . I want them to know that I care about

what I'm doing here. I think that I want them to get the message that they are important, that what they do is important. I guess my expectations are high, but, you know, I am here to help them move that way. I'd like them to have goals, I'd like them to know that . . . what we're

> This school has been wonderful. As long as we look at outcomes, as long as the children do what they need to be able to do by the end of the year, however you get there . . . everybody does travel their own road. . . . Everybody gets there a different way . . .
> —Amanda Petrie

doing is serious, it's important, but yet I think that I like to have that attitude that this is our room, this is yours, and it's mine. . . . It's a happy place to be, and they're involved in things that they're learning, yet they're excited about what they're doing.

Although Beth acknowledges expectations for academic achievement, she has much more to say about her affective goals. She wants children to be happy, feel that they are valuable, and believe their school experiences are important.

Controlling one's choices. Discourses of teaching include frequent references to controlling the choices one makes. For example, Amanda Petrie speaks with pleasure of the freedom she is given to make instructional decisions:

> *This school has been wonderful. As long as we look at outcomes, as long as the children do what they need to be able to do by the end of the year, however you get there . . . everybody does travel their own road. . . . Everybody gets there a different way, and from year to year I don't do the same thing.*

On the other hand, Mary Ransom, a first-grade teacher, is critical of administrators who fail to allow for individual teachers' choices:

> *I think administrators . . . don't allow for teachers' differences in how they grow and how they teach. They say, "Well, we're gonna do this and this," and that everybody's got to do it. And then the people start resisting it, if it's not what's in them. If they don't feel good about it, they're not going to do a good job.*

Clare Hansen provides a different perspective on the same idea when she explains that, as a Title I teacher charged to work with disadvantaged students, she could not make classroom teachers change their instructional practices. In her collaborations with classroom teachers, she could only "offer a little encouragement" even though she knew "they needed something different." Thus, even though Clare works closely with other teachers and has her own views about what they might do, she believes that teachers must decide for themselves. In her view, it would be an infringement on teachers' right to control their own choices if she told other teachers what to do.

Teachers' Talk and Discourse

The ways teachers have spoken to me about changes they made are reflective not just of these individual teachers' experiences but of a discourse of teaching in which they all engage. In other words, the sense these teachers have of themselves and their work reflects a discourse—a way to be, think, talk, and believe about teaching—that shapes their work and yet, on the other hand, is shaped by their participation in the discourse. When teachers speak of caring for kids, focusing on affective considerations, and controlling their own decision making, they are defining and being defined by a discourse of teaching. This is how to be a teacher, how to fit in.

I support this claim in three ways. First, I depend upon my personal experience as a teacher and as someone who has talked with many other teachers. These themes run like a thread through educators' conversations. There are other possible explanations for this, but none are convincing to me. For instance, one could consider whether all teachers are directly instructed to think in these ways as they prepare to teach, but that is not the case at my university, which has one of the largest teacher education programs in the U.S., nor is it the case at other universities with which I am familiar. Another explanation would be that these themes are communicated directly to teachers through professional journals, staff development, or administrative directives. Certainly, ideas such as control over one's choices can be found in communications to teachers, but so can contradictory messages, such as having the curriculum and standards control one's choices. To me, a much better explanation for the occurrence of similar themes of change among many teachers' views is that such themes are part of a discourse of teaching.

Beyond personal experience, I support this idea of a discourse of teaching because similar ideas about change appear in published representations of teaching. For instance, Noddings (1994) spoke of the manner in which teachers care for their students by getting to know each one's needs and responding appropriately to those needs:

> *The first member of the relational dyad (the carer or "one caring")*
> *responds to the needs, wants, and initiations of the second.* Her
> *mode of response is characterized by* engrossment *(nonselective*
> *attention or total presence to him, the other for the duration of the*
> *caring interval) and* displacement of motivation *(her motive*
> *energy flows in the direction of the other's needs and projects). She*
> *feels with the other and acts in his behalf. The second member (the*
> *one cared for) contributes to the relation by recognizing and re-*
> *sponding to the caring. (p. 174; emphasis in original)*

Noddings's use of gendered pronouns is notable. The carer is generally female, in the same way that teachers are still more often female than male, especially at the elementary level, which is the level of the teachers I have cited. In this way, Noddings participates in a discourse of teaching that includes the idea of teachers engaging in a gendered practice of caring for students, just as many teachers participate in the same discourse.

The media are similarly full of examples of this discourse of caring. The teacher-hero of movies is often the one who cares beyond the call of duty for her students and as a result accomplishes what no one else could on their behalf. Public service commercials on television remind us as well that teachers accomplish great things through their care for children. As a society we construct teachers as carers who engage with children, just as we construct women as people who engage with children, and teachers participate in these discourses as well when they speak of their reasons for changing practices.

My third argument for the discursive nature of teachers' beliefs and practices is based upon the contrast among documents related to school reform. Those documents aimed at teachers or written by teachers frequently use a discourse that parallels the one I have outlined. Those documents aimed at policy makers, legislators, or the public at large frequently use a very different kind of discourse.

Others' Talk of Change

The teachers I have cited were all speaking of changes in literacy instruction. Two documents, both released in the year 2000, address practices in literacy instruction as well, and the contrast between them is marked, because each uses different discourses.

THE NATIONAL EDUCATION ASSOCIATION (NEA) REPORT

One document is the *Report of the NEA Task Force on Reading 2000* (National Education Association, 2000). This report was issued by the NEA in February 2000 in response to a mandate from the 1999 NEA Representative Assembly that a task force of NEA members with classroom experience in teaching reading be formed to "develop comprehensive guidelines on the teaching of reading" (p. 2). The task force consisted of 11 members, all teachers.

I have carefully examined the NEA report for signs of a discourse of change, and I found in the report numerous references to themes that were discussed by the teachers I interviewed.

Decision making based on engagement with students. This report makes frequent reference to the need for a teacher to know students' individual needs. The report discusses students as individuals, noting the diverse "strengths, needs, backgrounds, interests, and ways of learning that students bring to school" (p. 7). According to the report, small class sizes are necessary in order for teachers to understand students as individuals and to provide the interaction and instruction their students need.

Concern for children's affect. The NEA report suggests that students should derive pleasure from reading and should have a positive attitude toward reading. It maintains that "learning to read should be enjoyable, attractive, and developmentally appropriate. Powerful learning experiences involve engagement, choices, success, and personal connections" (p. 23).

Controlling one's choices. The need for teachers to make their own decisions about instruction is emphasized. The report recognizes the expertise of teachers in knowing their students and the ability of teachers to develop a repertoire of classroom practices. The report also argues that teachers must

> The [NEA] report recognizes the expertise of teachers in knowing their students and the ability of teachers to develop a repertoire of classroom practices.

influence their own professional development and the direction of programs in their buildings and districts.

The themes found in teachers' talk of change run like threads through the NEA report as well. It is perhaps unsurprising that a teachers' organization would participate to some degree in the same discourse as that of teachers themselves. However, the significance of this idea is evident after looking at a competing report.

THE NATIONAL READING PANEL (NRP) REPORT

The second document is the report of the National Reading Panel (2000), which examined certain kinds of research related to reading and in April 2000 issued a report on its findings. The U.S. Congress mandated the formation of this panel in 1997 and appointed the National Institute of Child Health and Development to oversee its development. Membership on the panel consisted of 14 individuals: nine university professors, two university administrators, a middle school reading teacher, an elementary school principal, and an accountant. Thus, most members of this panel are likely to be entrenched in discourses removed from classroom teaching. What's more, the language of the report reflects this difference in discursive orientation. The themes that run through teachers' talk of change are virtually nonexistent in the NRP report.

Decision making based on engagement with students. There are two references to the need for teachers to respond to individual students' needs, but these references are outweighed by the more numerous references to the need for objective research to rule

teachers' decision making. For instance, immediately after suggesting that "teachers should be able to assess the needs of the
individual students and tailor instruction to meet specific needs,"
implying perhaps a kind of engagement with children, this report
claims,

> *It will also be critical to determine objectively the ways in which
> systematic phonics instruction can be optimally incorporated and
> integrated in complete and balanced programs of reading instruc-
> tion. Part of this effort should be directed at preservice and in-
> service education to provide teachers with decisionmaking
> frameworks to guide their selection, integration, and implemen-
> tation of phonics instruction within a complete reading program.
> (NRP, 2000, p. 11)*

Thus, teacher educators and staff developers are being trusted to
determine what students need, rather than individual teachers
who understand individual students.

Concern for children's affect. The NRP report makes one mention of student interest in books. This is the only statement that
focuses on students' affective response to instruction or to engagement in literate activities. There is one mention of student motivation and one mention of the need for teachers to keep students
engaged, but I would argue that these statements refer to the goal
of on-task student behaviors and not to an interest in the feelings
of children.

Controlling one's choices. The report discusses teachers as
"consumers" of the information in the report, describing them,
along with "parents, stu-
dents, university faculty,
educational policy ex-
perts, and scientists," as
"the ultimate users and
beneficiaries of the
research-derived findings
and determinations of the
Panel" (p. 2). Thus, rather than teachers controlling their choices
or creating their understandings, teachers become passive in the
discourse of this report. Teachers themselves also need to be

[R]ather than teachers controlling
their choices or creating their
understandings, teachers become
passive in the discourse of this
[NRP] report.

motivated, according to the report, particularly when providing phonics and phonemic awareness instruction. This discourse views teachers as the subjects of some other group's influence rather than in control of their professional work.

Summary

The discourses of change found in two national reports on reading instruction vary greatly. The report published by the NEA reflects teachers' discourses on several counts. The emphasis is on teachers' control of their work and their engagement with their own students to make instructional decisions. Consistent with teachers' own talk, this report suggests that instructional change takes place when teachers see the need in their own localized situations and act to implement the changes they desire. The report of the NRP represents a discourse of change that is markedly different from teachers' discourses. It focuses on research data removed from individual teachers' experiences and suggests that programs should change when teachers are given "objective" data and motivated to apply conclusions drawn from this data in their own classrooms.

So What?

Competing discourses. The manner in which change is talked about reflects more than just a choice of words, an opinion, or even a cultural effect. It reflects a discourse, meaning that it reflects a way of thinking, talking, and acting that signals who is in and who is out, who is in the know and who isn't, what knowledge matters and what doesn't. In other words, these discourses of change are connected to power. This is important in considering school change.

The language of the National Reading Panel report reflects a discourse of change that is rooted in a belief in objective knowledge existing outside the local context and beyond any individual teacher's awareness. It positions teachers on the receiving end of change and sees children as variables in research studies. On the other hand, the language of the National Education Association report, and the language of many teachers, reflects a discourse that positions change in the hands of individual teachers in response to their engagement with their own students, often in relation to children's affective concerns.

The discourse represented by the NRP report is a discourse found in a great deal of discussion about school change. Policy makers, administrators, and others often situate school change within the need to obtain the best science that will yield the best results and then are confused or angry when teachers don't respond favorably to these changes. On the other hand, the discourse of teachers and their union often considers the most worthy changes to be those that come from considering children's needs in particular situations, and thus they see policy makers and others as cold-hearted or out of touch when they suggest other sources of decision making. Is it any wonder that everyone in education seems frustrated by the school change puzzle?

When issues of power arise, issues of gender, class, or race are often evident. In the case of school change, gender is significant. Teaching, especially elementary school teaching, is still a gendered profession, and policy makers and administrators are still predominantly male. Engaging with children and attending to their affective needs are "womanish" concerns, and as such they are valued by many teachers. I am not suggesting that policy makers and administrators, male or female, do not value caring for children; in fact most would say, I am sure, that teachers must be caring and must engage with children. However, when one considers the discourse of change found in policy documents such as the NRP report, one finds that power is given to those who possess "clear, objective, and scientifically based information" (p. 2). Decisions are based on information other than that gathered by teachers in their own classrooms as they engage with their own students. Therefore, where does power lie? What is really important?

Implications

The practical reader looking for ways to apply these ideas might decide that these competing discourses of change indicate a need for someone's discourse to change. In other words, it may be tempting to see my argument as a call for administrators and policy makers to talk about change differently, or for teachers to do the same. However, the nature of discourses makes this idea seem unrealistic. Because discourse is so closely connected to power, the user of a discourse usually doesn't want to give it up. This is especially true when there is a lot of power associated with a discourse, as in the case of the discourse of the NRP report, which is sanctioned by the National Institute of Child Health and Development along with other government agencies, and therefore is being widely publicized and promoted. However, I would argue that teachers would not participate in their own discourse of change unless it, too, provided them with power. The power of teachers' discourse is in its elevation of teachers' own work and in the way it connects teachers with one another. This discourse provides teachers with a way of viewing teaching, learning, and change that serves as an "identity kit," in Gee's (1996) words; it is one way that teachers belong to the group called "teachers," and by privileging certain kinds of knowledge, this discourse creates a space in which only teachers can do the work as they believe it can be done.

So there may be little desire for altering one's discourse of change. Another tack would be to co-opt an alternate discourse of change. In other words, although teachers participate in a discourse unique to them, they might use the language of an alternate discourse when dealing with policy makers or administrators, say, by speaking

> [P]olicy makers might frame scientific evidence to show how it supports what teachers see in their own students' needs.

of scientific, objective evidence while nonetheless valuing their own decision making related to individual students' needs. Conversely, policy makers might frame scientific evidence to show how it supports what teachers see in their own students' needs. These co-optations would be, in a sense, the marketing of one's discourse: One would shape the discourse of change so that it fit into an alternate discourse.

I see attempts at such marketing as likely. The history of school change efforts is one of a search for a better technology.

Educators and others have manipulated the variables in school change—the innovations, the change processes, the leadership, the teachers, the larger community—in continued attempts to "get it right," despite the considerable documentation that school change efforts nearly always don't work, at least not as intended or not over the long run (e.g., see Gibboney, 1994; Hatch, 1998; Sarason, 1990; Tyack & Cuban, 1995). Some folks will no doubt see discourse as another variable to manipulate. This seems ill-advised, given the nature of discourse. Remember, discourses are not just opinions or ways of talking. As I am using the term, *discourse* refers to ways of being, reflected in words, actions, and beliefs, that are connected to power. Attempts to borrow another discourse in order to accomplish one's aims would be dishonest and manipulative, and probably not successful.

If we won't change our discourses of change, and if it is not appropriate to accommodate an alternate discourse, what can we do? I would suggest working in full awareness of competing discourses and developing a metadiscourse in school settings. Educators, policy makers, and others will benefit from open acknowledgment of the competing discourses in which they work. At minimum, this will create honesty in educational work; better, it may enable us to honor one another while preserving our sources of knowledge and power, and at best it will maximize the ability of educators to move beyond difference to a space in which the work of learning and teaching can be improved upon.

The NRP report on reading instruction provides a good example. This report has created consternation among some educators. Charges of faulty science and political positioning have been rampant (Krashen, 2000; Manzo, 1998), and it is important to consider this report from scientific and political perspectives. However, what these considerations often lead to is a kind of debate that can be reduced to, "Oh yeah?" "Yeah"—an argument in which each side claims it is more correct than the other. The public cries for an end to these debates and demands a return to the facts, which is, at least in part, what led to the formation of the NRP in the first place. Meanwhile, many educators ignore this report; in fact, one member of the NRP, who identifies herself as the only member who has spent a career in elementary education, filed a minority report that declared the NRP report to be, "to some extent, irrelevant" (NRP, 2000).

Consideration of discourse is another way to address the report. If educators, policy makers, and others make visible the NRP's discourse of change and contrast it with teachers' discourse of change, a new kind of conversation might take place. This conversation would acknowledge that the NRP, and apparently the Congressional mandate that led to this panel, privileges evidence conducted in experimental studies outside of teachers' everyday classroom experiences, and that many teachers privilege individual knowledge garnered by teachers through engagement with their own students, often with attention to student affect. Then, if all involved can resist the urge to argue for the superiority of their own discourse, a dialogue might result about the differences between these discourses. Some questions for consideration would be the following: What are the effects of empowering certain kinds of knowledge—for example, teachers' experience or experimental evidence—over others, in schools and in classrooms? How do we make room for difference in the profession of education and in the public sphere in which educators work? Will resistance be the result of privileging one discourse over another, and what are the effects—positive or negative—of such resistance? Are there kinds of research that honor teachers' decision making in relation to their own contextualized work, yet are respected as sound according to accepted notions of science?

Let me be clear: This kind of work is extraordinarily difficult. There is a great deal of attention right now on collaborative groups among educators (and others concerned with education), and these efforts have potential. However, all too often the discourses of these groups themselves lead to power imbalances and have tremendous potential for dishonesty (Anderson, 1998; Hargreaves, 1994). For instance, some elementary school teachers, as women in U.S. society, operate within a discourse that says it is "normal" for a woman to be polite and yielding to others, and this influences their interactions in study groups. Disagreement may be a struggle for some, and participants may resort to silence or counterproductive resistance as a result.

A key consideration in shaping the success of meta-discourses about school change is how educators deal with difference. This must be an essential part of any dialogue on change. Some questions for consideration might be the following: How is difference recognized and how is it responded to? What is a "safe" difference in any group? What does a person do if her or his difference from the group is so great that she or he finds it difficult to function in that group? What does the group do when it recognizes difference between it and another group, be it a group of educators, parents, or policy makers?

This is not a cry for smoothing over points of disagreement; I am not asking, "Can't we all just get along?" Issues surrounding literacy instruction, school change, and reading research reflect broader issues about how literacy is constructed, who controls what goes on in classrooms, and the kind of world we want to have in the future (Hoffman, 2000; Shannon, 2000). We cannot afford to minimize these issues or to smooth over our disagreements. What I am arguing for is a new way to conceptualize the issues, a way that might open up new ground for debate and for moving ahead.

Better science is not going to lead us to a utopian condition in which all educators know the answers to all of education's difficult questions. The fights will continue. Power will always be at play, and some will always be privileged over others. We can improve our work as educators, though, if we continually bring these issues to the fore and create dialogue about how we work within these constraints. The arguments about how to move beyond them have not gotten us far. Perhaps it is time to open up a new discourse.

> Better science is not going to lead us to a utopian condition in which all educators know the answers to all of education's difficult questions.

References

Anderson, G.L. (1998). Toward authentic participation: Deconstructing the discourses of participatory reforms in education. *American Educational Research Journal, 35,* 571–603.

Gee, J.P. (1996). *Social linguistics and literacy: Ideology in discourses.* London: Taylor & Francis.

Gibboney, R. (1994). *The stone trumpet: A story of practical school reform.* Albany, NY: State University of New York Press.

Hargreaves, A. (1994). *Changing teachers, changing times: Teachers' work and culture in the postmodern age.* New York: Teachers College Press.

Hatch, T. (1998). The differences in theory that matter in the practice of school improvement. *American Educational Research Journal, 35,* 3–31.

Hoffman, J.V. (2000). The de-democratization of schools and literacy in America. *The Reading Teacher, 53,* 616–623.

Krashen, S. (2000, May 10). Reading report: One researcher's "errors and omissions." *Education Week* [Online]. Available: <http://www.edweek.org/ew/ewstory>.

Manzo, K.K. (1998, February 2). New national reading panel faulted before it's formed. *Education Week* [Online]. Available: <www.edweek.com/ew/1998/23nichd.h17>.

National Education Association. (2000). *Report of the NEA Task Force on Reading 2000.* Washington, DC: Author.

National Reading Panel (2000). *Teaching children to read: An evidence-based assessment of the scientific research literature on reading and its implications for reading instruction.* Washington, DC: Author.

Noddings, N. (1994). An ethic of caring and its implications for instructional arrangements. In L. Stone (Ed.), *The education feminism reader* (pp. 171–183). New York: Routledge.

Sarason, S. (1990). *The predictable failure of educational reform.* San Francisco: Jossey-Bass.

Shannon, P. (2000). "What's my name?": A politics of literacy in the latter half of the 20th century in America. *Reading Research Quarterly, 35,* 90–107.

Tyack, D., & Cuban, L. (1995). *Tinkering toward Utopia.* Cambridge, MA: Harvard University Press.

PART II

*Politics, Policies, and Profits:
The Political Context of the
National Reports*

8 ■ The Politics of Phonics

Frances R. A. Paterson
Valdosa State University,
Valdosa, Georgia

As this article details, Frances Paterson found that phonics policy making was most popular in states where the Republican Party was in power. Now that the Republicans control the White House and House of Representatives (at least as of this writing), I don't think we should be surprised that phonics is on the national legislative agenda. Phonics has long been part of Republican platforms, although I'll leave it others to explain why. Given the historical links between phonics teaching and Republicans, no one should be surprised by the current push for phonics instruction. Phonics mandates could be viewed as the spoils of electoral war, but passage of recent federal bills that focus on emphasizing teaching phonics has largely been a bipartisan affair. How is it that so many politicians are advocating an emphasis on phonics instruction?

Public opinion polls are the "evidence" that supports a push for phonics mandates (Allington, 1999). The general public believes that schools would be better if they taught more phonics. Of course, given the pro-phonics media blitz of the past decade— did any article in any popular magazine support any approach other than phonics-emphasis?—perhaps we shouldn't be surprised that the public (and the politicians) thinks that no one teaches phonics anymore.

However, the available research evidence creates a very different picture. Morrow and Tracey (1997) and Baumann, Hoffman, Moon, and Duffy-Hester (1998) find phonics instruction to be the most important priority of primary teachers. I'll bet that if we asked parents whether their child's teacher offers too little, too much, or just about the right amount of phonics, the vast majority would select the final option. But people rate their own schools far better than they rate schools in general. When it comes to phonics education, media reports may have shaped their responses so they believe that other *schools should put more emphasis on phonics—but not their school.*

Developing effective and efficient decoding proficiencies is important; that's not the issue. It is how to best develop those proficiencies that is at the root of the debate. The National Reading Panel offered damn little direction in that regard. It said that phonics instruction should be systematic and occur in kindergarten and first grade, and that intensive phonics does not work better than less intensive approaches. It did not mention, much less recommend, the use of decodable texts. The panel report said nothing about the content, structure, or delivery of a research-based phonics curriculum. When policy advocates and entrepreneurs suggest that the NRP report supports their *kind of phonics, ideology trumps evidence.*

For those interested in the politics of phonics, I'd recommend also reading James Moffett (1988), David Berliner (1997), and Boyd and Mitchell (2001).

Berlinger, D. C. (1997). Educational psychology meets the Christian Right: Differing views of children, schooling, teaching, and learning. *Teachers College Record, 98(3),* 381–416.

Boyd, W. L., & Mitchell, D. E. (2001). The politics of the reading wars. In T. Loveless (Ed.), *The great curriculum debate* (pp. 299–342). Washington, DC: Brookings.

Moffet, J. (1988). *Storm in the mountains: A case study of censorship, conflict, and consciousness.* Carbondale, IL: Southern Illinois Press.

The debate over methods of reading instruction has been a frequent subject of commentary in the popular press.[1] In recent years this debate has been cast in terms of whole language approaches that stress meaningful reading instruction based on immersion in authentic literature and the use of semantic, syntactic, and phonetic reading strategies versus methods that emphasize phonics and discrete lessons that teach particular decoding skills. Newspapers and magazines have published articles related to the "great debate," including prophonics pieces by nationally syndicated editorial writers and columnists Cal Thomas and John Rosemond.[2] Supporters and opponents of phonics have expressed their opinions by writing letters to their local newspapers. Finally, academicians have addressed not only the merits of reading methodology but also the educational implications of the issue.[3]

What has been missing from accounts of the "reading wars" has been a comprehensive examination of how the educational and political debate over phonics has been translated into political action in the form of proposed legislation (phonics bills). Political activism over educational issues generally or curricular reform specifically is an integral part of a democratic society; however, neither political activism nor the dynamics that underlie it are immune from scrutiny. The purpose of this study is to explore in some depth the politicization of reading instruction methodology by examining phonics bills introduced into state legislatures from 1990 through the end of 1997 and the substance and rhetoric of these bills. The study also analyzes the political and religio-political factors influencing the introduction of this type of legislation.

Proposed Phonics Legislation, 1990–97

From 1990 to 1997, 101 bills were introduced into state legislatures. From 1990 through the end of 1994, the mean number of such bills introduced annually was 3.2 (n=16). In 1995, 1996, and 1997, 18, 34, and 33 phonics bills were introduced, respectively. The mean number of bills introduced from the beginning of 1995 through the end of 1997 was 28.3 (n=85). The data indicate that

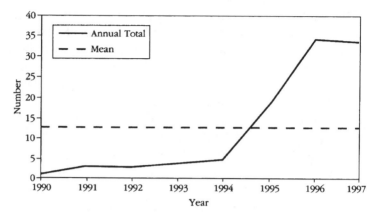

Figure 1.   State Phonics Bills, 1990–97.

1995 was a turning point with respect to the number of bills encouraging or requiring the use of phonics. Figure 1 shows the number of phonics bills introduced into state legislatures from 1990 through the end of 1997.

These 101 bills have been introduced into 26 state legislatures.[4] Through the end of 1994, bills had been introduced into 8 state legislatures. The following year phonics bills were introduced in 12 states. Bills were introduced in 13 and 14 legislatures in 1996 and 1997, respectively. Figure 2 shows the number of states with phonics bills, by year.

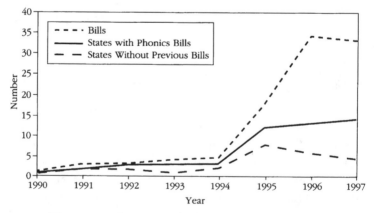

Figure 2.   States with Phonics Bills, 1990–97.

Eighteen states have had multiple phonics bills (either bills introduced into more than one legislative session or multiple bills within a given year). California has had the largest number of phonics bills (20). More than 5 phonics bills have also been introduced into the legislatures of Mississippi (10), Ohio (9), Oklahoma (10), and South Carolina (8).[5]

SUBSTANCE OF PHONICS BILLS

Fifty bills (49.5 percent) relate to the use of phonics as an instructional methodology. What is striking is the occurrence of directive language, for example, "shall be used," rather than permissive language encouraging the use of phonics. In a few cases, bills specify that phonics shall be the only method used. Thirty bills (29.7 percent) pertain to inservice or staff development, and 26 bills (25.7 percent) have provisions dealing with preservice training/certification. Miscellaneous provisions include the following:

- Requirements for parental notification (typically that schools must communicate the method of reading instruction and/or test results).
- Testing, with some bills requiring retention when students score below a certain level.
- The use of phonics in adult or bilingual education or both.
- An "opt-out" provision.
- The specification of specific curriculum/textbooks.[6]
- Funding for phonics-related materials.

Although the great majority require or encourage phonics, a few state bills have punitive provisions.[7] Two Tennessee bills would have stripped colleges and universities that failed to provide a course in phonics of their right to grant teachers certificates.[8] In 1995, two Washington state bills would have established legal remedies for parents living in districts that failed to use phonics in teaching reading—that is, the bills would have granted parents a statutory right to sue school districts for their failure to use a "synthetic, explicit approach to reading and writing instruction with intensive, structured sequential training in letter-sound associations and blending drills."[9]

LANGUAGE OF PHONICS BILLS

Early bills tended to use the term *phonics* without descriptors. Although such statements as "phonics shall be taught in all 1st grade classes" continue to be employed, many recent bills use a number of adjectives and descriptive phrases.[10] Such words and phrases as *systematic, early, direct, intensive, blending, word-attack skills, sound-to-symbol relationships, phonemic awareness,* and so forth are common. Even more recently, the term *decoding* or its variants, such as *decodable text,* have begun to appear. In one case, a bill specifies that text must be at least 95 percent decodable.[11]

The legislators who introduced bills using moderate and highly detailed language appear to have a clear and precise understanding of how schools should teach phonics. Language allowing for educator or school district discretion, such as that of an Iowa statute enacted in 1993 that provides for "reading instruction in phonics or whole language emphasis added," is not present in the bills introduced in 1994 through 1997.[12]

The 1994–97 phonics bills include such descriptions of legislative intent as the following:

> *systematic, intensive, direct, and early phonics that teaches children how to sound out and blend the letters that make up words in a specific sequence from the simple to the complex.*[13]

Virtually identical Mississippi bills introduced in 1995 and 1996 use the term SIDE phonics (systematic, intensive, direct, early) and list approved programs.[14] In Oklahoma,

> phonics *means reading instruction that teaches the sounds of the letters of the alphabet, how letter combinations form syllables, and how syllables form words.*[15]

A second 1994 Oklahoma bill defines phonics as a

> *teaching technique which teaches students how to sound out and blend the letters that make words in a specific sequence from the simple to the complex.*[16]

Washington state bills say that

reading and writing shall include a synthetic, explicit, phonetic approach with intensive, structured, sequential training in letter-sound associations and blending drills....[17]

Five 1995 and 1996 California bills use some variation of the phrase "phonemic awareness and systematically explicit phonics," for example, "beginning reading instruction, with an emphasis on phonemic awareness and systematically explicit phonics."[18] New York bills specify that "all instruction in the English Language shall be by the direct, systematic, intensive, phonetic system," which is defined as

a method of teaching students to read, write, spell, and speak by learning the sound association of individual letters, letter groups, and syllables and the alphabetic principles governing these associations.[19]

A Pennsylvania bill defines "direct intensive systematic phonics" as

an exact, concentrated, thorough, sequential presentation of phonetic knowledge through techniques and practices which are introduced incrementally, logically, systematically such that students are taught to read, enunciate, and spell accurately by learning the letter/sound associations of individual letters, letter groups, and syllables, as well as the principles governing these associations.[20]

The use of the term *sequential* would appear to preclude whole language approaches that teach children to sound out words as needed; that is, when they encounter words in text or when the teacher determines that phonetic cue strategy is appropriate for particular words encountered in text. California's Assembly Bill 1086 (1997) makes clear that the intent of its sponsors was to prohibit this method of instruction:

Systematic explicit phonics instruction does not mean "embedded phonics instruction" which is ad hoc instruction in phonics based on a random selection of sound and word elements.[21]

Both the substance and language of bills introduced after 1994 indicate an increased tendency on the part of state legislators to remove discretion over the methodology of reading instruction from state departments of education, local school boards, and individual schools and classroom teachers—in short, to prescribe instructional methodology in reading through state statutes.

The Ohio legislature recently extended this penchant toward micromanagement to the content of courses in the state's colleges and universities. In 1996 the legislature enacted a statute that required six semester hours of coursework in teaching reading for general elementary certification.[22] The statute mandates that applicants have a separate phonics course of at least three semester hours. The definition of phonics used in the statute is substantially similar to that employed by the majority of the recent phonics bills. Although this bill is not atypical of recent phonics legislation, what should give scholars pause is the fact that the legislature prescribed the required content of a college/university course in highly detailed language.[23] The enactment of this statute raises issues of academic freedom and faculty governance in higher education, characterized by Davis as an example of serious "governmental intrusion into higher education."[24] Academics in other disciplines—for example, history, political science, biology, geology, and so forth—would almost certainly object to legislatively mandated course content.

> Considering the bills as a whole, few mention comprehension.

Considering the bills as a whole, few mention comprehension. When comprehension is included, it is as a single phrase or sentence without descriptors, usually as part of a list of several phrases or sentences describing various aspects of phonics instruction. No bills address the transition from oral to silent reading or the need for access to high-quality children's literature.

Overall, the mean number of descriptors per phonics bill was 6.6. From 1990 through 1993, the mean number of descriptors per phonics bill was 0.89. In 1994, the mean number of descriptors per bill was 7.6, resulting in a mean of 2.93 descriptors between 1990 and 1994. In 1995, 1996, and 1997, the mean number of descriptors was 6.4, 6.7, and 8.4, respectively. Figure 3 displays the number of phonics bills superimposed on the mean number of descriptors, by year.

In addition to analyzing the bills according to their mean number of descriptors, the study identified the number of bills

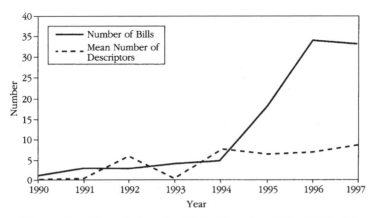

Figure 3.   Descriptors in State Phonics Bills, 1990–97.

in the categories of having mildly, moderately, and highly detailed language. For the purposes of analysis, bills were divided into these three groups. Those with fewer than three descriptors were considered to have mildly detailed language; those with three to six descriptors were considered to have moderately detailed language; and those with seven or more descriptors were considered to have highly detailed language. Eight states had a mean number of descriptors that fell into the highly detailed category.[25] Figure 4 shows the number of bills with mild, moderately detailed, and highly detailed language, by year.

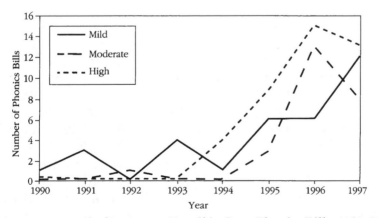

Figure 4.   Level of Language Detail in State Phonics Bills, 1990–97.

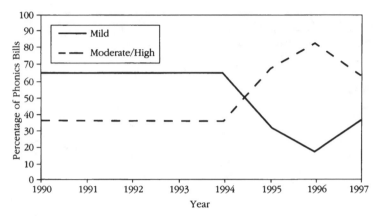

Figure 5.   Language Detail in State Phonics Bills in Percentage Terms, 1990–97.

Of the 101 bills introduced from 1990 through 1997, 33.7 percent (n=34) employed mildly detailed language, 25.7 percent (n=26) employed moderately detailed language, and 40.6 percent (n=41) employed highly detailed language. Figure 5 shows the clear trend toward more highly detailed language in recent phonics bills. In Figure 5, the mean number of bills with up to three descriptors (mildly detailed language) and of bills having more than three descriptors (both moderately detailed and highly detailed language) introduced from 1990 through 1994 has been combined.

Enactment of Phonics Bills

Before 1990, phonics language appeared in the statutes of three states: Arizona, New Mexico, and Ohio. Of those bills introduced in 1992 and 1993, one bill in each of two states—Louisiana and Mississippi—was enacted. No bills were enacted in 1994. Three bills introduced in 1995 were enacted (1 in Alabama and 2 in California), whereas 15 bills introduced in 1996 (5 in California, 1 in Delaware, 1 in Idaho, 1 in North Carolina, 5 in Ohio, 1 in Oklahoma, and 1 in Wisconsin), and 8 introduced in 1997 (3 in California, 1 in Delaware, 1 in Idaho, 2 in Louisiana, and 1 in Ohio) were enacted.

Factors Affecting the Introduction of Phonics Bills

Several factors appear to influence the introduction of phonics bills into state legislatures. First, such bills are disproportionately introduced by Republican lawmakers. Second, they are more likely to be introduced in states in which the Christian Right has substantial or dominant influence in the state's Republican Party.[26] Third, there is a positive relationship between challenges to Harcourt's whole language reading series Impressions and the introduction of phonics bills.[27]

PARTY AFFILIATION AND PHONICS BILL SPONSORSHIP

The first formal Republican involvement in the prophonics movement occurred in 1989 with the publication of the report of the United States Senate Republican Policy Committee entitled "Illiteracy: An Incurable Disease or Educational Malpractice?"[28] Like much prophonics literature, the report equates whole language and whole word approaches. Much of the material appears to be a greatly compacted summary of the arguments that have appeared over the years in books written by Samuel Blumenfeld and materials distributed by Phyllis Schlafly (see discussion below). The term *guessing* is used several times and "dumbed down" appears once.[29] The report uses the phrase *intensive, systematic phonics* (sometimes accompanied by the terms *direct* and/or *early*), which appears frequently in state-level phonics legislation.[30]

"Illiteracy" lays the blame squarely on college and university scholars in the field of reading instruction.[31] Among other "obstacles to reading reform," the report cites "lack of legal redress for malpractice in reading instruction" and "establishment of public schools and teacher education as a monopoly."[32] (This language is common in contemporary arguments in favor of tuition tax credits and vouchers for private school education.) The two 1995 Washington state bills granting parents a statutory right to sue districts that failed to teach reading by systematic, intensive phonics attempted to remedy the "lack of legal redress" mentioned in the report.[33] The report ends with a call to "propose legislation requiring teachers to be taught intensive systematic phonics as part of their training to teach in the public schools" and cites with approval an Ohio statute, enacted in 1989, requiring the use of phonics in grades kindergarten through 3 and providing for inservice training in phonics.[34]

With the exception of South Carolina's Senator Michael Rose, few Republican legislators immediately heeded the call to propose legislation. Nevertheless, examining the party affiliations of sponsors of phonics legislation shows that Republicans are disproportionally represented when compared with their overall membership in state legislatures.

The party affiliation of the bill sponsors could not be based on the 101 bills introduced between 1990 and the end of 1997 because (1) some bills were introduced by committees, (2) the party affiliation of some sponsors could not be discovered (primarily those who were no longer members of the state legislature), and (3) some bills were omnibus bills, which meant that it was not possible to affix with any degree of certainty a pro-phonics position to their sponsors. In addition, bills with more than three sponsors were excluded from consideration because of the difficulty of determining which of their multiple sponsors was responsible for the inclusion of the phonics-related provisions. Of the 89 bills whose sponsors could be identified and whose sponsors' party affiliation could be determined, 58 (65.2 percent) were introduced by Republicans, 26 were introduced by Democrats, and 5 by Independents. According to the National Conference of State Legislatures, as of July 12, 1996, 48 percent of all state legislators were Republicans.[35]

Of the 14 bills introduced between 1990 and 1994 whose sponsorship could be determined, 7 (50 percent) were introduced by Republicans. In 1995, 11 sponsors (64.7 percent) were Republicans. In 1996 and 1997, the Republican sponsorship was 69.2 (n=18) and 73.3 (n=22) percent, respectively. Thus, the sponsorship of phonics legislation appears to be becoming increasingly associated with Republicans. The mean number of descriptors used in bills with Democratic sponsors of phonics legislation was 6.1, whereas bills with Republican sponsors had a mean of 8.6 descriptors.

A second connection between state Republicans and phonics legislation is the inclusion of a phonics plank in state party platforms. The study examined 36 state Republican platforms or statements of resolutions.[36] Six platforms (those of California, Iowa, Kansas, Oklahoma, South Carolina, and Texas) mention phonics. The range of platform statements is illustrated by those of Kansas ("schools should return to a curriculum that stresses basic skills, such as phonics. . . .") and Oklahoma ("the primary goal of our public education system should be to teach the basic subjects of reading emphasizing the intensive systematic phonics method").[37] Of the 6 states with phonics included in the Republican Party platform, 83 percent (n=5) have or have had multiple phonics bills and/or phonics bills that employed moderately or highly detailed language.

THE CHRISTIAN RIGHT AND PHONICS LEGISLATION

Religio-political attacks on nonphonics-based reading instruction began before whole language approaches gained popularity among elementary teachers and schools. In 1980 Jerry Falwell deplored the illiteracy that he argued was symptomatic of "maleducated" students in American schools.[38] To Falwell, American education resembled Nazi indoctrination in Germany, and progressive education was the culprit.[39] In 1983 Tim LaHaye, a cofounder of the Institute for Creation Science, stated that whole word methodology was "a theory based on atheistic, humanistic beliefs" that was designed to "secularize our once God-conscious school system."[40] To LaHaye, "educrats" who resided in the "ivory-towered conference rooms of academia" saw "phonics textbooks as inculcating . . . too many acknowledgments of a Supreme Being."[41] Echoing LaHaye's views, an individual protesting the use of the Developing Understanding of Self and Others (DUSO) program stated that

> *phonics is Judeo-Christian, while look-see or decoding is a sign of Secular Humanism; rules of grammar, speech, and spelling are Judeo-Christian, while discovering language through discussion and reading indicate Secular Humanism.*[42]

Christian Right Commentators and Organizations

Samuel Blumenfeld. Although not affiliated with Christian Right organizations, Blumenfeld's 1973 work, *The New Illiterates,* anticipates their attacks on nonphonics-based instruction.[43] *The New Illiterates* criticizes whole word methods rather than whole language, which in later works Blumenfeld equates with whole word methods. Many of the issues raised in *The New Illiterates* appear in Blumenfeld's 1982 article published in *Reason* magazine; it is in this article that explicit references to Christianity in connection with the phonics–whole word debate first appear in Blumenfeld's writing.[44] Blumenfeld decries the "look-say syndrome" that was "turning children's brains into macaroni."[45] Polemics aside, Blumenfeld cites the increase of illiteracy and the necessity of remedial courses in college as evidence of the "educational malpractice" of "progressive educators" from Horace Mann to Ken Goodman. Blumenfeld raises the issue of conflict of interest by noting that "professor-of-education authors" of whole word series "were earning substantial royalties."[46] However, with the exception of the 1982 article, Blumenfeld's overtly religious criticisms of public education are confined to his more general discussions rather than those concerned with literacy and reading instruction methodology.

Blumenfeld's *NEA: Trojan Horse in American Education* contains the secular arguments against whole word methods plus allegations that public education was foisted on an unwilling and deceived American public by a group of anti-Christian "Harvard-Unitarians."[47] Subsequently, Blumenfeld was to expand this hypothesis and add material strongly critical of John Dewey and the Progressive movement, but the sections that discuss the whole word approach to reading instruction do so from the perspective of its historical development.[48] Blumenfeld's treatment of whole word techniques is relatively moderate in tone and contains no religious references. With the exception of the 1982 article, it is not until the 1990s that Blumenfeld combines both religious and secular arguments as reasons for his opposition to nonphonics methods.

Phyllis Schlafly and the Eagle Forum. As with other conservative Christian issues such as "family values," abortion, opposition to the Equal Rights Amendment, homosexuality, school prayer, and so forth, Christian Right groups differ in their degree of involvement with prophonics advocacy. Phyllis Schlafly's Eagle Forum has had a major role in the prophonics movement.

Schlafly has sponsored two national prophonics campaigns, and articles concerning phonics appeared in the Phyllis Schlafly Report in 1981, 1985, 1994, and 1996.

In 1981, citing her testimony before the Elementary, Secondary and Vocational Education Subcommittee of the United States House of Representative's Education and Labor Committee, Schlafly announced her Headstart Project. The Headstart Project was designed to teach children to read by using "the correct method (phonics-first) before the school confuses the child with any wrong methods."[49]

Schlafly mentioned an article in a 1981 edition of her newsletter as evidence of her long commitment to the issue of phonics; however, it appears that Eagle Forum's involvement in prophonics activities is increasing. During 1996 Eagle Forum published two articles, "Reading Experts Blast State's Endorsement of Whole Language" and "Phonics vs. Whole Language." Echoing Citizens for Excellence in Education (CEE), Schlafly reported California now requires districts to "give students systematic explicit phonics instruction, with phonemic awareness, sound-symbol relationships and decoding."[50] Variations of this language exist in many of the California bills. In July 1996, Schlafly announced that Eagle Forum was launching a nationwide project to combat illiteracy.[51] Unlike its earlier literacy campaign, the 1996 Eagle Forum's Literacy Project was overtly political in that readers were encouraged to influence legislators to take up the issue.

The Eagle Forum's 1996 campaign planned "massive distributions of the organization's First Reading Test by mail, radio spots, and the Internet."[52] In addition, the organization planned to provide "packets about the Literacy Workshops to churches and civic groups," increase staff, and establish a hot line.[53] Like her earlier Headstart Project, Schlafly urged her supporters to teach their children to read by purchasing her First Reader and attending or sponsoring Literacy Workshops, but unlike the earlier campaign, the Literacy Project "urged state legislatures to mandate phonics instruction" in the public schools.[54]

However, Eagle Forum's involvement in seeking state legislation to require the teaching of phonics predates the launching of Schlafly's national campaign. The Ohio Eagle Forum was active in the passage of a 1989 statute requiring the use of phonics in primary classrooms. State groups in Ohio, Tennessee, Alabama, and Texas have been involved in efforts of this nature during the 1990s. Their efforts have included drafting legislation, organizing petition drives, testifying before legislative committees, and organizing transportation for Eagle Forum members to attend legislative hearings.[55]

The Christian Coalition. During the 1980s, conservative Christian minister Pat Robertson, founder of the Christian Coalition, sponsored Operation Heads Up, employing Robertson's Sing, Spell, Read and Write curriculum.[56] Sing, Spell, Read and Write is produced by International Learning Systems. It is not clear if Robertson, unlike Schlafly and Blumenfeld, ever had a financial interest in the sales of this program. Sing, Spell, Read and Write is listed as an approved reading curriculum in bills in Mississippi and Alabama.

Although the national Christian Coalition appears to have little involvement in prophonics activities, the Wisconsin state chapter and at least one county chapter in Wisconsin appear to be engaged in prophonics political activities.[57] A 1995 Christian Coalition voters guide included the responses of candidates for the West Allis/West Milwaukee Board of Education to two questions about reading instructional methodology:

1. Should the phonics method (systematic decoding of sound-symbols/letters) be the primary method used to teach reading? and

2. Should the "sight" or "look say" method (memorizing whole words) be the primary method to teach reading?[58]

In February 1995, Leah Vukmir of Parents Raising Educational Standards in Schools (PRESS), a strongly conservative prophonics and "back-to-basics" group, addressed the Walworth County (Wisconsin) Christian Coalition.[59] In September 1995, the organization's newsletter advertised the second annual PRESS convention, which featured Robert Sweet of the National Right to Read Foundation as a keynote speaker.[60] In December 1995, the organization urged its members to contact their state senators in support of Wisconsin Assembly Bill 237, which would "require all licensed teachers who teach reading to be able to teach intensive phonics."[61] A flyer distributed by the organization referred to "a government study called 'What Works'" in stating that "reading must be taught by direct, systematic, intensive phonics," which "must be completed by the end of the first grade."[62]

Beverly LaHaye and Concerned Women for America. Although involvement of Beverly LaHaye's Concerned Women for America in the prophonics movement appears to be minimal, a November 1995 recruitment meeting of the Appleton, Wisconsin, chapter was organized around the theme of "'phonics only reading instruction."[63] The group showed a videotape, "Reading, Writing and Ripped Off" (distributed by the National Right to Read Foundation), which alleges that progressive education and nonphonics-based reading instruction are responsible for virtually all the problems in contemporary American education.[64] At the meeting a "Petition to Local and State Elected Officials to Restore Literacy Through Intensive, Systematic Phonics" was distributed to participants who were instructed to send completed copies to Concerned Women of Wisconsin.[65] The petition stated that it was a

> *fundamental and incontrovertible fact that written English is based on the alphabetic principle and that the public schools have abandoned systematic phonics for the "whole word" method.*[66]

THE CHRISTIAN RIGHT AND THE PROPHONICS STANCE OF STATE REPUBLICAN PARTIES

States with substantial or dominant Christian Right influence are more likely to have had phonics bills and to have phonics provisions in their Republican Party platforms.[67] Twenty-one (80.8 percent) of the 26 states with phonics bills have this degree of Christian Right influence in their Republican parties. In 13 (50 percent) of the 26 states with phonics bills, the Christian Right is dominant in the

Table 1.   Dominance of Christian Right in State Republican Parties with Phonics Bills, 1990–97

States	Percentage of Stages in Which the Christian Right Is Dominant	Percentage of States in Which the Christian Right Has Substantial Influence or Is Dominant
All	38	62
With phonics bills	50 (55)	69 (80)
With multiple bills	67 (64)	90 (79)
With bills containing moderately or highly detailed language	65 (53)	88 (73)
With multiple bills or bills containing moderately or highly detailed language	62 (55)	81 (78)

Note: Figures in parentheses are from a previous study showing the percentages through the middle of 1996. No parenthetical information is given for the "all states" category because the source for this information was Persinos's study. Thus, these figures would not vary. See John F. Persinos, "Has the Christian Right Taken over the Republican Party?" *Campaigns and Elections* 15 (September 1994): 21–24.

state Republican Party, as opposed to its dominance in only 38 percent of all state Republican parties. Eighteen states have had multiple phonics bills. Sixteen (88.9 percent) of these states have moderate or substantial Christian Right dominance of their state Republican parties. Fifty-seven percent (n=4) of 7 states whose mean number of descriptors per bill was greater than seven had dominant influence of the Christian Right in their state Republican parties. The Christian Right is dominant in 9 (52.9 percent) of the 17 states where the language was moderately detailed or highly detailed (the mean number of descriptors was greater than 3). Table 1 shows the relationships between Christian Right dominance of state Republican parties and proposed phonics legislation.

RELIGIOUS AND SECULAR BASES FOR PROPHONICS ADVOCACY

The preceding discussion and data have established that the Christian Right is a substantial force in the prophonics movement and in the movement's efforts to translate its advocacy of phonics into state statute. This activism raises the question of why elements of the Christian Right, a religio-political movement in which religion and politics are inextricably mixed, is involved in this area.[68] Arguments in support of phonics and, by extension, in opposition to nonphonics-based methods of reading instruction can be separated into three strands: those that are Biblically based, those that are faith based, and those that are primarily secular.

Scriptural Authority for the Teaching of Phonics The earliest use of a scriptural basis for the advocacy of phonics can be found in a pamphlet, "Why Not Teach Intensive Phonics?" published by A Beka books, one of the three leading publishers of textbooks used in fundamentalist Christian schools.[69] Chapman quotes Matthew 4:4: "Live by every word that proceedeth out the mouth of God" to support the proposition that children should learn phonics because "an emphasis on individual words is of paramount importance to those who believe in the verbal inspiration of the Scriptures."[70]

The most frequent use of scripture as a basis for the advocacy of phonics occurs in the writings of Samuel Blumenfeld. Blumenfeld has been an outspoken conservative critic of public education for a number of years and is cited in the Chapman pamphlet. His 1985 book, *Is Public Education Necessary?*, postulates that American public education developed as a result of a conspiracy among Harvard-educated Unitarians. Since 1986 Blumenfeld has published *The Blumenfeld Education Letter*, which has included such articles as "How Progressive Educators Planned to Socialize America" (March 1987), "Humanists Launch Attack on Christian, Fundamentalist Schools" (October 1987), "The Rivera Case: Why Is the State of Iowa Determined to Bring a Christian Home-Schooling Father to His Knees?" (June 1990), and "Dumbing Us Down: The Hidden Curriculum of Public Education" (May 1993).

Although many issues of the newsletter have dealt with the problem of illiteracy and the need for phonics instruction to solve it, Blumenfeld's advocacy of phonics actually began in 1973 with the publication of his book *The New Illiterates—And How You Can Keep Your Child from Becoming One*, a stinging attack on the whole word methodology of the 1950s.[71] In his most recent major work on the subject of reading instruction, *The Whole Language/OBE Fraud*, Blumenfeld develops a number of themes introduced in his newsletter articles.[72] Of particular note is the scriptural basis for the teaching of phonics that first appeared in his article "Whole Language, Linguistics, and the Wittgenstein Connection."[73] Blumenfeld begins by citing Webster's 1928 definition of reading:

> *Read: to utter or pronounce written and/or printed words, letters or characters in the proper order; to repeat the names or utter the sounds customarily annexed to words, letters or characters.*[74]

For Blumenfeld, the book of Genesis supports the primacy of oral language by describing how God brought "the fowls and beasts he had made, and that Adam gave them names. . . ."[75] Blumenfeld notes that Webster was an "orthodox Christian" who believed that language and speech were God's gifts to humanity. Blumenfeld explicitly reiterates the truth of Webster's view by stating, "By giving Adam the power of speech, God gave man the ability to know objective reality."[76] To Blumenfeld, instructional techniques that do not teach children to convert the printed word into speech or subvocal speech in silent reading fail to teach reading. Moreover, whole language approaches that appeal to "atheistic, cognitive psychologists or linguists" introduce subjectivity as the reader interacts with the text, and

> *such subjectivity is an anathema to adherents of the Bible who believe that God gave man language to enable him to know objective reality, not to create it.*[77]

Thus, in the beginning God gave man speech, not the ability to discern meaning from printed text. While not as strong a scriptural basis as religio-political conservatives find for their view of the sin of homosexuality, Blumenfeld's citation to scripture is at least as strong though not as widely repeated as the scriptural support for the prolife position.

Winters draws a distinction between inductive and deductive (termed "noninductive" by Winters) approaches to teaching reading.[78] For Winters, systematic phonics is a structured approach that is "the most noninductive method" because "it does not require the students to generalize any language concepts not directly taught."[79] Winters quotes I Corinthians 14:40 ("Let all things be done decently and in order") and Isaiah 28:10 ("For precept must be upon precept") to support his belief that a highly structured approach is the most desirable approach from a Biblical standpoint. The use of a highly structured methodology allows the selection of materials that are compatible with Biblical principles. The importance of selection of such materials is underscored by a second set of scriptural references: I Corinthians 1:5 ("That in everything ye are enriched by him, in all utterance, and in all knowledge") and Proverbs 19:27 ("Cease my son, to hear the instruction that causeth to err from the words of knowledge").[80]

Claggett also emphasizes the importance of selecting a phonics program with appropriate reading materials by citing direct scriptural authority[81]:

> *Finally, brethren, whatsoever things are true, whatsoever things are honest, whatsoever things are just, whatsoever things are pure, whatsoever things are lovely, whatsoever things are of good report; if there be any virtue, and if there be any praise, think on these things.*[82]

> *For as he thinketh in his heart, so is he: Eat and drink, saith he to thee; but his heart is not with thee.*[83]

Nonscriptural Religious Arguments for Phonics Religiopolitical attacks on nonphonics-based reading instruction began before whole language approaches gained popularity among elementary teachers and schools. As discussed earlier, in 1983, Tim LaHaye, a cofounder of the Institute for Creation Science, related whole word methodology to "atheistic, humanistic beliefs" designed to "secularize our once God-conscious school system"[84];

and another individual identified phonics and "rules of grammar, speech, and spelling" as "Judeo-Christian," and associated "decoding" and "discovering language through discussion and reading" with secular humanism.[85]

Two related issues of contemporary American public school curriculum are inherently problematic for fundamentalists whether or not they are political activists: (1) lack of absolute truth, that is, the existence of ambiguity or the presentation of the possibility of multiple truths; and (2) the danger that students instructed in whole language classrooms will not accept a literal or inerrant interpretation of the Bible. It is beyond the scope of this study to examine the myriad objections of Christian Right activists to such public school programs as values clarification and character education, sometimes termed *moral relativism* or *situation ethics*.[86] For Christian Right opponents, whole language is

a theory of knowledge based on the relativity of truth: there is no right and wrong; society develops it own standards, norms, and morality, and these are constantly changing.[87]

One might even say that such standards, norms, and morality are evolving, connoting an evolutionary process that is antithetical to the fundamentalist view of history as a struggle between the forces of good and evil and contemporary society as divided into believers and nonbelievers.

Blumenfeld raises the issue of literal interpretation of the Bible in a 1982 article, reprinted as a pamphlet by America's Future and subsequently reprinted by the Gablers.[88] "Most private schools, particularly the religious ones, where Biblical literacy is central, teach reading via phonics."[89] Both Chapman and Schlafly maintain that nonphonics-based approaches to reading diminish the likelihood that students will read the Bible literally.[90] Among the consequences of illiteracy listed in Eagle Forum's national prophonics Literacy Project materials for pastors is the "inability to read the Bible."[91] The materials warn pastors that "it won't be easy to carry the Gospel of Jesus Christ to people who can't read."[92]

For Claggett,

the ultimate goal of reading instruction is to equip Christ's precious lambs with the ability to read, comprehend and obey the Holy Scriptures that they may one day be equipped with a Biblical world view, godly character, and academic skills to fulfill God's calling and live for his glory.[93]

Using phonics, Claggett finds "the majority of 5-year-olds are able to find Scripture references quickly and read the verses fluently."[94]

Secular Arguments for Phonics Used by Religio-Political Conservatives Unlike the situation present in the evolution-creationism debate, direct theological grounds for the advocacy of phonics form only a small proportion of Christian Right literature on the subject of literacy. Articles, books, and nonprint media cite research establishing a rise in sexually transmitted diseases to support abstinence-based sex education or use crime statistics to argue that America needs to return to "family values." The issue is not only what research is being used but also which groups and individuals are using it and for what purpose. Failures attributed to American education, almost exclusively to public education, are viewed as the cause of a host of social problems that could be solved by the enactment of conservative initiatives, including a return to what is considered traditional education. The call for a return to traditional education encompasses a variety of conservative reforms, ranging from the disestablishment of the public schools to the discontinuation of innovations such as the use of portfolios in assessment and cooperative learning.[95]

The call for a return to traditional education encompasses a variety of conservative reforms, ranging from the disestablishment of the public schools to the discontinuation of innovations such as the use of portfolios in assessment and cooperative learning.

The use of secular arguments by religio-political conservatives builds on the work done in the 1980s by various Christian

Right elites. Citizens for Excellence in Education was a key player in the challenges to Holt, Rinehart and Winston's (now Harcourt's) whole language reading series Impressions.[96] More recently CEE has published a three-volume series of books called Reinventing America's Schools. The second volume of the series specifically addresses the issue of whole language.[97] To Hudson, "the lack of solid phonics instruction creates a major problem for many whole language students and can even result in a lifetime of illiteracy if phonics are completely neglected."[98] Hudson cites both newspaper accounts and three studies from the *Journal of Educational Research* casting doubt on the efficacy of whole language instruction. Hudson's tone is moderate, and she calls for a balanced approach. Most recently, *Education Newsline*, published by CEE, reported the passage of California's "ABC law, requiring state officials to give adequate attention to systematic, explicit phonics. . . ."[99]

The balanced approach and moderate tone of Reinventing America's Schools stands in contrast to Blumenfeld's *Whole Language/OBE Fraud*.[100] Throughout this work, the author assumes a highly sarcastic tone, castigating every theorist whose work has contributed to the development of the whole language philosophy. Blumenfeld's earlier work on literacy, *The New Illiterates*, employed considerably milder rhetoric.[101] In both books Blumenfeld makes a connection between whole word instructional methods and the progressive movement, whose chief architect, John Dewey, is virtually always identified as a socialist.

In *The Whole Language/OBE Fraud*, Blumenfeld describes whole language as a variant of whole word instruction. As is relatively common in Christian Right literature, persons who advocate a position in opposition to the views of the author are portrayed in religious terms. Thus, two relatively obscure documents, "The Humanist Manifesto I" and "The Humanist Manifesto II" are "bibles" of the religion of secular humanism. For Blumenfeld,

> *one gets the distinct feeling that whole language is a religious movement with its high priests identified as Yetta and Kenneth Goodman and Frank Smith, its sacred literature, its disciples and fanatics, its proselytizers.*[102]

Blumenfeld mixes articles and documents relating to the problems of illiteracy with citations to the work of Jean Chall and Rudolph Flesch and relatively long expository sections explaining how both whole language and whole word approaches impose an ideographic instructional system on an alphabetic code. Statements allowing for the fact that the whole word method might be effective with highly intelligent children because they are able to memorize large numbers of sight words are absent from the later work, *The Whole Language/OBE Fraud*. Missing, too, is the possibility of the balanced approach found in Hudson. To Blumenfeld, whole language and phonics are mutually exclusive. Methods of teaching reading other than systematic, intensive phonics will invariably produce readers who are crippled for life. Blumenfeld goes on to explain that such crippled readers would not even be aware of how they were victims of "an educational system that perversely functioned as a brain deforming instrument used to subjugate an entire people."[103] To Blumenfeld, "only the genius of American psychology could dream up something so evil, so diabolical, so efficient, and so ruthless."[104] The author blames graduate schools of education and what he describes as the "reading establishment" who have a financial interest in propagating inefficient methods of reading instruction. In particular, he singles out the International Reading Association and to a lesser extent the National Council of Teachers of English.

Blumenfeld himself does not have an organization as such, but his writings are frequently cited in Christian Right literature and are used by ostensibly secular prophonics organizations.[105] Blumenfeld's writings are also beginning to appear in the mainstream media. For example, John Rosemond, a family psychologist and syndicated columnist, cited *The Blumenfeld Education Letter* twice in 1996.[106] In a later column, Rosemond again approvingly cites not only Focus on the Family but also Of the People, "a nonprofit organization dedicated to the parents' rights movement," and the Separation of School and State Alliance.[107] Rosemond explicitly states his support for the Parental Rights Amendment, as opposed to the Children's Rights Amendment attributed to Hillary Clinton and Marian Wright Edelman.[108]

A second instance of religio-political conservative, prophonics advocacy appearing in the mass media is a series of columns on phonics and literacy by Cal Thomas, a syndicated columnist. From 1993 through 1996, Thomas wrote three columns on this issue.[109] Although Thomas's other writings make religious references, his columns on phonics are confined to short discussions of one or two studies and references to the "dumbing down" of American education, for example, the decline in SAT scores and the fact that elementary readers in wide use a hundred years ago included authors like Sir Walter Scott, Mark Twain, Shakespeare, Thoreau, John Bunyan, Samuel Johnson, Lewis Carroll, and Ralph Waldo Emerson.[110]

Thomas's attacks on reading instruction are linked to criticisms of Goals 2000 and the NEA (Thomas notes that the NEA "is for choice on abortion"), and disparagement of federal involvement in education.[111] Like other religio-political conservative commentators and some of the proposed phonics legislation, Thomas equates whole word and whole language approaches to reading. To Thomas, "see and say is thought to be better for a child's self-esteem even though it clearly isn't teaching them to read."[112] In the next sentence, Thomas describes primary grade students in Fairfax County, Virginia, as "trying to learn to read using fairy tales, fables, and classic stories," a whole language approach that Thomas fails to identify as such.[113] Whole word means "associating images, not reading words, or learning how to sound out the letters," whereas "whole language" teaches "word recognition by associating words and pictures."[114]

Like Blumenfeld and Schlafly, Mel and Norma Gabler of Education Research Analysts have advocated the use of phonics for a number of years. Although the Gablers' activism in the area of textbook content began in 1961, their prophonics position appears to date from 1980 to the present day:

> *The education establishment . . . seems literally to hate genuine intensive, systematic phonics—the only successful way to teach the English language.*[115]

Unlike Blumenfeld, the Gablers do not use overtly religious arguments to support their opposition to nonphonics-based approaches to reading instruction. However, the Gablers' publications frequently include scriptural quotations and often cite traditional Christianity as a motivating force behind their work and their objections to particular textbooks and contemporary curricular innovations. The Gablers share a number of concerns with other religiously conservative critics of contemporary education, for example, the teaching of evolution, the influence of secular humanism, advocacy of abstinence-based sex education, opposition to materials that allegedly denigrate free enterprise, and so forth. Gabler publications include copies of Blumenfeld's and Schlafly's articles on the efficacy of phonics.[116]

There can be little doubt that Education Research Analysts is a Christian Right organization, albeit one with a particularly narrow focus, and its prophonics position is an expression of the organization's highly conservative religio-political stance. Although other Christian Right organizations and leaders are not highly active advocates in the prophonics movement, without exception their publications support phonics or castigate nonphonics methods. For example, Focus on the Family's James Dobson and the Family Research Council's Gary Bauer exhort parents to "stand firm on phonics" in their polemic Children at Risk: The Battle for the Hearts and Minds of Our Kids.[117]

Conclusions

Much contemporary thinking on curriculum rests on the epigram "You can't feed them all from the same spoon." Although some evidence suggests systematic, intensive phonics may benefit some educationally disadvantaged children or children who have specific learning disabilities, at least temporarily, scholars must attempt to discover whether it benefits other groups of students as well.[118] Such an inquiry requires that reading and language arts educators as well as curriculum generalists address several issues. What do we mean by the word *reading*, and what is the goal of reading instruction? If reading is defined as decoding, then systematic, intensive phonics appears to be an efficient way to teach that skill. If the goal of reading instruction is comprehension and speed in silent reading, then we must ask what kind and amount of phonics instruction facilitates an early and smooth transition to silent reading.

Another question that flows from conclusions about the nature of reading itself is whether systematic, intensive phonics has any negative effects. Do all students taught using phonics-based or phonics-only methods make an early and smooth transition to silent reading? Do they practice reading of their own volition more or less than students taught using other approaches? In short, are they more or less likely to read for pleasure and thus practice the skills they will need for success in school?

The recent increases and changes in the nature of phonics legislation described in this article demonstrate that the "reading wars" have moved into the political arena. In some sense, disagreements about the nature of reading instruction have become yet another front in America's culture wars. No method works equally well for all students. The politicization of public school reading instruction demands that questions about the nature of reading and goals of reading instruction be addressed by scholars, policymakers, and practitioners in the political arena. Moreover, state-level curricular mandates with the amount of detail extant in recent phonics legislation raise many issues about who should control curricular content and instructional methodology. The phonics legislation described in this article essentially "leapfrogs" state departments of education and removes discretion from local boards of education, individual schools, and classroom teachers. One might properly ask why some state legislators have become proponents of phonics and on what sources of information and considerations they are basing their advocacy.

It would be a mistake to view these phenomena as restricted to phonics versus whole language or, indeed, to reading instruction. Ultimately, they call upon us to examine questions related to the shared governance of public education itself. In a democracy, policymakers, legislators, academics, administrators, teachers, parents, and members of the general public all have a role to play in determining curricular content and methodology. The recent changes in legislative activity related to public school curriculum in the area of reading instruction invite us to consider the proper roles of each of these constituencies. An informed consideration cannot begin without an understanding of the interaction of political activism and educational reform.

Notes

1. See James Collins, "How Johnny Should Read," *Time*, 27 October 1997, 78–81; Nicholas Lemann, "The Reading Wars," *Atlantic Monthly*, November 1997, 128–134; Lyn Nell Hancock and Pat Wingert, "If You Can Read This You Learned to Read Using Phonics, or So Its Supporters Say," *Newsweek*, 13 May 1996, 75; Cal Thomas, "It's a Crime Education Is No Longer Hooked on Phonics," *Seattle Post-Intelligencer*, 17 September 1993, sec. A, p. 15; Cal Thomas, "Federal Control of Schools Is One-Way Road to Illiteracy," *Philadelphia Daily News*, 4 April 1994, 22; Cal Thomas, "Back to the Future of Phonics," *New Orleans Times Picayune*, 30 May 1996, sec. B, p. 7; John Rosemond, "Studies Hint the Days of Whole Language Are Over," Norman (OK) Transcript, 10 May 1996, 4.

2. Diane S. Mancus and Curtis K. Carlson, "Politics and Reading Instruction Make a Dangerous Mix," *Education Week*, 27 February 1985, 29; Karen Diegmueller, "A War of Words: Whole Language Under Siege," *Education Week*, 3 March 1996, 1, 14, 15.

3. Diane Sirna Mancus and Curtis K. Carlson, "The Impact of the New Right on Reading Instruction in the United States," (Sioux Falls College, Sioux Falls, SD, 1984, photocopy); Ellen H. Brinkley, "Intellectual Freedom and the Theological Dimensions of Whole Language," in *Preserving Intellectual Freedom: Fighting Censorship in Our Schools*, ed. Jean E. Brown (Urbana, IL: National Council of Teachers of English, 1994), pp. 111–121; Ellen H. Brinkley, "Faith in the Word: Examining Religious Right Attitudes About Texts," *English Journal* 84 (September 1995): 91–98; Constance Weaver, "The Theology and Politics of Reading: Conflicting Views" (paper presented at the workshop of the Program in Language and Literacy, Tucson, AZ, December 1994); Constance Weaver and Ellen H. Brinkley, "Phonics, Whole Language and the Religious and Political Right," in *In Defense of Good Teaching: What Teachers Need to Know About the "Reading Wars,"* ed. Kenneth S. Goodman (York, ME: Stenhouse, 1998).

4. Alabama (1994, 1995), Alaska (1997), California (1995, 1996, 1997), Delaware (1996, 1997), Hawaii (1992, 1996), Idaho (1996, 1997), Illinois (1996), Indiana (1996), Iowa (1991, 1993), Louisiana (1992, 1995, 1997), Maine (1990), Mississippi (1993, 1994, 1995, 1996, 1997), Missouri (1994), New York (1995), North Carolina (1995, 1996), North Dakota (1997), Ohio (1995, 1996, 1997), Oklahoma (1995, 1996, 1997), Oregon (1997), Pennsylvania (1995), South Carolina (1991, 1993, 1995, 1997), Tennessee (1996), Texas (1995, 1997), Vermont (1997), Washington (1995, 1997), and Wisconsin (1996). Note that the years given are the calendar year the bills were introduced. The citations below give the legislative year of introduction.

5. See also Frances R. A. Paterson, *The Christian Right and the Prophonics Movement* (ERIC Document Reproduction Service, 1998), p. 4.

6. Open Court; Professor Phonics Gives Sound Advice; The Spalding Road to Reading; Distar; Sing, Spell, Read and Write; or Word Wise (H.B. 971, 1996 Leg., Reg. Sess. Miss).

7. See O. L. Davis Jr., "When Will the Phonics Police Come Knocking?" *Journal of Curriculum and Supervision* 14 (Spring 1999): 187–190.

8. H.B. 2908, 99th Leg., 2nd Reg. Sess. (Tenn. 1995); S.B. 2878, 99th Leg., 2nd Reg. Sess. (Tenn. 1995).

9. S.B. 5498, 54th Leg., 1995 Reg. Sess. (Wash.).

10. H.B. 835, 163rd Leg., 1996 Sess. (Miss.).

11. H.B. 1362, 164th Leg., 1997 Sess. (Miss.); S.B. 3004, 164th Leg., 1997 Sess. (Miss.).

12. Iowa Code Ann. (section) 294.14 (West 1993). This language implies the two methods are mutually exclusive and does not allow for the "balanced" approach.

13. Two Alabama bills specify which programs are acceptable to teach reading: Open Court; Professor Phonics Gives Sound Advice; The Spalding Road to Writing; Distar; Sing, Spell, Read and Write; and Word Wise. This bill creates a new term for this type of phonics instruction, SIDE phonics, and goes on to identify the method as "called the 'code approach' because it teaches the skills and logic needed to understand the English spelling system." S.B. 420, 1994 Reg. Sess. (Ala. 1994); H.B. 567, 1994 Reg. Sess. (Ala. 1994). Identical language appeared in H.B. 971, 110th Leg., Reg. Sess. (Miss. 1995).

14. H.B. 853, 110th Leg., Reg. Sess. (Miss. 1995); H.B. 567, 110th Leg., Reg. Sess. (Miss. 1995); H.B. 835, 111th Leg., Reg. Sess. (Miss. 1996); H.B. 971, 111th Leg., Reg. Sess. (Miss. 1996).

15. H.B. 1868, 45th Leg., 1st Reg. Sess. (Okla. 1995).

16. H.B. 1628, 45th Leg., 1st Reg. Sess. (Okla. 1995).

17. H.B. 1172, 54th Leg., Reg. Sess. (Wash. 1995); S.B. 5498, 54th Leg., Reg. Sess. (Wash. 1995).

18. A.B. 170, 1995–96 Leg., Reg. Sess. (Cal. 1995); A.B. 2265, 1995–96 Leg., Reg. Sess. (Cal. 1995); S.B. 2176, 1995–96 Reg. Sess. (Cal. 1996); A.B. 3075, 1995–96 Leg., Reg. Sess. (Cal. 1996); A.B. 2769, 1995–96 Leg., Reg. Sess. (Cal. 1996).

19. S.B. 6637, 219th Leg., 2nd Reg. Sess. (N.Y. 1996); S.B. 4359, 219th Leg., 2nd Reg. Sess. (N.Y. 1996); A.B. 9606, 219th Leg., 2nd Reg. Sess. (N.Y. 1996).

20. H.B. 2105, 179th Leg., Reg. Sess. (Pa. 1995).

21. A.B. 1086, 1997–98 Leg., Reg. Sess. (Cal. 1997).

22. Ohio Rev. Code Ann. (section) 3319.24 (Anderson, 1998). See <http://204.89.181.223/orc.htm>.

23. The course must include "phonological and morphological underpinnings of English spellings and the history thereof; the nature and role of word recognition in proficient reading; methods and rationale for the instruction of phonemic awareness (the awareness of sounds that make up spoken words) and the ability to use this awareness of sounds in reading, decoding, spelling, and the application thereof in reading and writing; methods and rationale for the assessment of phonemic awareness, decoding, spelling, and the application thereof in reading and writing; and the relation of deficits in phonemic awareness, decoding, spelling, and word recognition to reading disabilities." Ibid. The full text of the statute can be viewed at <http://204.89.181.223:80/cgi-bin/om_isapi.dll?clientID=21900&infob ase=ORC. NFO&softpage=Browse_Frame_Pg&x=31&y=10>.

24. O. L. Davis Jr., "When Will the Phonics Police Come Knocking?" *Journal of Curriculum and Supervision* 14 (Spring 1999): 188.

25. Alabama (3 bills, mean number of descriptors 8), Alaska (1 bill, 10 descriptors), California (20 bills, mean number of descriptors 8.05), Mississippi (10 bills, mean number of descriptors 10.4), Missouri (2 bills, mean number of descriptors 7), New York (3 bills, mean number of descriptors 8.33), North Carolina (3 bills, mean number of descriptors 9.33), Ohio (9 bills, mean number of descriptors 10.33).

26. A state Republican Party is considered to be "substantially dominated" by the Christian Right if the "Christian Right strength in the GOP is above 25 percent but less than a majority." The Christian Right is considered to be dominant in a state Republican Party if it "constitutes a working majority on major issues." John F. Persinos, "Has the Christian Right Taken over the Republican Party?" *Campaigns and Elections* 15 (September 1994): 21–24.

27. Holt, Rinehart, and Winston, the original publishers of Impressions, was acquired by Harcourt shortly after the company began U.S. publication of the series.

28. William L. Armstrong, Illiteracy: An Incurable Disease or Educational Malpractice? (report prepared for the Senate Republican Policy Committee, 13 September 1989).

29. Ibid., p. 4; Samuel L. Blumenfeld, "Dumbing Down America," *Blumenfeld Education Letter* 2 (November 1987): n.p.; Phyllis Schlafly, "Illiteracy: Its Consequences and Cure," Eagle Forum audiocassette; Eagle Forum, "A Proposal to Train & Equip Parents to Teach Their Children How to Read in Order to Reduce Illiteracy and Reduce Delinquency Among Minors" (brochure, Eagle Forum, Alton, IL, 1995).

30. William L. Armstrong, Illiteracy: An Incurable Disease or Educational Malpractice? (report prepared for the Senate Republican Policy Committee, 13 September 1989), pp. 4, 5, 8, 10, 11, 13.

31. State Eagle Forum leaders actively encouraging the introduction and passage of phonics legislation identified universities and professors of education as opposed to phonics. Both Cicil (Texas) and Smith (Alabama) identified specific universities as primary sources of opposition to phonics instruction. This view is entirely consistent with a general antipathy toward higher education prevalent in Christian Right literature. Stephanie Cicil, telephone conversation with author, 24 August 1996; Eunie Smith, telephone conversation with author, 23 August 1996.

32. William L. Armstrong, Illiteracy: An Incurable Disease or Educational Malpractice? (report prepared for the Senate Republican Policy Committee, 13 September 1989), p. 9.

33. S.B. 5498, 54th Leg., 1995 Reg. Sess. (Wash.).

34. William L. Armstrong, Illiteracy: An Incurable Disease or Educational Malpractice? (report prepared for the Senate Republican Policy Committee, 13 September 1989), p. 13; Ohio Rev. Code Ann. (section) 3301.07(M) (Baldwin 1989).

35. Brenda Erikson, telephone conversation with author, 23 July 1996. Taking figures for the 1995 legislative sessions does not appreciably alter the disparity. In that year, Republicans accounted for 48 percent of all state legislators.

36. Six states responded with the information that they did not have platforms or that they adopted the national Republican platform. Eight states did not respond to a request for a copy of their platforms.

37. Kansas State Republican Party, "Kansas Republican Party 1996 Handbook" (brochure, Kansas Republican Party, Topeka, KS, 1996), p. 62; Republican State Committee of Oklahoma, "Oklahoma Republican State Convention" (brochure, Republican State Committee of Oklahoma, Oklahoma City; OK, 1996), p. 16.

38. Jerry Falwell, *Listen, America!* (New York: Doubleday, 1980).

39. Ibid., pp. 182–184.

40. Tim LaHaye, *The Battle for the Public Schools* (Old Tappan, NJ: Fleming H. Revell, 1983), pp. 44, 50.

41. Ibid., p. 50.

42. Armstrong, Illiteracy, quoted in People for the American Way, Attacks on the Freedom to Learn: 1990–1991 Report (Washington, DC: People for the American Way, 1991), p. 29.

43. Samuel L. Blumenfeld, *The New Illiterates—and How You Can Keep*

Your Child from Becoming One (New Rochelle, NY: Arlington House, 1973).

44. Samuel L. Blumenfeld, "The Victims of Dick and Jane," *Reason* (October 1982): n.p.; reprint, Education Research Analysts, Handbook No. 9: Phonics (Longview, TX: 1995).

45. Ibid., p. 22.

46. Ibid.

47. The book is dedicated to Pat Robertson, among others, for Robertson's "giving America the hope of redemption." Samuel L. Blumenfeld, *NEA: Trojan Horse in American Education* (Boise, ID: Paradigm, 1984), n.p.

48. Samuel L. Blumenfeld, *Is Public Education Necessary?* (Boise, ID: Paradigm, 1985).

49. Eagle Forum, "How and Why I Taught My Children to Read," *The Phyllis Schlafly Report* 14 (June 1981): 1–4.

50. "Phonics vs. Whole Language," *The Phyllis Schlafly Report* 29 (July 1996): 1.

51. Phyllis Schlafly, letter to members of Eagle Forum (Eagle Forum, Alton, IL, July 1996); see also Roy Rivenburg, "Schlafly Adds Phonics to Long List of Causes," The (Cleveland) *Plain Dealer*, 9 July 1996, sec. E. pp. 1, 4.

52. Eagle Forum, "Help Eagle Forum's Literacy Project" (flyer, Eagle Forum, Alton, IL, 1996). Interested readers can access materials related to Eagle Forum's First Reader program via the Internet at <http://www.firstreader.com/> and can view the reading test at <http://www.firstreader.com/test/test.html>.

53. Eagle Forum, "Help Eagle Forum's Literacy Project" (flyer, Eagle Forum, Alton, IL, 1996).

54. Ibid., n.p.

55. See Frances R. A. Paterson, "Mandating Methodology: Promoting the Use of Phonics by State Statute," in *In Defense of Good Teaching: What Teachers Need to Know About the "Reading Wars,"* ed. Kenneth S. Goodman (York, ME: Stenhouse, 1998), pp. 110–111.

56. Alan D. Hertzke, "Echoes of Discontent: Jesse Jackson, Pat Robertson and the Resurgence of Populism" (Washington, DC: *Congressional Quarterly*, 1993), pp. 87–88, 102, 251; Pat Robertson, *The New Millennium: 10 Trends That Will Impact You and Your Family by the Year 2000* (Dallas, TX: Word, 1990), p. 171.

57. Katherine Sweet, telephone conversation with author, 7 August 1996. This lack of Christian Coalition activism is further supported by my personal observations. During the seven monthly meetings of the

Norman, Oklahoma, Christian Coalition that I attended, not one person addressed the issue of phonics or even literacy, although much discussion focused on other educational issues.

58. Wisconsin Christian Coalition, "Wisconsin Christian Coalition Voters Guide" (Wisconsin Research Center, Milwaukee, 1995, photocopy), n.p.

59. Walworth County Christian Coalition, "Agenda" (Wisconsin Research Center, Milwaukee, 28 February 1995, photocopy), n.p.

60. Walworth County Christian Coalition, "Things to Tune Into," Sandtree 1 (September 1995), (Wisconsin Research Center, Milwaukee, photocopy): n.p.; Dan Parks, "Conservative Reform Agenda: Education Group to Hold Convention, Rapidly Growing PRESS Plans Talks on Phonics, Local Control, Standards," *Milwaukee Journal/Sentinel*, 3 November 1995, 1.

61. "Walworth County Christian Coalition" (flyer, Wisconsin Research Center, Milwaukee, December 1995, photocopy).

62. Ibid. No further information regarding "What Works" is given in the flyer other than its identification as a "government study."

63. Planned Parenthood, "CWA Recruits in Appleton" (flyer, Wisconsin Research Center, Milwaukee, 31 January 1995, photocopy).

64. Ibid.; Pat Robertson, *The New Millennium: 10 Trends That Will Impact You and Your Family by the Year 2000* (Dallas, TX: Word, 1990).

65. Concerned Women of Wisconsin, "Petition to Local and State Elected Officials to Restore Literacy Through Intensive, Systematic Phonics" (flyer, Wisconsin Research Center, Milwaukee, 1994, photocopy).

66. Ibid., n.p.

67. See also Frances R. A. Paterson, *The Christian Right and the Prophonics Movement* (ERIC Document Reproduction Service, 1998), p. 13.

68. See also Ellen H. Brinkley, "What's Religion Got to Do with Attacks on Whole Language?" in *In Defense of Good Teaching: What Teachers Need to Know About the "Reading Wars,"* ed. Kenneth S. Goodman (York, ME: Stenhouse, 1998), pp. 56–71.

69. James A. Chapman, *Why Not Teach Intensive Phonics?* (Pensacola, FL: A Beka, 1986).

70. Ibid., p. 14.

71. Samuel L. Blumenfeld, *The New Illiterates—and How You Can Keep Your Child from Becoming One* (New Rochelle, NY: Arlington House, 1973).

72. Samuel L. Blumenfeld, *The Whole Language/OBE Fraud* (Boise, ID: Paradigm, 1995).

73. Samuel L. Blumenfeld, "Whole Language, Linguistics, and the Wittgenstein Connection," *Blumenfeld Education Letter* 10 (May 1995): n.p.

74. Samuel L. Blumenfeld, *The Whole Language/OBE Fraud* (Boise, ID: Paradigm, 1995), p. 13. Note the repeated reference to oral reading. Oral reading with an emphasis on recitation and elocution was the typical pedagogical technique employed by teachers during the 18th and 19th centuries. During and after the 1920s, an increased emphasis on silent reading and the need for standardized testing resulted in the development of various instructional methodologies to enhance comprehension during silent reading.

75. Samuel L. Blumenfeld, "Whole Language, Linguistics, and the Wittgenstein Connection," *Blumenfeld Education Letter* 10 (May 1995): n.p.

76. Samuel L. Blumenfeld, *The Whole Language/OBE Fraud* (Boise, ID: Paradigm, 1995), p. 15.

77. Ibid., p. 18.

78. David Winters, "Is There a Best Way to Teach Beginning Reading?" *Teaching Home* (November/December 1995): 48.

79. Ibid.

80. Ibid.

81. Doreen Claggett, "Simple Guidelines for Early Reading Instruction," *Teaching Home* (November/December 1995): 49.

82. Philippians 4:8, quoted in Doreen Claggett, "Simple Guidelines for Early Reading Instruction," *Teaching Home* (November/December 1995): 49.

83. Proverbs 23:7, quoted in Doreen Claggett, "Simple Guidelines for Early Reading Instruction," *Teaching Home* (November/December 1995): 49.

84. Tim LaHaye, *The Battle for the Public Schools* (Old Tappan, NJ: Fleming H. Revell, 1983), pp. 44, 50.

85. The comment was made by an individual objecting to the use of the revised version of "Developing Understanding of Self and Others," an elementary self-esteem program. People for the American Way, Attacks on the Freedom to Learn: 1990–1991 Report (Washington, DC: People for the American Way, 1991).

86. See Frances R. A. Paterson, "From Outside the Schoolhouse Gates: Christian School Parents Look at Public School Curriculum" (unpublished paper, Valdosta State University, Valdosta, GA, 1996), pp. 3, 11–12; Barbara B. Gaddy, William T. Hall, and Robert Marzano, *School Wars:*

Resolving Our Conflicts over Religion and Values (San Francisco: Jossey-Bass, 1996), pp. 34, 38, 52; Stephen Bates, *Battle-ground: One Mother's Crusade, the Religious Right, and the Struggle for Our Schools* (New York: Henry Holt, 1993), pp. 204, 211–213; Eugene F. Provenzo Jr., *Religious Fundamentalism and American Education: The Battle for the Public Schools* (Albany: State University of New York Press, 1990), pp. 40, 43.

87. Kathi Hudson, Reinventing America's Schools: A Practical Guide to Components of Restructuring and Non-Traditional Education, vol. 2 (Costa Mesa, CA: Citizens for Excellence in Education, 1992), p. 19.

88. Education Research Analysts, Handbook No. 9: Phonics (Longview, TX: 1995), p. E-2.

89. Samuel L. Blumenfeld, "The Victims of Dick and Jane," *Reason* (October 1982): 21.

90. James A. Chapman, *Why Not Teach Intensive Phonics?* (Pensacola, FL: A Beka, 1986); Eagle Forum, "Literacy Project Proposal to Pastors" (brochure, Eagle Forum, Alton, IL, 1996).

91. This material promotes Phyllis Schlafly's First Reader and includes a prepared "Notice to Our Congregation" form. Ibid.

92. Ibid., p. 1.

93. Doreen Claggett, "Simple Guidelines for Early Reading Instruction," *Teaching Home* (November/December 1995): 49.

94. Ibid.

95. It is interesting to note that religio-political conservatives are not pressing for a return to the whole word methods of instruction that dominated the teaching of reading from approximately 1930 through the early 1960s, but rather a return to the approach of the late 19th century with its emphasis on rhetoric, oral recitation, and elocution.

96. Louise Adler and Kip Tellez, "Curriculum Challenge from the Religious Right: The Impressions Reading Series," *Urban Education* 27 (July 1992): 152–173; Frances R. A. Paterson, "Challenges to Public School Reading Textbooks," *West's Education Law Reporter* 106 (7 March 1996): 10.

97. Kathi Hudson, Reinventing America's Schools: A Practical Guide to Components of Restructuring and Non-Traditional Education, vol. 2 (Costa Mesa, CA: Citizens for Excellence in Education, 1992).

98. Ibid., p. 16.

99. "California Struggles for Balance," *Education Newsline* (Summer 1996): 7.

100. Samuel L. Blumenfeld, *The Whole Language/OBE Fraud* (Boise, ID: Paradigm, 1995).

101. Samuel L. Blumenfeld, *The New Illiterates—and How You Can Keep Your Child from Becoming One* (New Rochelle, NY: Arlington House, 1973).

102. Samuel L. Blumenfeld, *The Whole Language/OBE Fraud* (Boise, ID: Paradigm, 1995), p. 197.

103. Ibid., p. 179.

104. Ibid.

105. Blumenfeld and Schlafly addressed the Texas Education Summit on 8 October 1994.

106. John Rosemond, "Studies Hint the Days of Whole Language Are Over," Norman (OK) Transcript, 10 May 1996, 4. That Rosemond may be sympathetic to the Christian Right is further evidenced by a July 1996 column that included James Dobson's (Focus on the Family) *Dare to Discipline* but excluded Benjamin Spock's *Baby and Child Care* from its annotated "recommended list of books on child rearing techniques." John Rosemond, "Columnist Recommends Books on Child Rearing Techniques," Norman (OK) Transcript, 26 July 1996, 4.

107. John Rosemond, "Best Newsletters on Parenting Aren't Politically Correct," Norman (OK) Transcript, 2 August 1996, 4.

108. Ibid.

109. Cal Thomas, "It's a Crime Education Is No Longer Hooked on Phonics," *Seattle Post-Intelligencer*, 17 September 1993, sec. A, p. 15; Cal Thomas, "Federal Control of Schools Is One-Way Road to Illiteracy," *Philadelphia Daily News*, 4 April 1994, 22; Cal Thomas, "Back to the Future of Phonics," *New Orleans Times Picayune*, 30 May 1996, sec. B, p. 7.

110. Cal Thomas, "It's a Crime Education Is No Longer Hooked on Phonics," *Seattle Post-Intelligencer*, 17 September 1993, sec. A, p. 15; Cal Thomas, "Federal Control of Schools Is One-Way Road to Illiteracy," *Philadelphia Daily News*, 4 April 1994, 22. The misuse of statistics by critics of American public schools is widespread. See David C. Berliner and Bruce J. Biddle, *The Manufactured Crisis: Myths, Fraud and the Attack on America's Public Schools* (New York: Addison-Wesley, 1995).

111. Cal Thomas, "Back to the Future of Phonics," *New Orleans Times Picayune*, 30 May 1996, sec. B, p. 7.

112. Cal Thomas, "It's a Crime Education Is No Longer Hooked on Phonics," *Seattle Post-Intelligencer*, 17 September 1993, sec. A, p. 15.

113. Ibid.

114. Cal Thomas, "It's a Crime Education Is No Longer Hooked on Phonics," *Seattle Post-Intelligencer*, 17 September 1993, sec. A, p. 15; Cal Thomas, "Back to the Future of Phonics," *New Orleans Times Picayune*, 30 May 1996, sec. B, p. 7.

115. "Whole Language vs. Phonics," The Mel Gablers' Educational Research Analyst Newsletter (December 1995): n.p.

116. Education Research Analysts, Handbook No. 9: Phonics (Longview, TX: 1995).

117. James C. Dobson and Gary L. Bauer, *Children at Risk: The Battle for the Hearts and Minds of Our Kids*, 2nd ed. (Dallas, TX: Word, 1990), p. 307.

118. See Richard L. Allington and Haley Woodside-Jiron, *Adequacy of a Program of Research and of a "Research Synthesis" in Shaping Educational Policy* (Albany: National Research Center on English Learning and Achievement, University at Albany, State University of New York, 1997).

9 ■ Decodable Text in Beginning Reading: Are Mandates and Policy Based on Research?

Richard L. Allington,
University of Florida
and Haley Woodside-Jiron,
State University of New York
National Research Center on English
Learning and Achievement

Decodable texts, with those "Nan can fan Dan" sentences, remain a hot issue among policy entrepreneurs. Since 1998, when Haley Woodside-Jiron and I wrote the article that follows, there has been no new scientific research that manipulated text decodability as a variable important to reading development (Allington, 2001). In other words, no scientific evidence yet supports the use of decodable texts.

One issue that has been largely decided is the regulatory definition of decodable text. The new policy standard is that from 80 to 90 percent of the words in a text must be decodable given the letter-sound relationships that have been taught. But that definition has no basis in science, only in ideology and political

195

mandates. Both Texas and California defined decodable texts in this manner prior to their recent adoptions of basal readers. Because of statewide controls and funding of textbook adoptions, Texas and California can set whatever criteria they like, scientific or not. And because these two large states are such huge textbook markets, most publishers just roll over and create products that fit their mandates. Textbook publishers market their products nationally, so whatever Texas and California want for textbooks is what the rest of the nation gets.

So, in this era of "evidence-based" decisions and reading programs based in "rigorous scientific research," textbook publishers are promoting reading curriculum materials that have no basis in science. None. How did this happen? Ideology trumps evidence every time politicians get involved in education. This article exposes the ways in which research on beginning reading materials has been misrepresented. Note that few of the state curriculum documents we looked at cite original research. That's because there was little such research for them to cite—and the research that was available did not support the states' decodable texts mandates.

I still believe, as we say at the end of the article, that it makes sense that children should encounter words in their reading that allow them to use their developing decoding skills. But there is no research evidence that supports my belief. And there is no research that suggests that beginning reading texts that have a large number of decodable words are useful, much less scientific. None.

Thirty years after the publication of the classic treatise *Reading: The Great Debate* (Chall, 1967), the profession and the public are again engaged in a vociferous, and sometimes rancorous, debate about how to best develop the reading proficiency of beginning readers. A public perception, or misperception (Berliner & Biddle, 1996; Bracey, 1997; Kibby, 1995), of a reading "crisis," a call for back to basics, and calls for an emphasis on phonics have created public concern over the nature and effectiveness of contemporary early reading instruction.

An interesting feature of the current debate is the focus on attending to the findings of "reliable, replicable research" in planning early reading instruction (Carnine & Meeder, 1997). We have encountered this phrase in a variety of sources including television programs, commentaries, journal articles, legislation, and Congressional testimony.

It is common for advocacy and policy documents to assert that "research shows . . ." in promoting education reform. In fact, one would almost be led to believe that there exists some set of "reliable, replicable research" findings that together map out the single most effective and efficient features of beginning reading instruction. Available research provides insight and guidance to good beginning reading instruction, but it does not provide an explicit blueprint for designing, or redesigning, beginning reading curriculum or instruction for all children.

Nevertheless, in the course of studying educational policy-making in four states (CA, NY, TX, WI) over the past two years, we have identified legislative proposals, legislation, or state education agency policies (or all of the above) that advocate or mandate certain aspects of beginning reading instruction (Allington & Woodside-Jiron, 1997). In each case, the policies and mandates focus on implementing instruction with a greater emphasis on teaching phonetic knowledge, and, in Texas and California, on supplying classrooms with certain types of beginning reading materials termed *decodable text*.

In this article, we report our detailed analysis of the research cited as supporting the implementation of policies recommending or mandating the use of "decodable texts" in beginning reading instruction.

Research-Linked Assertions Supporting Decodable Text

Early in the course of our study of policy making, we encountered various advocacy documents in both California and Texas that employed what were said to be researched-linked assertions about beginning reading instruction. We set out to locate and gather as many advocacy and policy documents as possible. Ultimately, we gathered a large set of documents—including background papers, research summaries, agency sponsored publications, policy statements, legislative testimony, authorizing legislation, education regulations, and teacher-training materials—used to recommend, urge, mandate, or implement the use of "decodable text" as part of instructional reform for beginning readers.

We found that many advocacy and policy documents simply asserted that "the research says," but provided no research citations. Others provided a general bibliography that did not link specific references to the various specific assertions. A few provided specific research citations tied to the assertions offered.

Here are some examples of research-linked assertions that we found, with the research citations also noted.

The words in the stories are based on the sound-letter relationships the children are learning . . . Research strongly asserts *that children benefit greatly from direct, systematic decoding instruction and that instruction should follow with practice in decodable stories. [emphasis added]* (Texas Reading Initiative, *p. 8. The document's bibliography lists Adams, 1990; Anderson et al., 1985; Beck and Juel, 1992; Juel, 1994, among other references.*)

Research strongly asserts *that from the beginning of first grade and in tandem with basic phonics instruction, the most appropriate materials for independent reading are decodable texts . . . most new words in these texts should be wholly decodable on the basis of the phonics that students have been taught. [emphasis added]* (California Department of Education, Teaching Reading, *p. 12. The bibliography lists Adams, 1990; Adams, Treiman, and Pressley, 1996[1]; and Anderson et al., 1985, among other references.*)

Neither the California or Texas document specifically linked any research citation to the assertions, though both included a bibliography. However, the California excerpt above also appeared in California State Board of Education (1996), *Guide to the California Reading Initiative of 1996*, p. 5, with these specific citations: Beck and Juel, 1995, and Adams, Treiman and Pressley, 1996 [sic].

Research shows *that it is important for children to practice the phonics they have learned. It is therefore essential that the initial books that children attempt to read on their own be composed of decodable text. [emphasis added] (California Department of Education, Teaching Reading, p. 7)*

The excerpt above also appears in California State Board of Education (1996), *Guide to the California Reading Initiative of 1996*, p. 4, with the following specific citations added: Beck and Juel, 1995; Adams, 1990; and Anderson et al., 1984 [sic], although no such citations appear in the published version of *Teaching Reading* and the Beck and Juel reference does not appear in the bibliography of *Teaching Reading*.

A similar assertion, illustrated below, appeared in materials produced to familiarize school board members and school superintendents with shifts in early literacy instructional policy.

In summary, nine important research findings. . . . The effects of phonics knowledge become significantly greater when children find the knowledge useful—that is, when they practice newly learned letter-sound correspondences successfully in decodable text. [emphasis added] (California State Board of Education, Read All About It, p. 24, and Board Members/Superintendents Kit on the California Reading Initiative of 1996, with Beck and Juel, 1995, cited as a source)

As illustrated by these examples of quotations from state education policy documents, assertions that research supports the use of "decodable texts" have been quite common. But what supporting evidence does the cited research provide, when it is examined?

What Is Decodable Text?

We first attempted to identify a common understanding of how the term "decodable text" is to be applied in the design and selection of instructional materials to be used in early reading instruction. In doing so, we identified and analyzed many recent advocacy and policy texts relevant to the question of operationalizing decodable text. The following is an example of the advocacy statements we found:

The rest of the lesson involves using these same phonemes in the context of words and stories that are composed of only the letter-

> *phoneme relationships the children know at that point ...*
> *Decodable text is composed of words that use the sound-spelling*
> *correspondences that children have learned to that point and a lim-*
> *ited number of sight words that have been systematically taught.*
> *(Grossen, 1997,* 30 Years of Research, *pp. 10–11)*

Our analysis of the various advocacy and policy documents suggests a general agreement that "decodable text" has two key features that distinguish it from other types of reading text: a) it is composed of words considered phonetically regular and b) those words are constructed from phonic elements that have been previously taught.

However, as indicated by the advocacy and policy document excerpts below, there is little agreement on the proportion or range of decodable words needed for a text to be considered "decodable."

- The best kinds of stories to give children practice . . . contain lots of words that use specific letter-sound relationships that have been taught
- Stories based on the sound-letter relationships the children are learning
- Text developed using words easily decoded using principles from that day's or previous days' instruction
- Meaningful material that includes many words that exemplify the sound-spelling patterns being introduced
- Text composed of words that use sound-spelling correspondences that have been systematically taught
- Words in the stories are based on the sound-letter relationships the children are learning
- Text contains a high percentage of words composed of letter-sound correspondences the children have learned
- Reading material in which a high percentage of words are linked to phonics lessons
- Most of the words are comprised of an accumulating sequence of letter-sound correspondences being taught
- Text comprised mostly of words containing the sounds and symbols being taught

What is left unclear is whether "decodable text" is comprised solely, or mostly, of "decodable" words (with a few sight words allowed) or whether "decodable text" is text that, more simply, offers some opportunity to apply the phonic skills taught in the context of a text reading activity. Clarifying this ambiguity would seem important, since official policy statements are emerging regarding early reading instruction that include recommendations or mandates not only for the use of "decodable text," but also for budgetary allocations for the purchase of "decodable texts" instructional materials.

The question becomes: Will policymakers, performance evaluators, and financial auditors consider texts that are comprised of 30 percent decodable words as "decodable"? Or would 70 percent decodable words meet the appropriate criterion? Or 90 percent? For instance, consider the following guides in Texas and California:

Use letter-sound knowledge to read decodable texts (engaging and coherent texts *in which* most of the words *are comprised of an accumulating sequence of letter-sound correspondences being taught)* . . . *[emphasis added] (1997 Proclamation of the Texas State Board of Education Advertising for Bids on Instructional Materials, p. 7)*

In addition to direct instruction, students must be able to practice what they have been taught in decodable text that is comprised mostly of words *containing the sounds and symbols being taught (Adams, 1990). [emphasis added] (California State University Institute for Education Reform,* Building a Powerful Reading Program, *p. 5, also cited in California State Board of Education (1996),* Guide to the California Reading Initiative of 1996, *p. 4)*

The policy sources we located offered no specific answer to the question of when a text becomes "decodable." At this point it seems that such texts could be composed of "some," "mostly," "a high percentage of," or "almost exclusively of" words that children could decode based on their previous phonics lessons.

Research References Cited in Advocacy and Policy Documents

Our examination of each of the research references cited in the various advocacy and policy documents as supporting the use of an instructional emphasis on "decodable text" found that only a few research reports were cited but some were referenced repeatedly. To expand our search, we posted queries about relevant research and requests for citations on several literacy listservs and in a professional newsletter, asking for citations of studies on the topic of decodable texts. We received two additional references, which we examined.

The analysis of the relative frequency with which specific publications were cited in the advocacy and policy documents as supporting the use of decodable texts is shown in Figure 1.

Figure 1.   Relative Frequency of Publications Cited in Advocacy and Policy Documents

---

Publications cited most frequently:

Adams (1990)
Anderson et al. (1985)
Beck and Juel* (1995)
NICHD-Supported Research**

Publications cited less frequently:

Adams, Treiman and Pressley*** (1998)
Foorman et al. (1997)
Juel (1994) *Original study*
Felton (1993) *Original study*
Publications identified by queries:
Juel and Roper/Schneider (1985) *Original study*
Honig (1996)

---

* This paper was originally published in 1992 and reprinted in another publication in 1995. We located citations to both publication dates and sources.
**These are a number of studies that have been funded over several years by the National Institute of Child Health and Human Development (NICHD).
*** This publication was cited in several policy documents as (1996) but apparently did not actually appear in published form until 1998. Differences could have resulted from availability of prepublication copies of article.

Most of the cited publications were not original reports of research studies, and of the research studies cited, none actually manipulated the use of "decodable text" as an experimental variable. Of all the references noted in the advocacy and policy documents and identified from our queries, only three were original research study reports—Juel and Roper/Schneider (1985), Felton (1993); and Juel (1994).

One other citation, Foorman et al. (1997), provided a summary of three studies completed by a single research team, but the original reports of these studies were to be published elsewhere and were unavailable for review.[2] The remainder were essays, discussions, or reviews of research. There was much cross citation of the reviews within the reviews, and, in some cases, citations of the original research studies. These reviews provided additional references that we also examined.

We found no reading research study cited in the advocacy and policy documents that defined "decodable text" using both phonics lessons taught and words used in text reading. When "decodable text" was studied in instructional research (which was a rare occurrence), only the phonetic regularity of the words occurring in the reading text was considered.

In other words, reading texts were considered "decodable" without reference to any linkage between the letter-sound correspondence instruction offered and the words being read in the texts. The only studies that examined both the letter-sound lessons and the words presented in the text were content analyses studies of the nature of different basal reading series (e.g., Beck & Block, 1979). But this sort of study tells us nothing about whether these reading materials actually ease reading acquisition or enhance early literacy learning of children.

> No research studies were identified that systematically manipulated the proportion of words in texts considered "decodable" to assess the efficacy of texts comprised of "some," "many," "mostly," or "exclusively" words that could be pronounced based on the lessons previously taught.

No research studies were identified that systematically manipulated the proportion of words in texts considered "decodable" to assess the efficacy of texts comprised of "some," "many," "mostly," or "exclusively" words that could be pronounced based on the lessons previously taught. Thus, the available research offers little if any guidance as to just what "decodable text" should be in order to foster optimum reading achievement among the largest number of children.

Analysis of Specific Research Cited

We analyzed the research specifically cited in advocacy and policy documents as supporting the efficacy of using "decodable texts" in beginning reading. The following are descriptions of the cited research plus our analyses of these specific citations. Our findings and comments are shown in italics to differentiate them from the quoted text and descriptions of the research cited.

Juel and Roper/Schneider (1985)

The Juel and Roper/Schneider (1985) study is especially important for two reasons: a) it is one of a very few studies that actually analyzed the nature of the texts children read and examined the effects of different text types on the development of reading proficiency, and b) it is the primary research source for several secondary citations contained in advocacy documents.

The study—titled *The Influence of Basal Readers on First Grade Reading*—compared the performances of two groups of first graders, both taught an identical, and locally developed, synthetic phonics curriculum but who received instruction using two different basal reader series. (Only first graders considered to be in the mid-range of reading readiness were included in the study.)

One basal reader series "was a phonics oriented series with text which emphasized primarily regular decodable words in the initial preprimer texts" (p. 139). The other basal reader series "focused more on high frequency words and whose text in the initial preprimers exhibited more equality between regular and irregular decodable patterned words" (p. 139).

The authors' analyses of the two basal series show that the phonics oriented series contained more regular decodable words, as defined by the authors. No mention is made of the specific relationship between the local phonics curriculum and the words introduced in either basal reader series.

In the study, words were identified as "decodable" based on the regularity of the word structure alone and not on whether children had been previously taught the phonic elements needed to decode the words.

The series of word and pseudo-word assessments completed during the school year showed a pseudo-word pronunciation advantage for children using the phonics oriented reader series. End-of-the-year assessment also showed that children using the phonics oriented series achieved a significantly higher score on an experimenter-developed test of the identification of words not common to both basal series.

However, the end-of-year assessments produced no significant differences between the two groups of children on either of the two standardized assessment measures used: a) the Bryant Phonics Test, a pseudo-word pronunciation test, or b) the Iowa Test of Basic Skills.

Juel and Roper/Schneider (1985) concluded with this statement: "The interpretation of the results of this study do not constitute advocacy of any one specific approach to beginning reading instruction" (p. 150).

Findings: This study does not offer good evidence of advantages from using a phonics oriented basal reader compared to a high-frequency-word-oriented basal reader. The study provides no evidence that would support a recommendation for using "decodable text" as defined in the several advocacy and policy documents we reviewed.

FELTON (1993)

This study reports the effects of three beginning reading curriculum approaches on the achievement of 81 students in grades 1 and 2. The experimental group used a phonics basal reader, while the other used a meaning-emphasis basal reader and the control group received normal classroom instruction. At the end of two years of instruction there were no significant differences between phonics and meaning approaches on non-word reading, word reading, or on a decoding skills test (except for a subtest of decoding polysyllabic non-words).

Findings: While this study compared the use of reading programs where the beginning reading texts differed in the proportion of words deemed "decodable," the study provides no support for the greater efficacy of such texts in developing beginning reading skills. That is, there were no differences in the reading performances after two years.

JUEL (1994)

The Juel (1994) study reported a four-year longitudinal study of children learning to read in one school. The first-grade teachers in this school used a locally developed phonics curriculum and one of two basal readers. Of the several conclusions from this study, the findings that seem most relevant are: a) phonics should not be taught separate from reading, and b) workbook activities fail to foster much decoding growth.

Findings: The research design did not manipulate children's access to decodable text nor were the phonics lessons taught linked to the words in the readers the children used. This study offers no empirical support for the efficacy of "decodable texts" in promoting reading achievement.

FOORMAN ET AL. (1997)

The Foorman et al. (1997) paper summarizes three reading intervention studies conducted by a single research team. It would appear from the summaries that decodable texts might have been used in some of the intervention designs. The study summaries offer no indication that "decodable text" was an experimentally manipulated variable or that the use of "decodable texts" produced reliable, replicable advantages.

Findings: The three original studies summarized in the article had not been published at the time of our analysis but were scheduled for later publication. We were unable to obtain prepublication copies of the three study reports. However, the Foorman et al. summary of the studies makes no explicit mention of "decodable texts" and the research designs apparently did not systematically manipulate or monitor the use of different text types. Thus, this summary offers no evidence of the efficacy of using "decodable text" and sheds no light on how "decodable text" might be defined.

ADAMS (1990) AND ADAMS, TREIMAN, AND PRESSLEY (1998)

Both Adams (1990) and Adams, Treiman, and Pressley (1998) recommend that texts used in early reading instruction should provide practice on the phonetic elements recently taught. Both reviews cite the Juel and Roper/Schneider (1985) study (described previously) as evidence supporting this recommendation. Adams (1990) states:

> *In concurrence with Juel and Roper/Schneider's conclusions, the National Academy of Education's Commission on Reading has strongly urged publishers to bring the structure and wording of their earliest readers into coordination with their phonics instruction. To do so may significantly increase the effectiveness of their series. (p. 282)*

But Adams then cautions:

> *Recall that Juel and Roper/Schneider's study included only students who were assigned to the middle reading group and who scored above 40 percent on the Metropolitan Reading Readiness Test that they took on entering the first grade. Properly, then, their results pertain only to children in the middle of the readiness distribution. (p. 282)*

Findings: *While some assessments conducted by Juel and Roper/ Schneider (1985) showed advantages for children using the phonics oriented reader series as compared to the high-frequency-word-oriented reader series, their study found no significant differences between the two groups of students at the end of first grade on either the standardized pseudo-word pronunciation test or on the broad standardized Iowa Test of Basic Skills. Their report closes with the note that their findings "do not constitute advocacy of any one specific approach to beginning reading instruction" (p. 150).*

ANDERSON ET AL. (1985)

A frequently cited source for support of the use of "decodable text" in beginning reading is the report of the National Institute of Education's Commission on Reading (Anderson et al., 1985).

This report, titled *Becoming a Nation of Readers*, suggests that in early reading materials a "high proportion of the words in the earliest selections children read should conform to the phonics" children have learned (p. 47).

Findings: Unlike the case with most other recommendations in the report, no research citations are offered for this one. The report goes on to also note that overzealous attempts to create "decodable text" are not recommended and no rigid criteria should be established. But the primary question remains: What was the research basis for the recommendation?

The report continues:

> When programs . . . seek perfect regularity between spelling and pronunciation, using only letter-sound relationships that have already been taught, the results can be selections for beginning readers comprised of deadly sentences such as, "Dan had a tan fan." Children do not require this much regularity to master the alphabetic principle. (p. 47)

Findings: There are no citations in the text regarding the amount of regularity required for children to master the alphabetic principle. However, earlier in the report, one of the series of studies by Beck and colleagues was cited, but those reports do not offer evidence of the efficacy of "decodable text" use.

Beck and McCaslin (1978) and Beck (1981)

Several sources we located cited one of the series of older studies conducted by Beck and her colleagues (e.g., Beck & McCaslin, 1978; Beck, 1981). These were content analyses of different basal reading series. They identified many of the differences in competing basal reader series and identified a number of instructional design concerns including the strength of the relationship between phonics skills taught and the application of these skills in reading basal reader selections.

Findings: These studies were not experimental, correlational, or observational studies of teaching or students learning to read. The studies offered no research evidence that using "decodable text" had any effect on the reading acquisition of students.

BECK AND JUEL (1995)

This paper offers an overview of beginning reading and contains a section on beginning reading materials. The authors report:

> *Problems arise when the relationship between what children learn in phonics and the stories they read is either too low or too high. When too few of the words are decodable it is questionable whether what is taught in phonics is of any use. On the other hand, when all but one or two of the words in a selection are constrained by letter-sounds introduced, it is virtually impossible to write interesting selections in natural sounding language . . . Is there an optimal relationship between the letter sounds children are learning in phonics and the words in their readers? Clearly, the answer is no. (p. 39, Beck & Juel, 1995)*

Findings: Note the question raised by the authors Beck and Juel concerning optimal relationships between the letter sounds children learn in phonics and the words in their basal readers. Also note their clear negative answer to the question. While offering a practical rationale for providing text containing at least some decodable words, the authors did not offer evidence *for identifying an optimal proportion of decodable words in the text.*

BECK AND BLOCK (1979)

Beck and Block (1979) report on characteristics of various beginning reading texts. They cite Chall (1967) as a source for their use of "opportunity to transfer newly learned correspondences to sentence and story reading" (p. 347) as a useful criteria.

Findings: Chall (1967) developed this as one of nine separate criteria for categorizing the "learning of letter-sound correspondences" in her earlier content analyses of basal reader series (along with others, such as: set for regularity or set for diversity, number of verbalized rules taught, etc.) (p. 347). These were criteria that differentiated reading programs of the 1960s and not important features of instructional texts drawn from reliable, replicable research with beginning readers. Neither Beck and Block nor Chall provides evidence for the efficacy of "decodable text" use.

Honig (1996)

The following statement regarding research concerning "de-codable text" is offered by Honig (1996) in his reading methods text:

> *Researchers have found that the existence of the right number and kind of decodable words in beginning-reading texts is one of the most important factors in developing children's word recognition. They also found that phonics lessons made little sense to children beginning to read if few of the words in their initial texts did not follow these regular letter/sound correspondences (Adams, 1990, pp. 276, 279–280). (Honig, p. 67)*

Findings: *No research, including that cited by Adams (1990) has studied the "right number and kind of decodable words in beginning reading texts." The pages cited in the quotation above pertain to Adams' description of the Juel and Roper/Schneider (1985) study described previously.*

NICHD-Supported Research

Research funded by the National Institute of Child Health and Human Development (NICHD) is frequently cited by advocates of an emphasis on "decodable text" in reading instruction. The following are two examples that cite NICHD-supported research as authority for points being made in advocacy documents and policy recommendations.

Grossen (1997) A publication frequently cited as supporting research regarding an emphasis on "decodable text" in literacy instruction is a review by Grossen (1997)[3], titled *30 Years of Research on Reading: What We Now Know About How Children Learn to Read —A Synthesis of the Research on Reading from the National Institute of Child Health and Development.* (This work was not funded by NICHD.)

Grossen offers a series of general recommendations for classroom instruction that are said to have been drawn from 30 years of research funded by the NICHD. For example, Recommendation Number 5 states: "Use connected, decodable text for children to practice the sound-spelling relationships they learn" (p. 11).

No direct citation of supporting research is given. The author simply states:

> *The findings from the NICHD research emphasize that children need extensive practice applying their knowledge of letter-sound relationships to the task of reading as they learn them. This integration of phonics and reading can only occur with the use of decodable texts. (p. 11)*

Findings: *Since no specific research studies were cited, we reviewed the whole set of NICHD-supported studies that Grossen cites throughout the "30 years of research" document and found no evidence to support the recommendation (Allington and Woodside-Jiron, 1997).*

We found no study cited that attempted to isolate or manipulate: a) the sequence of sound-spelling instruction, and b) the coordination of the instruction of sound-spelling with the materials read.

One cannot analyze the available NICHD-supported research and arrive at the conclusion that the integration of phonics and reading can only occur with the use of "decodable text," nor that most children need extensive practice in such materials, not from the NICHD research currently available.

National Right to Read Foundation (1996) The following advice was disseminated in both California and Texas by the National Right to Read Foundation:

> *Teach students sound-spelling relationships using connected, decodable text. Students need extensive practice applying their knowledge of sound-spelling relationships as they are learning them. This integration can only occur with the use of decodable text composed of words that use sound-spelling correspondences that have been systematically taught.* (Principles of Reading Instruction, *National Right to Read Foundation, 1996, p. 1)*

An accompanying note indicates that this principle was "distilled from $200 million in research, conducted over thirty years, under the direction of the National Institutes of Child Health and Human Development."

Findings: *While some NICHD studies have evaluated interventions that employed text that could be described as decodable, our search found* *no NICHD-supported study where "decodable text" had been experimentally isolated or systematically manipulated as a variable. At this point, the role that "decodable text" plays in beginning reading is simply not well understood.*

Discussion and Summary

Educational reforms have come round and round in reading instruction and have often been promoted as being "research-based." Policy statements and mandates requiring the use of "decodable text" in early reading instruction is a reform currently being advocated in several states and initiated in some states as being "research-based."

We have carefully traced the research citations noted in advocacy and policy documents to their original research sources and were unable to locate any "reliable, replicable research" concerning the use of "decodable text" upon which these policy decisions were based.

We have located no research studies that provided evidence that the use of "decodable text"—as defined in the California and Texas educational policy documents—actually enhances the reading development or the reading achievement of children. We have found no research evidence to support the two states' educational policy recommendations, which are purported to be based on research findings.

Many persons and agencies have made arguments and recommendations for the use of "decodable texts." And few would question that there should be some linkage between the phonics taught and the words contained in the texts used by children beginning to read. However, the fact is: there are no research studies cited in the advocacy and policy documents that shed light on the amount or range of text that should be decodable or that provide evidence of the relative efficacy of variations in "decodable texts" in helping most students develop specific reading skills.

The ambiguity and uncertainty of what constitutes "decodable text" can pose major problems when policies or mandates are made requiring teachers to use, evaluators to assess, school officials to purchase, financial auditors to verify, text book selection committees to approve, and text book publishers to produce "decodable texts."

Thus, the uncertainty of definition and the absence of research on what constitutes effective use of "decodable text" leads to confusion both on the part of persons and agencies required to use "decodable text" and on the part of those responsible for making sure that "decodable text" is being used in early reading instruction.

It is troublesome to learn that policies and mandates that do not have a foundation in research findings can become widely accepted as being "research based." The current emphasis on using reading instruction programs based on "reliable, replicable research" requires a greater emphasis on the rigor with which research is not only conducted and reported, but also increased rigor with which research is reviewed and greater care when attempting to translate research findings into instructional recommendations and policy.

> The current emphasis on using reading instruction programs based on "reliable, replicable research" requires a greater emphasis on the rigor with which research is not only conducted and reported, but also increased rigor with which research is reviewed and greater care when attempting to translate research findings into instructional recommendations and policy.

As it now stands, we have available two well-populated and geographically diverse locales—California and Texas—in which to carry out large-scale analyses of the role that "decodable text" plays in the acquisition of early reading proficiency by students.

But in neither state does there seem to be recognition that such research is needed. We have located no plans or any funding for research to address the questions, both practical and theoretical, about the effects on student reading proficiency of variations in phonetic elements taught and the use of different types of "decodable texts." Without several well-constructed longitudinal studies, we will remain unaware of whether there are optimal relationships between the letter-sounds various children learn in phonics instruction and the decodable words in their reading texts.

In making policy decisions as well as in future research, we must remember that the early acquisition of effective and efficient decoding skills and strategies, while important, is not the only factor that determines children's success in initial reading.

We have some 50 years of research that has identified important features of children, texts, and instructional settings that play crucial roles in beginning reading. If we are to be successful in our attempts to create more effective beginning literacy instruction, educational policy making must attend to this research, as well as the research on the acquisition of decoding skills.

Recommending broad policy and sweeping mandates for reading instruction without careful attention to existing and future research that is both relevant and meaningful undermines both the development of more effective reading programs and important academic discourse.

Notes

1. This publication was cited in several policy documents as (1996) but apparently did not actually appear in published form until 1998. The differences in dates could have resulted from the availability of earlier prepublication copies of the article.

2. These articles were reviewed in a later paper (Pressley & Allington, 1999). None manipulated text decodability in its research design. No conclusion about the utility of decodable texts can be drawn from those studies.

3. We have located three substantially identical versions of this publication. The earliest version was published in the summer 1996 issue of *Effective School Practices,* edited by Bonita Grossen. The second was downloaded from the Center for the Future of Teaching and Learning (CFTL) web site, December 20, 1996, and listed no author. The third was downloaded from the CFTL web site April 1997 and lists Bonita Grossen as author.

References

Adams, M. J. (1990). *Beginning to read: Thinking and learning about print.* Cambridge, MA: MIT Press.

Adams, M. J., Treiman, R., & Pressley, M. (1998). Reading, writing, and literacy. In I. Sigel & A. Renninger (Eds.), *Handbook of child psychology, Vol. 4. Child psychology in practice* (5th ed., pp. 275–355). New York: Wiley.

Allington, R. L. (1984). Oral reading. In P. D. Pearson (Ed.), *Handbook of reading research* (pp. 829–864). New York: Longmans.

Allington, R. L., & Woodside-Jiron, H. (1997). *Adequacy of a program of research and of a "research synthesis" in shaping educational policy* (Research Report No. 1.15). Albany, NY: State University of New York at Albany, National Research Center on English Learning and Achievement.

Anderson, R. C., Hiebert, E. H., Scott, J., & Wilkinson, I. A. (1985). *Becoming a nation of readers: The report of the Commission on Reading.* Washington, DC: National Institute of Education, U.S. Department of Education.

Beck, I. L. (1981). Reading problems and instructional practices. In G. E. MacKinnon & T. G. Waller (Eds.), *Reading research: advances in theory and practice, Vol. 2* (pp. 55–91). New York: Academic Press.

Beck, I. L., & Block, K. K. (1979). An analysis of two beginning reading programs: Some facts and some opinions. In L. B. Resnick & P. A. Weaver (Eds.), *Theory and practice in early reading, Vol. 1* (pp. 279–318). Hillsdale, NJ: Lawrence Erlbaum Associates.

Beck, I. L., & Juel, C. (1992/1995). The role of decoding in learning to read. In S. J. Samuels & A. Farstrup (Eds.), *What research has to say about reading instruction* (2nd ed., pp. 101–123). Newark, DE: International Reading Association. (Reprinted 1995 in *American Educator 19*, pp. 8, 21–25, 39 & 42).

Beck, I., & McCaslin, E. S. (1978). An analysis of dimensions that affect development of code-breaking ability in eight beginning reading programs. (No. 1978/6). Pittsburgh, PA: Learning Research and Development Center, University of Pittsburgh.

Berliner, D. C., & Biddle, B. J. (1996). *The manufactured crisis: Myths, fraud, and the attack on America's public schools.* White Plains, NY: Longmans.

Bracey, G. W. (1997). *Setting the record straight: Responses to misconceptions about public education in the United States.* Alexandria, VA: Association for Supervision and Curriculum Development.

California Department of Education (1996). *Teaching reading: A balanced comprehensive approach to teaching reading in prekindergarten through grade three.* Sacramento, CA: Author.

California Department of Education (1997). *Read all about it.* Sacramento, CA: Author.

California State Board of Education (1996). *Guide to the California Reading Initiative of 1996.* Sacramento, CA: Author.

California State Board of Education (1997). Comprehensive Reading Leadership Program board members and superintendents read all about it: One day workshop. Sacramento, CA: Sacramento County Office of Education.

California State University Institute for Education Reform (1996). *Building a powerful reading program*. Sacramento, CA: Author.

Carnine, D., & Meeder, H. (Sept. 3, 1997). Reading research into practice. *Education Week*, pp. 41, 43.

Chall, J. S. (1967). *Learning to read: The great debate*. New York: McGraw-Hill.

Felton, R. H. (1993). Effects of instruction on the decoding skills of children with phonological processing problems. *Journal of Learning Disabilities 26*, 583–589.

Foorman, B. R., Francis, D. J., Beeler, T., Winikates, D., & Fletcher, J. M. (1997). Early interventions for children with reading problems: Study designs and preliminary findings. *Learning disabilities: A multi-disciplinary perspective, 8*, 63–71.

Grossen, B. (1997). *30 years of research on reading: What we now know about how children learn to read—A synthesis of research on reading from the National Institute of Child Health and Development*. Santa Cruz, CA: The Center for the Future of Teaching and Learning.

Honig, B. (1996). *Teaching our children to read: The role of skills in a comprehensive reading program*. Thousand Oaks, CA: Corwin Press.

Juel, C. (1994). *Learning to read and write in one elementary school*. New York: Springer-Verlag.

Juel, C., & Roper/Schneider, D. (1985). The influence of basal readers on first grade reading. *Reading Research Quarterly 20*, 134–152.

Kibby, M. W. (1995). *Student literacy: Myths and realities* (Fastback No. 381). Bloomington, IN: Phi Delta Kappa Educational Foundation.

National Right to Read Foundation, California Division (1996). *Principles of reading instruction*. Cypress, CA: Author.

Texas Education Agency (November 7, 1997). 1997 Proclamation of the State Board of Education Advertising for Bids on Instructional Materials. Austin, TX: Author.

Texas Reading Initiative (n.d.). *Beginning reading instruction: Components and features of a research-based reading program*. Austin, TX: Texas Education Agency.

10 ■ Explicit and Systematic Teaching of Reading— A New Slogan?

Brian Cambourne
University of Wollongong, Australia

Brian Cambourne is an Aussie. His paper doesn't even mention the National Reading Panel—so why is it included here? Because he hits on a universal theme that runs through reading education in English-speaking countries, and especially through the current national reading campaign here in the U.S.: the focus on explicit *and* systematic *(and now* scientific*) instruction. How many times are those words repeated in the legislation that Frances Paterson summarizes in Chapter 8? How many times are those phrases used in various state curriculum documents and frameworks?*

What I like about Brian's short piece is how nicely he sets up the contrasts and forces the reader to think a bit beyond the obvious. Should instruction be explicit? Yes, some of the time. For some kids. On some days. The problem with always being explicit is that it leaves kids no room to figure things out for themselves. No room to develop self-regulation. No room for curiosity.

This article brings the issue of mindful *vs.* mindless *to bear on the question of effective and contextualized teaching. I like this piece because it reflects my own experience: The exemplary*

217

teachers we have observed (Pressley, Allington, Wharton-McDonald, Block & Morrow, 2001) were explicit when they needed to be, and they were often explicit about useful decoding strategies—what some would call embedded phonics, *though in a contextualized sense. And the children they taught, even the poorest readers, could decode as well as the best readers from less effective classrooms (the classrooms that used those explicit, systematic phonics kits).*

Good teaching is an expert activity. It is explicit when explicitness is needed. It is systematic, but not in the sense of following some publisher's idea of a model phonics lesson sequence. It is always mindful and usually contextualized. It is precisely the opposite of the one-size-fits-all scripted curriculum. Only in Alice's Wonderland could teaching from a script be labeled "scientific."

Pressley, M., Allington, R. L., Wharton-McDonald, R., Block, C.C., & Morrow, L. M. (2001). *Learning to read: Lessons from exemplary first-grade classrooms.* New York: Guilford.

Teachers through the ages have been bombarded with slogans that reflect the preferred methods for teaching reading. In the 1940s it was Look and Say or Whole Word. In the 50s it was Phonics First. Then came Language Experience, which merged into Reading for Meaning, then Whole Language. Direct Instruction was a slogan that challenged Whole Language during the 70s and early 80s.

In the mid-80s and 90s there has been a strengthening of support for Direct Instruction in most western democracies (e.g., U.S., Australia, U.K., Canada, New Zealand). This support for Direct Instruction seems to have brought with it a new slogan: Explicit and Systematic Teaching of Reading. In each of these countries the slogan (or some paraphrase of it) pervades, with monotonous regularity, curriculum, policy, and legislative documents, and a diverse range of other literacy-related texts.

Some time ago the prevalence of this slogan coerced me to pose myself a research question: When it comes to creating classroom conditions that support a relatively uncomplicated and barrier-free approach to the acquisition of literacy, what is the role of explicit and systematic teaching? I revisited the classroom data archives I've been building for several years to address this question. Here is what has so far emerged from this retrospective incursion into the data.

The teaching-learning events and activities that took place in those classrooms that seemed to produce effective readers and users of texts could be described in terms of four categories of learning and teaching. These four categories—explicit teaching, systematically planned teaching, mindful teaching, and contextualised teaching—were really concepts that had opposites. If their opposite concepts—implicit teaching; unsystematically planned, unstructured teaching; mindless teaching; and decontextualised teaching—were placed so that they formed imaginary continuums, a potentially useful framework for understanding the teaching and learning that occurred in such classrooms emerged. I decided to call this framework the Four Possible Dimensions of Learning and Teaching: explicit, as opposed to implicit; systematic, as opposed to unsystematic; mindful, as opposed to mindless; contextualised, as opposed to decontextualised. Here's how I defined each of these dimensions.

Explicit—Implicit

Explicit teaching refers to the practice of deliberately demonstrating and bringing to learners' conscious awareness those covert and invisible processes, understandings, knowledge, and skills over which they need to get control if they are to become effective readers. Implicit teaching refers to the practice of deliberately leaving it to learners to discover or work out these things for themselves.

What sorts of things were made explicit in effective classrooms? While this varied from classroom to classroom, in the classrooms I observed there seemed to be a high incidence of teachers making explicit such things as (a) **What sort of things were made explicit in effective classrooms?** personal dislikes, enthusiasms, tastes in literature, and other kinds of texts; (b) the reasons for engaging in the reading events and activities that they prepared; and (c) the implicit, often invisible, processes that make successful reading (and writing, spelling, and learning) possible. Each of these forms of explicit teaching seemed to serve the following purposes.

- By making explicit their personal likes and dislikes about the texts they read, and even sharing some of their personal lives (e.g., what their children and relatives were doing, or the things they did with their families on the weekend), teachers were able to create an ethos that supported the establishment of the kind of personal relationships they believed were at the core of the learning cultures they were trying to create.

- By making explicit the invisible, often taken-for-granted, processes and knowledge that effective literacy behavior entails, teachers were helping learners in at least two ways. First, for those who did not come from home cultures that provided repeated opportunities to discover these processes, teachers were providing repeated demonstrations of the skills, understandings, and know-how their students might not otherwise get the opportunity to understand. Second, teachers were providing opportunities for students with a confused understanding of how reading and writing worked to clarify their confusions.

- By making the reasons for asking students to engage in the learning activities that were introduced into the setting explicit, teachers were constantly helping students understand how all the bits of what they did in the course of a school day fit together to achieve the purposes of school and school learning.

Systematic—Unsystematic

I defined systematic instruction as that which is based on proactive rational planning. It was evidenced by formal planning documents indicating that teachers had thought ahead, developed, and documented a set of plans or blueprints of future lessons, activities, resources, and assessment procedures that they intended to use. Unsystematic instruction was unplanned or showed little evidence of rational planning.

A teacher's position on this continuum reflected the coherence, rationality, and proactive nature of a teacher's planning and preparation. Two interdependent indicators were used to locate teachers along this continuum. One was the degree to which the planning documents they prepared reflected proactive rational planning. The other was each teacher's ability to articulate this rationale. Teachers who were judged to be high on "systematicity" were those who could explain in confident and coherent ways why they'd planned to use the teaching-learning activities and processes they'd included in their planning documents and how such activities facilitated their students' learning.

Teachers who were judged to be more toward the unsystematic end of this continuum were those whose planning documents were sparse or difficult for another professional to understand, and those who could not explain and justify their planning decisions in anything but superficial ways ("I don't know why I have Show and Tell each day. Isn't it good for kids?"). My data strongly indicated that teachers who were successful (according to my criteria) at creating effective reading classrooms were more toward the systematic end of this continuum.

Mindful—Mindless

The concept of mindful, as opposed to mindless, learning is the brainchild of Ellen Langer (1989, 1997). She argued that the way we take in information or learn skills ultimately determines how we use it or them later. Thus, if we learn something like reading, writing, or indeed any of the accoutrements of literacy in a mindful way, we are more likely to use it in mindful ways, and vice versa.

Langer equated mindless learning with learning that encourages and develops nonconscious automaticity. Such automaticity, she argued, usually develops as a consequence of mindless repetition and practice. Automaticity results in responses and meanings that tend to be nonconscious, invariant, and fixed, regardless of context. This kind of learning creates a mindset that inhibits critical awareness. Langer equated mindful learning with an openness to other possibilities. I equate it with metacognitive awareness; that is, the state of being consciously aware of what's going on, of being consciously aware of other possibilities, given the context. Mindful teaching and learning were more obvious in those classrooms I judged to be producing more effective readers.

Contextualised—Decontextualised

Contextualised learning is learning that makes sense to the learner. Because it makes sense, such learning is not only less complicated, it is more likely to result in robust, transferable, useful, and mindful learning. In contrast, learning that learners can't make much sense of leads to automatic, rigid, mindless learning. The degree to which learners can make sense of any learning situation is a function of the degree to which they can place it in a context that helps them make connections. In those classrooms that I judged to be producing effective readers, teachers consciously strove to contextualise their students' learning.

My data also showed that these teachers tried to contextualise the learning activities associated with learning to read by employing a mix of such strategies as (a) creating meaningful and authentic purposes for engaging in reading behaviour; (b) giving the message that reading helps us get control of information and information is a source of power in our culture; and (c) making the learning activities associated with reading as much like the reading, writing, learning, and problem-solving behaviours that highly literate adults would demonstrate in the world outside school.

> My data also showed that these teachers tried to contextualize the learning activities associated with learning to read by employing a mix of such strategies . . .

A Word of Caution

From this retrospective revisiting of classroom data, I drew this conclusion: The new slogan—Explicit and Systematic Teaching of

Reading—is potentially a dangerous one for teachers to implement. This is not because there is anything wrong with teachers being both explicit and systematic. On the contrary, it is when explicit and systematic teaching is also mindless and decontextualised that it becomes dangerous because it makes learning much more complex than it ought to be.

On the other hand, my data suggest that mindful, contextualised teaching that is also implicit and unsystematic would also create serious barriers for many learners. Perhaps a so-called balanced approach to teaching reading is one that needs teachers to create the optimum mix of these four dimensions of learning.

References

Langer, E. (1989). *Mindfulness*. New York: Addison-Wesley.

Langer, E. (1997). *The power of mindful learning*. New York: Addison-Wesley.

11 ■ The Will of the People

Jacqueline Edmondson
and Patrick Shannon
Pennsylvania State University,
University Park, Pennsylvania

*Maybe I agree with the National Reading Panel, because I don't
believe that reading a book is reading instruction. Instead, it is
practice; it is enjoyable; it is interesting; it is the reason I put up
with reading instruction in the first place. Perhaps some self-
teaching is going on as I talk to myself about plot development,
or the character's motives, or the author's political stance. I might
talk with myself about the probable meaning of a new word I've
encountered, or its likely pronunciation.*

*Personally, I think the whole idea of "instruction" is over-
rated and largely misunderstood. Much of what passes for instruction in schools and in the experiments the NRP reported on
is at best guided assessment. Filling out phonics worksheets is
not instructional. It is decontextualized practice at best, and isolated assessment at worst. No one learns phonics from a work-
sheet. No one learns to decode proficiently from phonics drills. I
spent a couple of years observing some of the nation's best first-
grade teachers, and I hardly saw a "phonics" program. What I
saw was expert teachers teaching children how to decode (or
spell) the words they encountered in the texts they read and*

wrote, and in the context of books, not decodable texts. Most of this teaching was conducted with teacher and student working side-by-side, not through whole-group chanting. These exemplary first-grade teachers had their children read and write all day long. Like the exemplary fourth-grade teachers I studied later, they had kids reading three, five, ten times as much material as less effective teachers did.

So, like Jacqueline Edmondson and Patrick Shannon, I reject the NRP's assertion that there isn't enough evidence to support using extensive reading as a path to improved reading. We have reliable, scientific evidence that extensive reading produces children who read better. The NRP just ignored it. Perhaps the panel should have focused on what good teachers do, rather than on what crafty experimental psychologists have decided they should do.

"We're not supposed to do that anymore." "Not supposed to have your students read children's literature silently?"

"Our curriculum supervisor is gearing us up for the Reading First initiative, and we are only supposed to do research-based instruction."

"Sustained Silent Reading is to stop?"

"During reading instruction. We can't count it as part of our instruction because there isn't a solid research base for it."

"What about the research that shows a correlation between the amount of students' recreational reading and achievement-test scores?"

"What about it? I'm telling you that my coordinator is telling my principal that silent reading does not bring test results. My principal, who always worried what parents would think when they wandered into the building and saw everyone reading, just told us to stop SSR and start teaching more."

"You're kidding."

"Give him a call if you don't believe me."

And so we did. The conversation with the principal was brief and enlightening. Kelly (pseudonym), one of the school's reading teachers, was correct that silent reading would not be considered reading instruction next year at her school. In the past, silent reading was encouraged because the previous state curriculum for English Language Arts had recommended it as a primary means for helping students learn to read. In fact, the length of time devoted to silent reading was increased over the years and grades. Kindergarten students were up to 10 minutes a day, and third graders in this primary school were reading at least 30 minutes a day. Although the achievement scores in this U.S. school district were improving steadily, they still were not above the state levels. According to the latest research, we were told, redirecting the silent reading time to direct instruction should bring better test results. More reading instruction didn't mean that students wouldn't read books; rather, teachers would need to find other time during the day for silent reading. Administrators wanted a research-based reading program in line with the state and federal guidelines.

Reading First and Sustained Silent Reading

Worried that we might be considered out of step in our teaching, we started to trace those guidelines, beginning at the only point of reference given in our two conversations—U.S. President George W. Bush's Reading First initiative. It wasn't hard to find. Part of the No Child Left Behind educational program, the Reading First initiative is intended to make sure that all school children in the United States learn to read by third grade. To pursue this intention, the Bush Administration will make US$900 million available to elementary schools eligible for grants, if their K–2 reading programs are "anchored in scientific research." (An early Reading First initiative is designed for preschool programs, Head Start in particular.) According to the No Child Left Behind homepage (http://www.ed.gov/inits/nclb/part4.html), the basic architecture for design of scientifically based programs is the National Reading Panel report (2000).

Effective reading instruction includes teaching children to break apart and manipulate the sounds in words (phonemic awareness), teaching them that these sounds are represented by letters of the

*alphabet which can then be blended together to form words (phon-
ics), having them practice what they have learned by reading aloud
with guidance and feedback (guided oral reading), and applying
reading comprehension strategies to guide and improve reading
comprehension.*

When U.S. Senator Thad Cochran of Mississippi introduced
Senate Bill 939 (The Successful Reading and Instruction Act) in
July 1997, to establish the National Reading Panel, he offered four
reasons why his fellow senators should approve the appropriation. The National Assessment of Educational Progress results
suggested that 20% of elementary school children in the U.S. cannot read at a basic level and that nearly 60% read below the proficiency level.* The National Institute for Child Health and
Human Development (NICHD) research concluded that appropriate early intervention would lower those rates substantially.
The U.S. Department of Education has not made these findings
known to schoolteachers and parents. Finally, many teachers and
parents he talked with are frustrated and confused about what
method of reading instruction is best.

Accordingly, the National Reading Panel was charged by the
U.S. Congress in 1997 to (a) conduct a thorough study of the research and knowledge relevant to early reading development and
instruction in early reading, (b) determine which research findings and what knowledge are available in the nation's classrooms,
and (c) determine how to disseminate the research findings and
knowledge to the nation's schools and classrooms.

The panel was expected to accomplish these goals in 9
months. The panel first met on April 28, 1998. NICHD Director
Duane Alexander presented a more detailed charge to the group.
According to Alexander,

> *the Congress of the United States directed the panel to assess the
> status of research-based knowledge of reading development and dis-*

---

*Editor note: The NAEP 4th grade reading reports have offered steadily de-
clining numbers of children failing to achieve the Basic level of reading proficiency across the past decade (from 47% in early 1990s to 37% in the most
recent NAEP administration) <http://nces.ed.gov/nationsreportcard/>.

*ability, including the effectiveness of various approaches to teach-
ing children to read. . . . [T]he panel is charged to conduct an extensive and critical review, analysis, and synthesis of the research
literature on how children learn to read, and on how the components
of skilled reading behavior are developed by various approaches to
reading instruction for children of differing backgrounds, learning
characteristics, and literacy experiences taking into account the
relevance, methodologic rigor and applicability, validity, reliability
and replicability of the reported research, the panel should. . . .*
(Alexander, minutes of NRP, pp. 2–3, April 28, 1998)

The panel took it from there and "looked only at research
that presented what it described as clear scientific evidence that
a particular practice was causally linked to a particular outcome"
(Manzo, 2000, p. 14). During the 2001 annual convention of the
International Reading Association in New Orleans, USA, panel
member Timothy Shanahan put the nail in the coffin for silent
reading in primary grades when he told *Education Week* reporters that anecdotal and qualitative evidence was not good enough
any longer: "If it isn't proven to work through research, you can't
count it towards instruction" (Diegmuller & Manzo, 2001, p. 18).

Trying to trace the rationale for removing Sustained Silent
Reading from reading instruction is like calling a phone company
about a mistake on your bill. No one accepts responsibility, and
there is always someone else that you need to talk to. Kelly must
inform the teachers in her school that Sustained Silent Reading
is not instruction anymore. If they ask why not, she'll refer them
to the principal. If the
teachers repeat the ques-
tion, then the principal
will refer them to the
Reading First initiative.
Should the teachers have
enough gumption to call
the Department of Educa-
tion of the Bush adminis-
tration, then they will be
referred to the National Reading Panel's report. Ask about the
report, and they'll be referred to the integrity of the science upon

> It can't be that science proves that
> Sustained Silent Reading isn't
> reading instruction, because in
> 1985 the National Academy of
> Science's *Becoming a Nation of
> Readers* recommended the practice
> enthusiastically.

which the report was based. Question the omnipotence of science (very brave indeed), and reference to the charge from Congress will be mentioned. Examine the charge from Congress and the rhetoric that surrounded it in 1997, and they'll be referred to the "many teachers and parents . . . frustrated and confused." In the end apparently, they should talk to themselves. They are parents and teachers, and we are now frustrated!

What's Going on Here?

Just who or what has the authority to turn Sustained Silent Reading into noninstruction? It's not the will of the people. People (yes, parents and teachers are people) aren't confused about reading books. They know that reading books independently is valuable to reading instruction. They might quarrel over which books to read, but virtually all teachers and parents want students to read books. There's nothing in the charge from Congress about Sustained Silent Reading, and we think even members of Congress would agree that reading books is a good practice. For that matter, there's nothing in the Congressional charge to the panel about science, only "research and knowledge." It can't be that science proves that Sustained Silent Reading isn't reading instruction, because in 1985 the National Academy of Science's *Becoming a Nation of Readers* recommended the practice enthusiastically. "Research suggests that the amount of independent, silent reading children do in school is significantly related to gains in reading achievement" (Anderson, Hiebert, Scott, & Wilkinson, 1985, p. 76).

Clearly the National Academy of Science knows science.

Clearly the National Academy of Science knows science. That leaves the National Reading Panel and a lesson in power. As member Thomas Trabasso argued during its second meeting, this isn't a case of being objective:

> *I think it is impossible to be quote "objective" unquote. You are going to have—You always have some. . . . Everything is interpreted, okay? Everything is constructed. The question is whether*

or not we get some degree of support independently of our own opinions. That is what we are looking for. (Trabasso, lines 25–30, minutes of NRP, July 24, 1998)

This quote is useful in coming to understand who has the power to name instruction and how that power can be used. In this case, the interpretation (which Trabasso mentions) began with Duane Alexander's reading of the Congressional charge. During his interpretation, Congress's assessing research and knowledge became the panel's "taking into account the relevance, methodologic rigor and applicability, validity, reliability and replicability of the reported research" (Alexander, minutes of NRP, p. 3, April 28, 1998). The construction of official reality began when the panel decided that in order for a stimulus to be considered instruction it must have a demonstrated causal link with a desired response, denigrating and excluding many types of research and much of what teachers know about reading instruction from its consideration. In the first mention of the need for a panel before Congress, Senator Cochran named the opinions to be supported by independent sources—NICHD research reports on reading. In the end, the panel's report obliged, and there won't be any Sustained Silent Reading as reading instruction in Kelly's school next year.

A Brief Aside

Just so there is no confusion about whether this is a demonstration of power and not some natural expression of science, we include this brief aside. The Bush administration's Reading First initiative has a preschool component with the intention of revamping the federally funded Head Start program. According to Reid Lyon, a reading expert at NICHD, there is little data on how best to prepare Head Start kids for reading. "I have some thoughts, but no validated data," he told *The Wall Street Journal* (Davis, 2001, p. A24). According to the panel's construction, without research data showing direct links, there can be no reading instruction. Yet Lyon is urging lawmakers to award grants to states that revise Head Start programs so kids are taught skills such as recognizing letters and connecting them with sounds. Trabasso was correct—it is impossible to be objective.

So, apparently we are out of step with our teaching because we recommend and use many practices that have not been validated by NICHD studies or the panel's selective logic. It's quite easy for us to justify being out of step, when the one who pays the fiddler and calls the tune hasn't helped many children learn to read. Yet many children *have* learned to read well by finding the time during the school day to read a good book. We know because we've watched some do it.

References

Anderson, R., Hiebert, E., Scott, J., & Wilkinson, I. (1985). *Becoming a nation of readers*. Washington, DC: National Academy of Science.

Davis, B. (2001, April 23). Phonics maven is at center of Bush's education push. *The Wall Street Journal*, p. A24.

Diegmuller, K., & Manzo, K. (2001, May 9). IRA attendees flock to sessions on applying reading research. *Education Week*, 18.

Manzo, K. (2000, April 19). Reading panel urges phonics for all in K–6. *Education Week*, 14.

National Reading Panel. (2000, April). *Teaching children to read*. Washington, DC: National Institute of Child Health and Human Development.

CONCLUSION

*An Unwarranted Intrusion:
The Evidence Against a
National Reading Curriculum*

12 ■ Accelerating in the Wrong Direction: Why Thirty Years of Federal Testing and Accountability Hasn't Worked Yet and What We Might Do Instead

Richard L. Allington
University of Florida

I magine watching an automobile turn onto an exit ramp and rapidly accelerate into the oncoming traffic. The driver isn't looking at you, he's headed in the opposite direction. You feel sick to your stomach as you see that a disaster is about to unfold. You might even close your eyes and pray for divine intervention.

Today, I feel the gut-wrenching horror of knowing that an accident is in the making—but I'm watching American politicians engaged in their version of stimulating educational reform. At the crux of their "new, new" plan for improving American schools is the testing of students. But there is nothing new about mandated federal testing. The government has for thirty years or more required schools that receive federal funds to test students (Wise, 1979). In fact, the U.S. Office of Technology Assessment (1992) noted that federal education program requirements had dramatically increased the amount of testing in American schools since the 1970s. It reported a decade ago that most elementary school children were tested annually, and some twice a year, in order to meet federal program evaluation requirements.

The children most likely to be tested frequently are poor children, who attend schools that are eligible for that smorgasbord of federal education program dollars. Part of the price of accepting federal funds has always been submitting children to annual testing and meeting federal accountability requirements. The rules have required that *all* students in schools that receive federal funds be tested, not just students who participate in, say, a remedial reading program funded with federal dollars (LeTendre, 1996).

The No Child Left Behind bill, PL 107–110, expands the testing requirement to the few schools that didn't already test for federal programs compliance, primarily schools serving an almost exclusively middle-class population of students. It is difficult for me to see this minor, but expensive, shift as truly "new." Politicians' touting the passage of the No Child Left Behind bill as some sort of new day in education is simply what newspeople call "spin."

It's difficult to understand just how spending federal dollars testing America's rich kids is going to improve the achievement of poor kids. And in this era of "evidenced-based" educational planning, I'm puzzled that, so far, no federal official has made it clear which theory or scientific evidence supports expanding testing to middle-class kids. Or what evidence supports testing, in general, as the route to improved achievement—that testing is a "scientific" means for narrowing the rich/poor reading achievement gap (Strauss, 2002).

This is an era of political rhetoric routinely punctuated with the phrase "scientific evidence." The new law proscribes the use of any effort to improve reading that is not based in "scientific" research. But there is no research evidence to support that the mandates the law does prescribe represent a scientific strategy for improving schools (Allington, 2001; McGill-Franzen, 2000; Pogrow, 2002). In fact, the evidence suggests just the opposite: Mandates routinely undermine the likelihood of reliable school improvement.

In his book *Standardized Minds*, journalist Peter Sacks (2000) offers some plain-language criticisms of the push for federalized accountability. "Common sense might further tell one that if teachers are teaching to the test via rote teaching styles, rushing through lots of drills and worksheets and practice tests . . . shortchanged are thinking, analyzing, synthesizing, performing, articulating, and other modes of in-depth learning. Call it the dumb down (p. 130). . . . While the rhetoric is highly effective, remarkably little good evidence exists that there's any educational substance behind the accountability and testing movement" (p. 155).

I have noted that politicians seem most enamoured with research that supports their political agendas (Allington, 1999, 2001). At the same time, they seem to be fully capable of ignoring scientific research that violates their political ideologies. The most recent example of this occurred when new federal funding for sex education programs clearly did not follow the scientific research. *Newsweek* magazine (February 11, 2002) reported that when asked about this, a presidential advisor shrugged and said, "Values trump data," and noted that there would have been political hell to pay had any sort of sex education other than abstinence programs been funded.

The major thrust of the recently passed education legislation (PL 107-110) isn't based on "scientific evidence," even though it invokes that phrase more than a hundred times. In fact, the accumulated weight of thirty years of scientific evidence on the effects of federal testing and accountability requirements indicates that this approach is largely devoid of any positive effects on student achievement. Is this new law another case of values trumping data? Of ideology trumping evidence?

The Effects of Thirty Years of Federal Testing and Accountability

The best evidence on the achievement of students in the U.S. comes from the National Assessment of Educational Progress (NAEP). The national assessments in reading were initiated in the 1970–71 school year and have been administered regularly since that time. The good news is that the most recent reading assessments indicated that students at each of the grade levels tested (fourth, eighth, twelfth) read just as well as (maybe a little bit better than) students did thirty-plus years ago (Donahue, Voelkl, Campbell, & Mazzeo, 1999). In other words, even though the past thirty years have brought us a variety of school reform efforts (the effective schools movement, mastery learning, whole school reform models, proven programs) and an array of new reading curriculum models, reading achievement has remained largely stable across the period.

Because the last thirty-plus years have been the heyday of the federalized accountability movement, the same period has brought more testing. By federalized accountability I mean the centralization of authority and decision making—removing decision making from local education agencies and giving it to state and federal governmental agencies.

Accountability per se is not new. Schools have always been accountable to parents and taxpayers—that's local accountability. The federalized accountability movement was spawned by purported concern for improving the nation's schools and raising students' achievement. Local decision makers—boards of education, superintendents, parents—were seen as being too naive to make good decisions. Chester Finn (1991), former federal education official and now associated with the for-profit Edison Schools and the conservative Fordham Institute, said it straightforwardly:

> *The shortcomings of American education don't stem from malevolence . . . they arise from the maintenance of archaic practice . . . and cumbersome governance arrangements (such as entrusting decisions to fifteen thousand local school boards at a time when the entire nation is imperiled). (p. xiv)*

Since the mid-1980s federal officials and corporate chiefs have campaigned on the premise that American schools are producing unsatisfactory products. At the same time, though, local stakeholders have been generally satisfied with the quality of their schools. Even today, most parents give *their own child's school* a grade of A or B, but at the same time, those parents grade *schools in general* in the C or D range (Bracey, 2002).

Clarifying what the NRP said about independent reading

Tim Shanahan, one of the members of the National Reading Panel, recently expressed some surprise at the controversy surrounding the NRP's position on independent reading. He noted that "much of the discussion is based on an evident misunderstanding of what the National Reading Panel actually did in this area." He notes that the NRP did not study independent reading and continues . . .

"What the panel did study was the efficacy of various procedures and programs used to encourage children to read more. The issue that the NRP studied was not whether independent reading had value, but what school efforts lead children to increase their amount of reading. The NRP examined the research on procedures like SSR and DEAR which set aside time within the school day for free reading, commercial programs aimed at encouraging more reading, and various incentive plans.

"The conclusion: None of these programs or procedures has proven it effectively gets students to read more and, consequently, to read better. The NRP did not reject the possibility that some procedures might succeed in encouraging reading, and it called for more research on the issue . . . no matter what the benefits of reading—and they appear extensive—not all plans for encouraging kids to read more are likely to work. Schools should be cautious about adopting such uncharted schemes on a large scale . . ." (p. 38)

So, is everyone clear now on what the NRP studied and what it reported?

These comments are from Shanahan's published letter to the editor, *Education Week*, May 22, 2002.

In other words, those closest to the schools—parents of school-aged children—typically see their child's school as offering an education of a fairly high quality. When they are asked to rate schools they do not know except through media accounts and political rhetoric, they see schools as the politicians do—as offering something less than a high-quality service. Either most parents are wrong—the schools their children attend are not very good—or the media and political rhetoric have convinced them that most schools aren't much like the one their child attends.

In order for the thirty-year federal campaign to gain greater control over schools to be a success, the public had to be convinced that most schools were not very good. If parents and other taxpayers could be convinced that most schools didn't offer a very good education, it would perhaps make sense to them that the federal government should take action. If most kids are not really reading very well, then maybe the nation is at risk. Obviously, the disinformation campaign to convince the public that U.S. schools were not doing a good job of teaching children to read has been successful. Both the public and politicians have been convinced that students' reading achievement is not up to par. But could the many parents who believe their child's school is good be that wrong?

A major shift in education is under way in America—from a tradition of local control of schools to the federalization of the education system, with decisions about teaching and learning more often being made by legislators or bureaucrats in faraway offices. Testing is not new: The federal government has required testing since the first federal education programs began. Accountability is not new: Schools have always been accountable to parents and taxpayers. Even federalized accountability, in the sense of reporting progress toward meeting specified goals, is not really new: Federally funded education programs have for almost thirty years set and required schools to meet outcome targets or lose the funding. Working to close the rich/poor achievement gap is not new: That was the specific purpose of the original Elementary and Secondary Education Act of 1966. The *new, new* education bill (and accompanying federal plan) is actually the *same old, same old* when it comes to the basic design. What has changed with the new law is the locus of decision making, especially decisions about curriculum and instruction.

Why More of the Same Is Likely to Get Us More of the Same (or Less)

For the past thirty years the federal government has attempted to improve public education through a steady erosion of local control. More federal funding has meant more decisions controlled by federal agencies. The major complaint that school superintendents and principals have about their positions isn't testing and accountability concerns. It is that they feel hamstrung when it comes to making decisions about the process of education in the schools they supervise. Federal and state educational regulations substantially reduce the available alternatives. And these regulations have more often targeted inputs than outcomes, though now they often target both.

Input regulations tell *who must be hired* to work with *how many kids* for *how long* in *what location*. These regulations govern the design of remedial reading, bilingual education, summer school, and special education programs. They are typically set at the state education agency level but emanate from the federal legislation that provides some portion of the funds that support such programs.

Schools have typically responded to such rules with what I dub "minimum compliance models" (Allington, 1994), making whatever minimum effort was required to qualify for federal funding. The result, according to the federal evaluation team, was that "the level of instructional assistance Title 1 students generally received was in stark contrast to their levels of educational need" (Puma et al., 1997, p. iii). In other words, the combination of federal input regulations and the lack of full funding (roughly half the eligible poor children received any services) fostered the creation of educational programs that spent huge amounts but could not be expected to make much of a dent in the rich/poor reading gap problem.

The accountability components of the federal laws failed, historically, to have much impact on the design of reading interventions because federal mandates undermine local accountability. If I must select a "proven" program from a bureaucratically approved list, it will be easy to blame that program for any failure to educate the participating children well. Accountability without autonomy is no accountability at all. When someone tells you how you must do something, it is quite unlikely that you will feel accountable for the results should that approach fail to work.

Imagine for a minute that you've taken your car in to have new tires installed. You ask the mechanic whether it is true that over-inflating your tires will result in better gas mileage. He tells you that it's true, but that the downside is that, first, you will wear out your tires faster and, second, over-inflated tires give you less control as a driver. You tell the mechanic to seriously over-inflate the tires anyway. He will probably refuse to do this, saying something to the effect of "If you want over-inflated tires, you do it. I won't accept that responsibility." Even if the mechanic did as you asked, when your tires wore out quickly he wouldn't be likely to say anything but "I told you so."

When an external authority tells a school administrator or a teacher how to design their instructional program, the same thing happens. The principal or teacher may follow the externally approved plan, but if it doesn't work out they say, "I told you so."

Instead of accountability without autonomy, what might improve schools is building and supporting the development of greater professional responsibility. But as Peter Johnston (1992) notes:

> To arrange for responsibility, you focus on building communities, involvement, trusting relationships, and self-assessment. . . . To arrange for accountability, you focus on building external assessment, a power differential, and some means for those in power to mete out consequences. (p. 61)

As publicly funded institutions, it is appropriate for schools (and the administrators and teachers who work in them) to be responsible for the quality of the instruction they provide. I can even support a focus on estimating the quality of instruction from instructional outcomes, as demonstrated by student achievement. Schools are already responsible, in parents' eyes, for instructional outcomes. When the outcomes do not meet parents' expectations, parents don't typically wonder what is wrong with the federal education plan, they wonder what else the teacher and school might have done.

When I say that I support a focus on student outcomes, I do not mean that they should meet mandated cut points on a standardized achievement test. Such testing has little to recommend it. Besides, it's usually not just test scores that upset or thrill parents—it's the daily work that their children accomplish, or fail to accomplish, and the way the school and the teachers respond to their child. Years ago, before I was a parent, I told my preservice teachers that I did not care if the teacher loved my child, that I preferred a teacher who could teach him. Now I'd take the teacher who loved my child any day. Of course, I'd rather have a teacher who loves my child *and* who can teach him expertly. I've come to understand how much caring matters in good teaching, and how observant children are about the attitudes their teachers display. Can children learn from a teacher who does not care about them? What can they learn? Is any of this scientifically testable?

I am not opposed to using test scores as one component of a plan that addresses the issue of schools and teachers acting in an instructionally responsible manner. But test scores tell only a part of the educational story—and it's usually not the most important part, especially for individual students.

THE FALLIBILITY OF TEST SCORES

The financial spotlight these days shines brightly on the publishers of standardized achievement tests. "Bush's education bill seen as a boost for publishers" shouts a Reuters news service headline (January 8, 2002). According to the article, the new law will double the volume of testing, providing a major "earnings opportunity" for test publishers. Unfortunately, psychometric evidence has been tossed out when it comes to the achievement testing plans mandated by this new law.

Psychometrics is the science of test construction. It is primarily a quantitative science, one focused on issues such as reliability, validity, and standard error of measurement. The central problem, from the standpoint of psychometrics, is that the tests we have cannot accomplish the grand goals the politicians have set for them. According to Robert Linn (2000), a senior researcher at the National Center for Research on Evaluation, Standards, and Student Testing:

> *In most cases the [assessment] instruments and technology have not been up to the demands that have been placed on them by high-stakes accountability. Assessment systems that are useful monitors lose much of dependability and credibility for that purpose when high stakes are attached to them. The unintended negative effects of high-stakes accountability uses often outweigh the intended positive effects. (p. 14)*

When teaching to the test becomes common, the test, or at least the kind of tests that are commonly used to meet the new education bill's mandates, loses much of its usefulness as a measure of learning (much less teaching). Linn also reinforces a major point made by the National Research Council in its report on high-stakes testing (Heubert & Hauser, 1999): Group standardized achievement tests are simply not reliable measures of individual student achievement. In other words, psychometric scientists agree that it is unscientific to use a single test performance to make decisions about individuals, including decisions about grade promotion or retention and about what a child knows, what needs to be taught, and how to teach it.

> [P]sychometric scientists agree that it is unscientific to use a single test performance to make decisions about individuals, including decisions about grade promotion or retention and about what a child knows, what needs to be taught, and how to teach it.

This isn't new information. The test publishers themselves have always noted, albeit typically only in the technical manuals that accompany their tests, that group standardized achievement tests were not reliable measures of individual achievement. This limitation is a primary reason that schools employ psychologists to test students individually for participation in special education classes: Those individually administered assessments are more reliable measures of individual performance.

But someone in Washington, D.C., has not done their homework. The U.S. Department of Education's website says:

Annual testing . . . provides the sort of information needed to determine what works, what doesn't, how well students are achieving, and what to do to help those who need help. <www.ed.gov/nclb>

As Linn (2000) points out, when annual achievement testing becomes part and parcel of an accountability system, the usefulness of the tests is compromised. The testing no longer provides much reliable information on "what works, what doesn't, how well students are achieving." Not one of the group standardized achievement tests provides reliable information on "what to do to help those who need help." None. Nada. As the scientists writing for the NRC so pointedly noted, these tests just cannot provide reliable information on individual students.

Unfortunately, the same sorts of unscientific claims about the power of tests and testing were made by Secretary of Education Rod Paige (2001) in his address to the Education Writer's Association and again in a featured article in Phi Delta Kappan (Paige, 2002). I will hope that Secretary Paige is simply naive concerning the limitations of group standardized achievement tests, and so was ill-advised in misrepresenting the properties of the assessment tools now in use. Nonetheless, both America's education reporters and a broad educational audience were fed what can only be characterized as misinformation. Nearly a year after Secretary Paige's speech, the USDE website continues to misrepresent the technical capacity of standardized tests.

If we are pursuing accountability, why not try to be sophisticated about it? Richard Rothstein (2001) notes that until recently, "Congress assumed accountability was best left to the states. That way, superior systems might be copied elsewhere; inferior ones could be abandoned without imposing the mistake on the entire nation" (p. 2). He points out that this is the major shift found in the federalized accountability plan mandated by the new education bill. The new law puts in place a rather unsophisticated accountability scheme that's like the one Texas uses—unsophisticated at least compared to the schemes that many states have developed. Thus this push for federalized accountability would undo more-sophisticated educational accountability schemes. For instance, Maryland assesses all students using a matrix sampling process that is somewhat akin to the process used in the NAEP system. Different kids are tested on different parts of the curriculum so as to get a reasonable estimate of school effectiveness, broadly conceived. In other words, different students take different tests. Since individual test scores are not reliable measures of student achievement, this system makes sense as a way to estimate school effectiveness across the curriculum. In North Carolina the accountability system tracks the progress of cohorts of students because it makes little sense to compare two different groups of kids (last year's and this year's fourth graders). The system expects that each cohort of students will do progressively better with each year in school. In other words, school effects are judged by continuous improvement, reducing the number of low achievers in the cohort each year. In Kentucky the assessments measure achievement in writing, science, and social studies, as well as in reading and math, at different grade levels. This ensures that the curriculum is not narrowed to just the two subjects tested in the federalized accountability plan.

Federalized accountability, like federalized curriculum planning, is a bad idea for a number of reasons, not least those that Rothstein points out. But what is even more difficult to understand than congressional support for federalized accountability is the support for a poorly designed federalized accountability plan. Is it possible that the government's educational bureaucrats and education advisors were wholly unaware of the flaws in the Texas accountability system (Haney, 2000)? If so, they could not have been paying much attention to research literature on the topic of accountability schemes. If they *were* aware of the flaws, is this another case of ideology trumping evidence?

Controlling Curriculum Choices

So we have a "new, new" educational reform law that simply perpetuates and expands the federal tradition of testing and accountability. What this new bill does add is an acceleration of the recent trend toward federalized curricular specification. It is this feature that led the Council of State Legislatures and the American Association of School Administrators to oppose the bill (Conk, 2002). Historically, federal education programs have been banned from recommending, specifying, or mandating the use of particular curriculum content, methods, or materials. One finds a similar ban even in the new bill:

> *Local Control. Nothing in this section shall be construed to: 1) authorize an officer of the Federal Government to mandate, direct, review, or control a State, local education agency, or school's instructional content, curriculum, and related activities. [Sec. 9526 (b) of PL 107.101]*

The recent efforts at federalizing control over education—and federalizing reading instruction especially—seem an abrupt shift away from local control of curriculum and instruction. In the new law federalization seems focused on controlling instructional decisions through appeals to "scientifically based reading research":

> *Moreover, Reading First differs from earlier initiatives by establishing clear, specific expectations for what can and should happen for all students. Reading First specifies that teachers' classroom instructional decisions must be informed by scientifically based reading research. (<www.ed.gov/offices/OESE/readingfirst/faq.html>, p. 3)*

The problem is, as the National Reading Panel pointed out, there is 1) a wealth of research the panel could not review due to time and fiscal constraints and 2) substantial gaps in research on teaching reading. Most instructional decisions teachers must make cannot be informed by research. Even more cannot be informed by the limited body of research reviewed by the NRP.

At other times the push for control seems targeted at curriculum materials and packaged programs. The Executive Summary of the new federalization plan opens with the heading "Transforming the Federal Role in Education so No Child is Left Behind" (<www.ed.gov/inits/nclb/part2.html>). This document later proclaims that the initiative is focused on "investing in scientifically-based reading instruction programs in the early grades." And we've been told that "the Department of Education will send education officials around the country guides that will carefully content analyze all core reading programs to see whether or not they are scientifically based" (Schemo, 2002, p. 2). All of this points to the push for a national reading curriculum and to an expansion of centralized control to include the curricular and instructional decision making that was historically out of the reach of federal bureaucrats, politicians, or reading czars. The ideological distortions of the NRP report found in both the Summary of that report and the more recent *Put Reading First* booklet provide good evidence of the dangers of federal intrusions into curriculum and instruction.

I do not want politicians and policy makers making decisions about what I will teach or how I will be allowed to teach. I don't want bureaucrats writing regulations on which instructional methods or curricular tools my grandchildren's teachers will be allowed, much less required, to use. I don't want bureaucrats making curricular decisions, especially bureaucrats who don't seem to understand that curriculum materials don't teach, that teachers teach. Who don't understand that there are no "proven" programs, just programs that might help teachers learn to teach more expertly. Who don't understand that investing in the development of teacher expertise is the one "scientifically based" strategy that could work over the long haul.

The strength of the U.S. education system has been its diversity, its commitment to local problem solving and local decision making. Like Harold Hodgkinson, America's foremost educational demographer, I worry that the standardization—the federalization—of education will undermine what we have achieved to this point. Hodgkinson noted at the sixth annual Conference on Teaching and Learning, sponsored by the Association for Supervision and Curriculum Development, that states are becoming more dissimilar. For instance, ten states have 90 percent of the Hispanic population, and other minority groups are similarly concentrated in a few states and regions. Six states have large recent immigrant populations and six have almost none. In some states most of the citizens were born there, and in others four out of five citizens moved in from somewhere else. Some states have twice the proportion of college graduates that other states have. Hodgkinson concluded:

> *Therefore, to have a single national standard, measured by a single national test . . . would not be a good thing for America. . . . All the demographics suggest that we need to give states more leeway in how they accomplish their educational objectives.*

The International Reading Association grew so concerned about the commercialization of advice from officials at the U.S. Department of Education that on April 15, 2002 the president and executive director co-signed a letter to Secretary of Education Rod Paige that opened as follows:

Dear Secretary Paige:

We write to express our concern about the implementation of Reading First. As we interact with International Reading Association members across the country, we are increasingly being asked the question, "Will I have to buy a commercial program?" Or even, "Will I have to buy X?" (which is filled in with various combinations of Open Court, SRA Direct Instruction, and others).

Many of the writing teams for the SEA application have gained the understanding that approval will be expedited if, in their state competitions, they indicate a competitive preference for particular commercial programs. This belief has been fostered by comments and examples offered by Department staff at public meetings and events. We are gravely concerned about this. . . .

The most immediate response seems to have been that every major official of the U.S. Department of Education who was scheduled to speak at the annual IRA meeting, which opened two weeks later, suddenly found that they had scheduling conflicts and none attended the IRA meeting.

The IRA found alternative speakers to fill the slots scheduled for USDE officials. Mike Pressley was one of those replacements and he drew a standing ovation for his pointed question about who was supposed to be serving whom in the education department.

It seems that many federal education officials do not understand the term "public servants." When key officials of the federal education agency cannot be bothered to attend the meeting of the largest literacy organization in the world, priorities are out of whack. When nonattendance is used as punishment for raising questions concerning questionable federal policies, those same public officials should be asked to resign by the administration that appointed them.

Standardization is, of course, the hallmark of fast-food chains, global corporations that guarantee that the burgers you buy in Peoria will taste virtually identical to the one you buy in Prague. Some folks find great comfort in that.

But has anyone ever suggested that food preparation and nutrition are of routinely higher quality as a result of this sort of standardization? I think not.

The point to standardization is to ensure a minimum standard at a low cost. Fast-food chains do not need chefs. They don't even need cooks. They don't need anyone to select from the market the meats and vegetables that will go into preparing today's menu. They don't need anyone who knows the difference between making soup and making a soufflé. Standardization invariably leads to a dumbing down—of food, of teaching, of education.

Almost a quarter-century ago, Arthur Wise (1979) noted that goal reduction—dumbing down—is a reliable result of bureaucratic centralization. Setting goals results in minimal expectations: standards that are likely to be attainable by almost everyone. Setting goals includes excluding some goals, the ones that not everyone would agree on or the ones that aren't amenable to measurement. In addition, preeminence is given to goals that seem to address pressing national social problems vs. individual goals (such as improvement in the nation's economy vs. individual fulfillment). He argued that

> In the drive to make educational institutions accountable, goals have become narrow, selective, and minimal. That which is measurable is preferred to that which is unmeasurable. (p. 59)

I would add that federalization of accountability has, indeed, accomplished all this and now seems aimed to accomplish even more: the standardization of the teaching of reading. But standardized teaching, as Darling-Hammond (1997) pointed out, is educational malpractice. Further, instructional mandates produce consistently negative effects:

> What they [teachers] felt they needed were supports and protections from the unhelpful demands of current policies. Detailed

prescriptions for practice, it turns out, not only constrain teacher decision making but also undermine the knowledge base of the profession and its ability to recruit and keep talented people. (p. 92)

Darling-Hammond was discussing how the teachers she studied responded to the unhelpful prescriptions and demands of local bureaucrats. Imagine the impact of standardized national prescriptions for teaching children to read. Yet that seems to be what is being passed off these days as "scientifically based" reading instruction.

Intensive, Expensive, Expert Instruction as the Scientific Solution

Largely ignored in the hoopla surrounding the new education law and the new mandates is the research demonstrating the power of expert, intensive instruction. Much of the legislative impetus for the new law came from a recent policy consensus that 90 to 95 percent of poor readers can be reading on grade level if provided with appropriate instruction. This mantra can be found in news magazines, political advocacy, congressional testimony, political press releases, and floating easily about the statewide "reading summits" that have so suddenly become popular, at least among Republican governors.

What evidence was drawn upon to produce the assertion that 90 to 95 percent of poor readers would be reading on grade level simply by receiving "appropriate" instruction? What does that instruction look like? What does it mean to be "on grade level"? What would it cost to provide every child who needed it with access to such instruction?

90 TO 95 PERCENT READING ON LEVEL

Locating the source of the 90–95 percent figure was easy. G. Reid Lyon, head of the Dyslexia Division of the National Institute of Child Health and Human Development (NICHD), provided that figure in his testimony before the U.S. Senate Committee on Labor and Human Resources in April 1998, and that figure has stuck like glue.

> *We have learned that for 90 percent to 95 percent of poor readers,*
> *prevention and early intervention programs that combine instruc-*
> *tion in* phoneme awareness, phonics, fluency development,
> and reading comprehension strategies, *provided by well-*
> *trained teachers, can increase reading skills to average reading*
> *levels. [Emphasis added] (Lyon, 1998, p. 7)*

I find it interesting that Lyon set out four components of "evidence-based" reading instruction (emphasized above) a full two years before the National Reading Panel reported that its exhaustive review of the research had identified precisely the same components.

What research did Lyon use to establish the 90 to 95 percent success rate? No citations were provided in his testimony, but in that same year he coauthored a paper with Jack Fletcher that offers two studies to support this assertion: Vellutino et al. (1996) and Torgeson, Wagner, Rashotte, Alexander, & Conway (1997). Let's take a closer look at these two reports on reading intervention studies.

Vellutino et al. (1996) studied at-risk students in six suburban districts. These students were split into two groups, treatment and control. The treatment students got one-on-one expert tutoring, typically for thirty minutes daily for one semester (for a total of seventy to eighty sessions), although some students continued to receive tutoring for a longer period. Almost half (44.7 percent) of the tutored students scored at average reading levels (45th percentile) after tutoring. The 45th percentile figure seems appropriate to represent the "average reading level" standard, since most laypersons, including, I suggest, U.S. senators, understand "average" levels of achievement to mean "on grade level" or the ability to read, for instance, grade-level materials independently.

Torgeson et al. (1997) provided twenty-minute tutoring sessions four days a week for two and one-half years. Half the sessions were offered by teachers, half by trained paraprofessionals. Tutoring varied, with students receiving one of three possible interventions. The three intervention plans produced similar outcomes on word-reading tests. The explicit phonics group did better on "alphabetic reading skills," but this advantage in reading nonsense syllables did not transfer to reading real words. Nowhere close to 90 to 95 percent of the students were reading, even just words in isolation, on grade level, and a quarter remained substantially below grade-level achievement.

While the Vellutino et al. (1996) and Torgeson et al. (1997) interventions did provide a strong demonstration of the power of intensive, expert tutoring, the outcomes offered nothing close to 90 to 95 percent of the poor readers reading at "average reading levels."

Perhaps Lyon misinterpreted the data in the two studies. I suggest this because after the intervention the proportion of very poor readers in the total population largely matched Lyon's 90 to 95 percent figure. In other words, the intensive, expert tutoring of struggling readers (plus other efforts by the schools) reduced the proportion of poor readers to something like 10 percent of all children. In the Torgeson et al. (1997) study, after intervention the very poor readers accounted for approximately two and one-half percent of the total population and the students reading below the 45th percentile accounted for approximately 8 percent. In the Vellutino et al. (1996) study, 3 percent of the original suburban students in the larger sampling population had very poor reading after tutoring, with 9 percent of total population still falling below the 45th percentile. So 91 percent of all readers would be at "average" achievement levels using the 45th percentile criteria. But 90 percent of all children reading at or above "average" achievement levels is something quite different from 90 percent of poor readers having their achievement normalized.

To clarify, imagine Normal Elementary School with 1,000 children whose reading achievement just happens to be perfectly distributed along the traditional bell curve. Thus, 450 children fall below the 45th percentile and 200 fall below the 20th percentile (a typical cutoff point for identification as a struggling reader). To get 90 percent of the struggling reader population (200) above the 45th percentile, we would need a program that solved the problems of 180 of the 200 struggling readers. But to get 90 percent of the total population (1,000) above the 45th percentile, we would have to solve the reading problems of only half, or 100, of the struggling readers. In the first scenario the school is left, after the tutoring intervention, with 20 children with reading problems; in the second, the school is left with 100 struggling readers. Lyon (1998), it seems, inaccurately calculated the impact of the NICHD studies.

So even with expert intensive remedial tutoring supplementing good classroom reading instruction, we might still expect half of the poor readers in any given suburban elementary school to lag behind their peers, unable to read grade-level texts independently. Additionally, Vellutino and his colleagues removed from the poor reader pool all students with measured IQs below 90. However, almost 40 percent of all schoolchildren have measured IQs below 90, and the historical evidence suggests that many of these students struggle to attain "average" achievement levels. In other words, that NICHD study demonstrated that half of the struggling readers with higher measured IQs could have their literacy development accelerated through intensive expert tutoring, achieving average levels of reading proficiency.

> So even with expert intensive remedial tutoring supplementing good classroom reading instruction, we might still expect half of the poor readers in any given suburban elementary school to lag behind their peers, unable to read grade-level texts independently.

These studies demonstrated that many children who are instructionally needy are being incorrectly identified as learning disabled. That was a primary intention of the researchers. But neither study demonstrated that 90 to 95 percent of poor readers will achieve average reading levels with appropriate instruction, even when that instruction is expert intensive tutoring.

THE POTENTIAL COSTS OF SCALING UP THE TUTORING

The Vellutino et al. (1996) and Torgeson et al. (1997) intervention studies provide additional evidence of the potential for expert tutoring as an early intervention (see also Shanahan, 1998). But what might it cost to provide tutoring of this sort—appropriate reading instruction following Lyon's (1998) characterization—to every child who struggles with early literacy learning? In these two studies the children received thirty to seventy-five hours of expert tutoring, and the children in the Torgeson study received an additional thirty hours of tutoring provided by a paraprofessional. The expert tutors were typically certified teachers, including several with M.S. degrees and advanced certification in reading remediation. We might set a conservative estimate of $50,000 per teacher (salary, plus retirement and other fringe benefits).

If each tutor followed the Vellutino model, they would work with ten kids a day (thirty minutes of tutoring plus six minutes of transition per child produces a six-hour instructional day, which is typical of most U.S. school instructional workdays—omitting planning time and noninstructional duties). We would need approximately twenty full-time tutors for a semester, or ten full-time tutors for the year, to teach the 200 students who qualified for tutoring at Normal Elementary (if we followed the Torgeson model, the expert tutors would work with four more children each day for an additional year and a half at about the same cost, but you would need to also hire an equal number of aides). In either case, it would take at least half a million dollars to implement the intervention.

In the NICHD studies other poor readers who did not qualify or who were not selected for tutoring still received small-group remedial or special education instruction, as did some of the tutored children after they completed the tutoring. We will assume that existing revenues at Normal Elementary will continue to fund those services.

But few schools have a normally distributed student population. Consider that in a recent study of children enrolled in urban, high-poverty schools (McGill-Franzen, Allington, Yokoi, & Brooks, 1999), the *average* pretest performance—the 11th percentile—of this group of randomly selected kindergarten children was below the cutoff both Vellutino and Torgeson used for tutoring eligibility. The costs of tutoring can be staggering. For instance, if the 1,000-student Abnormal Elementary School serves a high-poverty neighborhood where two-thirds of the students qualified for tutoring, we would have 667 students to be tutored. That would be work for thirty-four additional expert tutors at a cost of some $1.7 million dollars every year. And even with this added tutoring we could still expect about half of the tutored kids to have measured reading achievement below "average"—below grade-level expectations.

> "Dick argued that phonics is being oversold. I tend to agree with him, for I'm not convinced that systematic phonics is the panacea its advocates take it to be. If it were, it's hard to see why [our study] . . . (Juel, Griffith, and Gough, 1986) found that a year long, systematic, intensive phonics program left nearly twenty percent of first graders all but illiterate." p. 1
>
> From: Gough, P. B. (1998, December). Overselling phonemic awareness? Paper presented at the National Reading conference, Austin, TX.

One final consideration. While Vellutino et al. (1996) and Torgeson et al. (1997) provide powerful testimony on the potential of early, intensive, expert instructional intervention, we have no data that suggest how permanent or temporary the effects of such tutoring might be. If the data from Reading Recovery (Hiebert, 1994) can be generalized, many children will remain on this normal achievement track. But many will also gradually but steadily fall behind without continued instructional support. This should not surprise anyone. Early intervention is not a vaccine that can protect children from further difficulties.

It is time to face the fact that some children will need expert, intensive intervention for sustained periods of time—even across their whole school career—if they are to continue to develop "normal" reading proficiencies. But without continued tutoring some children will fall behind and escalate the costs of achieving the elusive (and expensive) goal of "all children on grade level."

SUMMARY

The implied promise of emphasizing evidence-based instruction—that 90 to 95 percent of poor readers or 98 percent of all children would be reading on grade level if only classroom teachers would follow the research—is a misrepresentation, a distortion and exaggeration of what the evidence actually reports.

- No intervention has brought the achievement of 90 percent of poor readers to the 50th percentile level. None.
- The most successful studies that accelerated the literacy development of struggling readers relied on expert intensive tutoring. Tutoring raised the achievement of roughly

half of the poor readers to average (50th percentile) levels. This occurred at a substantial cost, and cannot happen unless a sufficient supply of expert tutors is available. If tutors need to be trained, training costs will be added to the intervention outlay.

• No longer-term evidence on the durability of the intervention effects is available. The extra funding needed to maintain the gains for the half of the population that was successfully remediated may be substantial.

Given the potential costs of initiating tutorial intervention for all struggling readers, it is little wonder that details of what research has revealed have been conveniently neglected in policy advocacy, which emphasizes *more efficient* reading instruction, not necessarily *more effective* instruction. Little mention, if any, has been made concerning those research-based tutorials that demonstrated promise for accelerating the reading development of low-achieving students. Buying new "scientific" reading materials is surely less expensive than providing expert, intensive reading tutorial instruction would be. Buying new phonics kits costs less than building teacher and tutor expertise.

If Congress and the Department of Education are to be true to the research on "scientifically based" reading interventions, then a substantial reordering of the federal budget priorities will be necessary in order to generate the needed funds (the billions of extra dollars have to come from somewhere). I am not a big fan of federalization, as must be clear. But if the politicos are going to mandate programs based on "scientific evidence," then I say that they should fully fund the research-based tutoring that proved reasonably successful in the NICHD studies. In addition, an evidence-based federal plan would provide the funds needed to reduce class size, at least in schools serving higher poverty neighborhoods, and the funds to provide salaries that will attract well-qualified teachers to those schools. Finally, an evidence-

> [I]f the politicos are going to mandate programs based on "scientific evidence," then I say that they should fully fund the research-based tutoring that proved reasonably successful in the NICHD studies.

based education reform plan would provide the funds to build the expertise of the teachers who already work in U.S. schools.

High-quality classroom instruction is an essential feature of any good reading program, but there is no research suggesting that if only classroom teachers knew a lot more about phonology, or used a scripted curriculum, or taught systematic phonics, or followed a "proven" program, virtually all children would have grade-level reading proficiency. None. Nada. We can improve the quality of classroom reading instruction. We should work to that end. But the research doesn't indicate that new reading materials can accomplish that goal. The research doesn't show that good classroom instruction alone can solve the problems of children who find learning to read difficult.

Is it possible that the folks who run the U.S. Department of Education are so unfamiliar with the research on reading that they don't even realize the extent of the misrepresentation that is occur-

---

Richard Elmore, senior research fellow at the Consortium for Policy Research, analyzed the new education bill and concluded that it represents an "unwarranted intrusion" into educational policy making by the federal government. "In other words, there is no genuine opposition in Washington to accountability rules that simply fail to understand the institutional realities of accountability in states, districts, and schools. And the law's provisions are considerably at odds with the technical realities of test-based accountability. Never, I think, in the history of federal education policy has the disconnect between policy and practice been so evident, and possibly never so dangerous. What's particularly strange and ironic is that conservative Republicans control the White House and the House of Representatives, and they sponsored the single largest—and the single most damaging—expansion of federal power over the nation's education system in history. . . . Thus the federal government is now accelerating the worst trend of the current accountability movement: that performance-based accountability has come to mean testing, and testing alone. . . . this shift is based on little more than policy talk among people who know hardly anything about the institutional realities of accountability and even less about the problems of improving instruction in schools."

From "Unwarranted Intrusion" in *Education Next*, a magazine of educational commentary published by the Hoover Institution. Available at <www.educationnext.org/20021/30>.

ring? Personally, I hope that is the case, because the only other scenario I can conjure up involves the purposeful misrepresentation of the research for reasons of ideology (or career advancement). In either case, the misrepresentation is horrible for reading researchers and other reading professionals—and for our children.

Conclusion

Thirty years of a failed federal educational policy is enough. The federalized accountability strategy for improving reading achievement has not worked. Super-sizing the same old fast-food meal does not give us a more nutritious dinner. Super-sizing the same old, same old educational policy will not give us better teaching or improved achievement. Peter Sacks (2000) writes:

> *The lesson from history is that political motivations and the exercise of political power by those in positions of authority, rather than sound educational reasons, have driven the nation's use of standardized tests in schools. Indeed, whatever the perceived problems with the nation's schools, the answer has always been the same: more testing. (p. 70)*

Another common answer has been increased federalization of the educational process. But in this era of "evidence-based" educational decision making, too little attention has been paid to the evidence on the effectiveness of federalization or the evidence on how instruction might be improved.

Federalization of American education is precisely the wrong school-improvement strategy. There are few things that federal governments do well, and fewer still that they do better than local agencies do when given the appropriate capacity. I was worried back when the federal government served primarily an advisory role, if only because politics always loomed so large in federal advice. I was more worried when the federal government began to advocate for competition for public schools as an improvement strategy. I worried about the financial and ideological links between politicians and the for-profit education industry gurus who were such vocal supporters of increased privatization. I also worried about national standards, and I supported having any such standards developed by those in the profession.

I was truly worried when the federal government terminated funding for the standards-development project cosponsored by the International Reading Association and the National Council of Teachers of English. As a member of the IRA board of directors I reluctantly voted to devote a huge sum of the organization's money to continue that project through to the end. I was worried because I still wasn't convinced that national standards were a good idea, no matter who developed them. In the end, I decided that if there are going to be national standards—and there are—it is best for education professionals to have a go at developing them, rather than leaving the task to a federal bid winner.

I still worry that even while the national reading/language arts standards remain largely ignored, this new "evidence-based" rhetoric does nothing more than get policy makers what they had hoped to get with national reading standards—federal control of education. And, worse, that corporate federalism (Edmondson, 2002)—federal decisions driven by corporate concerns—becomes standard operating procedure, all in the name of "evidence-based" education.

The "evidence-based" framework focuses primarily on the lowest level literacy proficiencies—the ones that are easiest to accomplish and easiest to measure. The push for a national reading curriculum has already dumbed down expected achievements to the lowest common denominators (phonemic segmentation, pseudo-word pronunciation, words correctly read per minute, etc.). The most recent initiatives seem targeted to dumbing down teaching as well, by further limiting the instructional options teachers can select from.

After thirty years of a failed federalization strategy, one might expect that someone of influence, somewhere, might just say, "Here we go again." After thirty years of increasingly restrictive federal control with little to show for the effort, one might expect that even the Washington politicos would begin to question the sanity of the federalization strategy.

After thirty years increasingly restrictive federal control with little to show for the effort, one might expect that even the Washington politicos would begin to question the sanity of the federalization strategy.

One might expect that someone would take measure of the scope of the failure of the federalization strategy and say, "This isn't working, Bubba; it's time to change direction." But, so far, no such luck. Instead, our politicians—of all stripes and persuasions (liberal Democrat Ted Kennedy did broker the new education bill after all)—have handed us a warmed-over but super-sized serving of the same old failed education reform strategy.

It seems obvious that someone in the U.S. Department of Education would have noticed not only that increasing federalization wasn't working, but that ideologues were making a mockery of the "scientific research" that the department has funded over the past three decades. It just seems obvious that someone in the department would have mentioned that the emperor is naked. And if not someone in the department, then some education writer or influential policy analyst or congressional staffer. But no. Instead, I see the bureaucrats and too many reading professionals simply avert their eyes and move along.

Maybe it is all about power rather than improving schools. Maybe it is more about making education more "efficient"—read, cheaper—than about making schools richer and more engaging places for children to spend their young lives. Maybe it is about corporate federalism (Edmondson, 2002) and the globalization phenomenon (Boyd & Mitchell, 2001). Maybe we—you and I—have been enormously gullible and really believed that education policy making was about more than test performance, profits, and pandering for votes.

Maybe we were wrong.

References

Allington, R. L. (1994). What's special about special programs for children who find learning to read difficult? *Journal of Reading Behavior, 26* (1), 1–21.

Allington, R. L. (1999). Crafting state educational policy: The slippery role of educational research and researchers. *Journal of Literacy Research, 31,* 457–482.

Allington, R. L. (2001). Does state and federal reading policymaking matter? In T. Loveless (Ed.), *The great curriculum debate* (pp. 268–298). Washington, DC: Brookings Institution.

Boyd, W. L., & Mitchell, D. E. (2001). The politics of the reading wars. In T. Loveless (Ed.), *The great curriculum debate* (pp. 299–342). Washington, DC: Brookings.

Bracey, G. W. (2002). *The war against America's public schools: Privatizing schools, commercializing education.* Boston: Allyn & Bacon.

Conk, M. (February 2002). Four benefits of ESEA fall short of district needs. *School Administrator, 59,* 76.

Darling-Hammond, L. (1997). *The right to learn: A blueprint for creating schools that work.* San Francisco: Jossey-Bass.

Donahue, P. L., Voelkl, K. E., Campbell, J., & Mazzeo, J. (1999). *NAEP Reading 1998: Reading report card for the nation and the states.* Washington, DC: U.S. Department of Education, Office of Educational Research and Improvement.

Edmondson, J. (2002). Asking different questions: Critical analyses and reading research. *Reading Research Quarterly, 37* (1), 113–119.

Finn, C. E. (1991). *We must take charge: Our schools and our future.* New York: The Free Press.

Haney, W. (2000). The myth of the Texas miracle in education. *Education Policy Analysis Archives,* Available at: http://epaa.asu.edu/epaa/v8n41/

Heubert, J. P., & Hauser, R. M. (1999). *High stakes: Testing for tracking, promotion and graduation.* Washington, DC: National Academy Press.

Hiebert, E. H. (1994). Reading Recovery in the United States: What difference does it make to an age cohort? *Educational Researcher, 23* (9), 15–25.

Johnston, P. H. (1992). Nontechnical assessment. *Reading Teacher, 46* (1), 60–62.

LeTendre, M. J. (1996). The new Improving America's Schools Act and Title 1. *Journal of Education for Students Placed at Risk, 1*(1), 5–8.

Linn, R. L. (2000). Assessments and accountability. *Educational Researcher, 29* (2), 4–16.

Lyon, G. R. (1998, April 28). *Overview of reading and literacy initiatives: Statement of G. Reid Lyon,* [Testimony before the Senate Committee on Labor and Human Resources; Washington, DC]. Available: http://156.40.88.3/publications/pubs/jeffords.htm.

McGill-Franzen, A. (2000). Policy and instruction: What is the relationship? In M. Kamil, P. Mosenthal, P. D. Pearson, & R. Barr (Eds.), *Handbook of reading research: Vol. 3* (pp. 891–908). Mahwah, NJ: Erlbaum.

McGill-Franzen, A., Allington, R. L., Yokoi, L., & Brooks, G. (1999). Putting books in the room seems necessary but not sufficient. *Journal of Educational Research, 93* (2), 67–74.

Office of Technology Assessment (1992). *Testing in America's schools: Asking the right questions.* Washington, DC: U.S. Government Printing Office.

Paige, R. (2001, April 27, 2001). *Remarks as prepared for delivery by U.S. Secretary of Education Rod Paige.* Paper presented at the Education Writers Association, Phoenix, AZ.

Paige, R. (2002). An Overview of America's education agenda. *Phi Delta Kappan, 3,* 708–713.

Pogrow, S. (2002). Avoiding comprehensive school reform models. *Educational Leadership, 58,* 82–83.

Puma, M. J., Karweit, N., Price, C., Ricciuti, A., Thompson, W., & Vaden-Kiernan, M. (1997). *Prospects: Final report on student outcomes.* Washington, DC: U.S. Department of Education, Office of Planning and Evaluation Services.

Rothstein, R. (2001, December 19). The education bill: Many trials ahead. *New York Times,* p. A12.

Sacks, P. (2000). *Standardized minds: The high price of America's testing culture and what we can do to change it.* Cambridge, MA: Perseus.

Schemo, D. J. (2002, January 9). Education bill urges new emphasis on phonics. *New York Times.* (www.nytimes.com/2002/01/09/politics/09EDUC.html, date accessed, January 13 2002.)

Shanahan, T. (1998). On the effectiveness and limitations of tutoring. In P. D. Pearson & A. Iran-Nejad (Eds.), *Review of research in education, Vol. 23* (pp. 217–234). Washington, DC: American Educational Research Association.

Strauss, S. (2002). Politics and reading at the National Institute of Child Health and Human Development. *Pediatrics, 109,* 143–144.

Torgeson, J. K., Wagner, R. K., Rashotte, C. A., Alexander, A. W., & Conway, T. (1997). Preventive and remedial interventions for children with severe reading disabilities. *Learning disabilities: A multi-disciplinary perspective, 8* (1), 51–61.

Vellutino, F. R., Sipay, E. R., Small, S. G., Pratt, A., Chen, R., & Denckla, M. B. (1996). Cognitive profiles of difficult-to-remediate and readily remediated poor readers: Early intervention as a vehicle for distinguishing between cognitive and experiential deficits as basic causes of specific reading disability. *Journal of Educational Psychology, 88* (4), 601–638.

Wise, A. E. (1979). *Legislated learning: The bureaucratization of the American classroom.* Berkeley, CA: University of California Press.

13 ■ Why We Don't Need a National Reading Methodology

Richard L. Allington

There is a federal policy push to make education an evidence-based profession and to mandate evidence-based reading methodologies. But what evidence counts? And whose interpretation of that evidence? Consider the discrepancies between two recent reviews of research on beginning reading. The National Research Council's *Preventing Reading Difficulties in Young Children* (referred to here as the PRD report) (Snow, Burns, & Griffin, 1998) "plain-language" summary offers the following research-based instructional recommendations—recommendations you will not find in the NRP report (in point of fact, some of the PRD recommendations actually contradict the NRP recommendations):

- instruction that highlights the relations between print and speech (interactive writing lessons, language experience chart stories, invented spelling during meaning-focused writing)
- book reading shared by an adult and a child (big-book read-alouds, trade book read-alouds)

- daily independent reading of texts selected to be of interest to the child and beneath the child's frustration level ("drop everything and read")
- daily writing with invented spelling supported to foster phoneme awareness and segmentation and sound-spelling relationships
- reading instruction designed to *integrate* attention to the alphabetic principle with attention to the construction of meaning and opportunities to develop fluency (emphasis in the original)
- instruction for children who are having difficulties that is not substantively different than instruction for children who are "getting it"

How is it that two panels of educational researchers, predominantly psychologists, reviewing the research on beginning reading didn't reach the same conclusions? Scarr (1985) argues that:

We do not discover scientific facts, we invent them. Their usefulness to us depends both on shared perceptions of the "facts" (consensual validation) and on whether they work for various purposes, some practical and some theoretical. (p. 499)

Achieving a professional consensus was a goal of the groups that developed the PRD and NRP reports, but neither produced a professional consensus. Nonetheless, somewhere along the way a *political* consensus was achieved. That political consensus means we are now confronted with political mandates that the reading-education profession does not consensually support. Regardless of the perceived flaws in the manner in which the NRP invented its "facts" about what the research says (and the papers in this book point out many of those flaws), the language of its report was, generally, appropriately cautious and considered. The same cannot be said for many of the "plain language" inventions of what the NRP concluded. I suggest that the push for evidence-based reading instruction is but a thinly disguised ideological push for a national reading methodology, for reading instruction that meets the "phonics-first" emphasis of the Republican Party platform and the direct-instruction entrepreneurs, those who profit financially when federal and state governments mandate the use of curricular materials like the ones they produce.

Elaine Garan (Chapter 4), especially, points to a number of discrepancies between what the National Reading Panel concluded and what its Summary reported its conclusions to be. A similar invention of "facts" seems to be widespread and ongoing among phonics-first supporters. For example, in the National Institute for Literacy (NIFL) booklet, *Put Reading First* (Armbruster, Lehr, and Osborn, 2001 p. 18), it says

> *The research is quite convincing in showing that phonics instruction contributes to comprehension skills rather than inhibiting them.*

But then that

> *The effects of phonics instruction on students in second through sixth grades are limited to improving their word reading and oral test reading skills. The effects do not extend to spelling and reading comprehension.*

These two contradictory statements are followed by this bulleted summary on page 19:

> *Systematic and explicit phonics instruction significantly improves children's word recognition, spelling, and reading comprehension.*

With this kind of self-contradiction within a single short publication, is it any wonder that teachers find "research" of little use? Perhaps if the authors of the *Put Reading First* booklet had

---

What the NRP Report Doesn't Say

It does not support any particular phonics program.
It does not talk about decodable text.
It does not support intensive phonics instruction.
It does not talk about the content of a phonics program.
The NRP report does not support any one phonics program.
It does not support the use of phonics programs with older, poor readers.

(From Steven Stahl's keynote address at the Michigan Reading Recovery Conference, Detroit, January 2002. Available at <www.ciera.org>.)

been a bit more specific they could have avoided this sort of contradictory mumbo jumbo. Perhaps they would have had fewer difficulties in developing their plain-language interpretation of the NRP's findings had they adhered to the more circumspect language of the original NRP report. Perhaps there would have been less confusion about what the research supports if there had been at least some agreement on which research-based findings the PRD committee and the NRP agreed upon, or if the NRP had been more consistent in applying rules of evidence, or had allowed itself a broader evidence base. Still, a reliable summary of even a flawed report would not have to introduce additional distortions, as the NRP Summary did.

Other inventions of the "facts" about phonics instruction occur in the *Put Reading First* booklet (Armbruster et al., 2001). For instance, the authors offer various criteria for evaluating effective phonics instruction (pp. 16–17), including a definition of *effective phonics* as *synthetic phonics* (sound and blend). They list various program components, including decodable texts, activity sheets, precise directions for teachers, and so on. The disturbing fact is that the NRP said *nothing* about the content of effective phonics programs. Nothing. Yet the afterword to the *Put Reading First* document states: "The findings described in this document were drawn from the report of the National Reading Panel." This is not scientific consensus. This is not summarization. This is misrepresentation. This is simply invention of "evidence-based" evaluative criteria. This is ideology trumping evidence.

A similar invention of NRP "facts" by the Learning First Alliance (LFA) (2000) illustrates an even more powerful ideological distortion. From the LFA's plain-language interpretation of the NRP report:

> *The Report of the National Reading Panel states that explicit, systematic synthetic phonics (in synthetic phonics, children are taught to blend individual speech sounds into words) is significantly more effective than other types of phonics. (p. 14)*

The NRP offered no such conclusion. The panel compared the research evidence for three types of phonics programs: synthetic phonics, onset-rime, and miscellaneous. The NRP asks,

Are some types of phonics instruction more effective than others? *The analysis showed that effect sizes for the three categories of programs were significantly greater than zero and* did not differ statistically from each other. . . . *The conclusion supported by these findings is that* various types of systematic phonics *instruction are more effective than non-phonics approaches. (p. 2-132, emphasis added)*

How is it that neither the NIFL nor the LFA could find folks who could read and understand the research and then write reliable summaries? What makes it so difficult to reliably summarize what the NRP reported? As I noted in an earlier publication (Allington, 1999b), the LFA's *Every Child a Reader* booklet wholly misrepresents the findings of a study on the use of decodable texts. I wondered if anyone at the LFA had actually read the research they cited. I pointed out that when an author closes an original research article on teaching children to read by noting that no support was found for the particular approach studied, it shouldn't be too difficult for someone to simply report that conclusion accurately. And yet the LFA authors (unnamed) and the NRP report Summary authors (unnamed) and the *Put Reading First* booklet authors (Bonnie Armbruster, Fran Lehr, and Jean Osborn) all seem to have been stricken with a malady that makes reliably representing the research an enormously difficult task.

I will acknowledge that there are occasions when the NRP report might lead to confusion about what is being recommended. For instance, it states:

The Panel cannot conclude that schools should adopt programs to encourage more reading if the intended goal is to improve reading achievement. (p. 3:27)

Both Cunningham (2001) and Krashen (2001) address other problems with the NRP's conclusions on extensive reading (procedural inconsistency and procedural omission), but I find the report's inconsistency about instructional recommendations more interesting. The NRP report concludes that vocabulary is important to comprehension and that most vocabulary is developed "indirectly"—to use the panel's terminology—through extensive assigned and independent reading (p. 4:27). But because they found few "scientific" studies of the effects of extensive reading, the panel members could not recommend independent reading as a method for improving reading achievement. But they couldn't really recommend *against* it, either (p. 3:3). And they say that independent reading did seem to be important to vocabulary development.

It is perhaps this sort of confused thinking in the NRP report that led the authors of the *Put Reading First* booklet to state:

> *Rather than allocating instructional time for independent reading, encourage your children to read more out of school. (Armbruster et al., p. 29)*

One has to wonder why a teacher would encourage a child to read outside of school but not in school. Is there scientific evidence that supports the recommendation for out-of-school reading? The NRP report doesn't discuss out-of-school reading. It doesn't examine the research on out-of-school reading. Just six pages later, the *Put Reading First* booklet, like the NRP report, indicates that children learn word meanings by "reading extensively on their own" (p. 35). But not in school? Is there scientific evidence that extensive reading improves a child's vocabulary? Is there evidence that out-of-school independent reading improves reading achievement but in-school reading doesn't? Going by the NRP and NIFL inventions, it's hard to disentangle what the research actually says.

> One has to wonder why a teacher would encourage a child to read outside of school but not in school.

There is, of course, a good reason that there is little "scientific" evidence (as defined by the NRP) on the impact that extensive reading has on achievement. Given the extent of acknowledged correlational evidence, what school administrator would allow a "scientific" study of extensive reading to be conducted? Imagine that I propose randomly assigning children in your school to one of four instructional treatments in grades one through five. The four treatments systematically vary the volume of reading children are allowed to do. The first group will read for sixty minutes each day, the second for thirty minutes, the third for ten minutes. The fourth will be a no-reading control group. For five years children's reading at school and at home will be controlled. Even if the school administrator agrees to participate, I must still obtain parental permission—informed consent—so I'll have to inform parents that if their child is randomly selected for the no-reading group, the available evidence suggests that he or she will be illiterate upon exiting fifth grade. How many administrators or parents would sign on to such a study for the sake of science?

The NRP should have been experienced enough to understand why we have few experimental studies of the relationship between reading volume and reading achievement (but as Jim Cunningham notes in Chapter 2, functioning as a group seemed to make the panel members dumber). There are no experimental studies of child language acquisition for the same reason. No experimental studies of diet and growth in babies. No experimental studies of the effects of different quantities of insulin on normal children's growth and development. There are many aspects of human learning and development that are not amenable to random-assignment control-group research experiments. How, then, can we explain the current federal fascination with evidence, with evidence-based education?

Should Education Be More like Medicine?

There has been much made about the need for education to become more like medicine—more of an "evidence-based" profession. Lyon (2001) wrote that "When we give our children medicine to improve their health, we make sure it is scientifically proven; should we ask anything less regarding their educational development?" First of all, relatively few medicines have actually been tested on children. That itself is a current issue in the medical community. But even the general medical field has been far less evidence based than Lyon seems to imagine it has. Shortly after Lyon posed this question in the *New York Times*, that newspaper published a short piece on a new, new trend in the medical field: evidence-based medicine. According to a medical researcher quoted in that article, something close to 80 percent of medical decisions are based on experience, tradition, and intuition, not on any scientific evidence (Hitt, 2001). The article noted that certain long-standing therapies, such as bed rest for lower-back pain, have recently been shown to exacerbate the medical problem rather than promote healing.

More recently, the press has been full of reports about evidence on the usefulness of mammograms in mitigating deaths from breast cancer. Even though virtually every medical organization has supported the practice, at least for women over age fifty, a meta-analysis of the research suggested there was no positive impact from getting annual mammograms (Kolata, 2002). But then another research team reanalyzed those study data and concluded there was a significant benefit (Parker-Pope, 2002). The National Cancer Institute recommends that women continue to have mammograms given the competing evidence. The *New York Times* editorialized (January 27, 2002) about the scientific community's "uncertainty" over mammograms. The editorial noted that because mammography is a long-standing practice that is endorsed by the "cancer establishment" and because it is a significant source of income for doctors and hospitals, it would be difficult to get a "truly independent review" of mammography study data. The editorial suggested that it will be difficult to eliminate mammography from women's health care without "overwhelming evidence that it is dangerous."

Joanne Silburner, a National Public Radio reporter, interviewed the researcher who conducted the original meta-analysis. He argued that random assignment in clinical trials is the only scientific strategy for determining the effectiveness of mammography. Not surprisingly, none of the women Silburner interviewed were willing to participate in such trials. Silburner concluded that "absolute truth" about mammography is hard to come by, science notwithstanding.

Similar debates about the effects of hormone replacement therapy, the value of vitamin E in mitigating heart disease, and even the role of sodium in hypertension have graced the pages of not only our newspapers and magazines, but our medical

---

Drug testing and children

"A month after suspending a federal regulation that required drug makers to test their products to dermine whether they are safe and effective on children, the Bush administration yesterday reversed its position . . . The turnabout was welcomed by public health groups and legislators who were incensed by the FDA's decision, made public last month, to suspend the pediatric testing rule. It had been adopted in 1997 to address the fact that most drugs come onto the market without any information about whether they are safe for children and without an understanding of how children's dosages might differ from adults'."

The reinstatement was hailed by Mark Isaac, policy director of a pediatric foundation, because, "Seventy-five percent of drugs used in America have never been tested for use by children at all."

From: Marc Kaufman and Ceci Connolly, U.S. backs pediatric tests in reversal on drug safety. *Washington Post*, April 20, 2002, p. A3.

---

journals as well. Concerns about the adequacy of drug testing, especially the inadequacy of current procedures for safeguarding children from drugs that have been tested only on adults, or women from drugs that have been tested only on men, ripple through the medical literature.

In other words, medicine is not quite as scientific as many would like educators to believe—but we still get all these educational policy advocates suggesting that teaching should be more like healing: based on scientific evidence. Lyon isn't the only who advocates this shift. So does direct-instruction guru and policy entrepreneur Doug Carnine, who has written on the topic for the Fordham Foundation (1998b). So does his colleague, direct-instruction author and entrepreneur Bonita Grossen, who made the argument for the American Federation of Teachers (1996). Perhaps it is some sort of stethoscope envy or something.

Learning Disabilities, Special Education, and Patent Medicine

Jim Cunningham (Chapter 2) notes that the NRP used the wrong medical analogy. Research on reading instruction should be more like research on healthy human development, not research on disease. Perhaps the wrong analogy was selected because all of the direct-instruction policy entrepreneurs who so vigorously push the disease analogy come from the learning disabilities field. Coles (1987) long ago noted that this field was attempting to enhance its professional status by linking bad reading to some mysterious (and unmeasurable) "neurological disorder." Coles argued that affiliating with the medical field provided a sort of professional cover for a profession that has no scientific base. So learning disabilities professionals started talking about neurology, adopted some medical lingo, and almost invented attention deficit disorder as an explanation for why children didn't pay attention to the mind-numbing direct-instruction drill-and-skill lessons that were routinely prescribed for struggling readers who had been given the learning disabled label.

Given that direct-instruction programs for children identified as learning disabled have been just about the most disastrously unsuccessful educational efforts offered in American schools (Kavale, 1988; NYSUT, 1997), it seems almost lunacy that so many of the entrepreneurs of that approach are now offering advice on improving classroom instruction. One could argue that the current campaign emerged out of the Learning to Read, Reading to Learn project developed under Carnine's direction at the National Center for Improving the Tools of Educators (NCITE, 1996). This project was funded by the U.S. Office of Special Education and Rehabilitation Services (OSERS). The NCITE team reviewed the learning disabilities research funded by both OSERS and NICHD and concluded that

> *This body of research suggests that the relatively recent swing away from phonics instruction to a singular whole language approach is making it more difficult to lift children with learning disabilities out of the downward learning spiral and, in fact, may impede the progress of many students in learning to read with ease. (p. 3)*

The NCITE team argued that the increase in the numbers of children being identified as learning disabled was the result of the move away from phonics instruction. However, the team's review cited no studies that documented such a shift in instruction, and it ignored available research showing that the rise in the numbers of students identified as learning disabled paralleled the implementation of high-stakes testing (Allington & McGill-Franzen, 1992; McGill-Franzen & Allington, 1993; Potter & Wall, 1992). That is, using a time-series analysis, the researchers linked the increasing "learning disabled" identification rate to accountability mandates that make school test scores public and involve assigning schools grades or ratings. In every such accountability scheme, the achievement of pupils with disabilities was excluded from the ratings, a substantial incentive for labeling low-achieving students as learning disabled. And because there was no reliable method for identification, almost any student with low achievement could be labeled learning disabled (Allington, 2002; Lyon, 1995).

Federal policy makers were so concerned about the exclusion of pupils with disabilities that they changed the law in 1997 so that those students were required to participate in state testing programs (McGill-Franzen & Goatley, 2001). But while participation in testing is required, states still exclude these students' achievement scores from school ratings. Thus the incentive still exists, and the numbers of students being labeled learning disabled continue to rise. Pupils with disabilities are still rarely taught to read proficiently (Fine, 2002). There is no evidence that phonics instruction ever vanished from classrooms or special education resource rooms. In fact, if the research on teaching special education students to read is any indication, intensive phonics teaching continues to predominate in special education settings. But special education students couldn't read a decade ago, and they seem to be doing no better today.

> The people the media now tout as "leading reading researchers" are folks who cut their teeth and made their names advising the profession to offer code-emphasis direct instruction to children identified as learning disabled.

The people the media now tout as "leading reading researchers" are folks who cut their teeth and made their names advising the profession to offer code-emphasis direct instruction to children identified as learning disabled. These folks serve on the editorial boards of special education journals, not reading research journals (Allington, 1999). Never mind that their efforts have already led to instructional programs that consistently created juvenile illiterates, let's call them reading researchers and have them advise us on how teach all children to read.

If we are going to go with evidence, let's start with the evidence on the "success" of school programs for students identified as learning disabled. Now that National Institute of Child Health and Human Development (NICHD) researchers have found that there seems to be no such thing as dyslexia or learning disabilities (Shaywitz, Escobar, Shaywitz, Fletcher, & Makuch, 1992), maybe we should ask just why anyone should adopt the direct-instruction phonics interventions that have been part and parcel of failed learning disabilities interventions for the past thirty years. The failure of direct instruction to teach learning disabled children to read seems to be related simply to bad instructional design, not to dysfunctional neurology. Even the NRP found no evidence that systematic direct-instruction phonics helped older (grades two through six) poor readers develop general reading proficiencies (p. 2:133). And yet the NCITE direct-instruction entrepreneurs continue to argue for mandated intensive phonics for all kids, but especially for those who find learning to read difficult (Grossen, 1997).

Given the almost complete failure of phonics-intensive direct instruction in programs for children identified as learning disabled, we might ask whether we have invested more funding in any other educational program and ended up with less to show for it. It would have made sense to me if the politicians had stepped in and eliminated the NICHD and the Office of Special Education and Rehabilitation Services because of their almost complete failure to educate the learning disabled children entrusted to them. But putting the special education direct-instruction gurus in charge of reforming American reading instruction—even Orwell wouldn't have imagined such an outcome.

MEDICINE, EDUCATION, AND FOR-PROFIT INFLUENCES

There are other problems with comparing education to the medical field. The troubling relationship between big pharmaceutical companies and continuing medical education providers, for instance (Sternberg, 2000; Vergano, 2000). Is it continuing medical education that is being provided—or a sales pitch for new products? The evidence suggests the latter. There are financial conflicts of interest, as the General Accounting Office noted, between university researchers and drug company sponsors (Strope, 2001). And there are financial conflicts of interest when a federally funded university researcher stands to benefit from patent rights on a new medicine or treatment that's being studied.

G. Reid Lyon of the NICHD seems to understand this problem. He argues that some of the antagonism toward evidence-based reading instruction stems from "people investing in careers, in products, in ways of making a living that have frankly been found wanting" (Schemo, 2002). Likewise, direct-instruction entrepreneur Doug Carnine (1998a) stated,

> *Specialists who claim objectivity . . . should appear reasonably disinterested, or at least should not be expected to speak authoritatively where their own individual or professional interests are at stake. (p. 110)*

I agree with both Lyon's and Carnine's sentiments. But Carnine is both an advocate for and an author of direct-instruction materials, and he is an advisor to many of the politicians and policy makers who are now mandating the use of those very same materials. Jean Osborn, as primary author of the Texas "Little Red Book" on what the research says, advocated for decodable texts (Ellis, 1998) and for reading curriculum materials that just happen to contain decodable texts—and there is no evidence supporting the use of such materials. Osborn, like Carnine and like Grossen, is an author of direct-instruction materials. Osborn and her colleagues (Armbruster et al., 2001) have continued to make the same argument more recently, but now with a national venue and a federal sponsor, the National Institute for Literacy. What are the hallmarks of a "scientific" reading program? The NIFL's *Put Reading First* says,

> *These materials include books and stories that contain a large number of words that children can decode by using letter-sound relationships they have learned and are learning.*

Well, scientific research still provides no scientific evidence of a positive effect from the use of decodable texts. But Osborn is still the author of direct-instruction curriculum materials (SRA Reading Mastery, published by McGraw-Hill) that use decodable texts as the mainstay of beginning reading. The NRP report, which the *Put Reading First* advice is suppose to draw from, said nothing about the use of decodable texts. Nothing said because there is no scientific research supporting the use of decodable texts. Ideology trumps evidence.

There is a similar problem with the current push for "proven programs": Most education initiatives are "researched" by their own developers, education entrepreneurs who earn substantial income from curricular materials and assessments developed with federal dollars (Allington, 2001). One troubling trend is the use of publishers to "train" teachers in the latest research, as Florida is doing (Wasson, 2002). How likely is it that the publishers will focus on what the research actually says, versus what the politicians say it says? How likely is it that the publishers will demonstrate how to teach expertly without using their products?

Perhaps more worrisome about using the medical field as a model for education are indications that new medical accountability measures are leading to denial of treatment for certain high-risk patients. Jauhar (2001) describes a case in which the accountability measures had to do with tracking surgical outcomes for cardiac patients—basically, tracking survival rates. The intent of the tracking was to identify doctors and hospitals with unacceptably low patient-survival rates. The net effect, however, was that high-risk cardiac patients are now being denied a potentially lifesaving procedure because they are too likely to die and thus lower the survival rate.

What's the parallel in education? There are already complaints that too many for-profit, charter, and private schools are unwilling to enroll those students who are the most difficult to educate (Bracey, 2002). As accountability pressure rises, classroom teachers, too, will become more reluctant to have harder-to-teach children in their classrooms. Fewer teachers will be willing to work in schools that enroll many children who need extraordinary educational services in order to thrive academically.

And then there is the profit problem. Health maintenance organizations (HMOs) have not actually improved medical services, at least in my experience. I rather liked having my own physician, as opposed to whichever physician the corporation assigns me today. I rather preferred that my physician got rich for providing a needed service in a manner that attracted patients. Personally, I don't much care how much money MetraHealth or any other HMO makes.

Suddenly no one wants to run hospitals located in higher poverty neighborhoods or rural areas. There's no money to be made there. And actually providing high-quality care that is conveniently close to consumers is just too expensive for the health-care insurers: It cuts into profits.

Some kids are expensive to educate, but public schools do try to educate them all. There are lots of reasons I wouldn't use medicine as the model for education reform. But more to the point, those who make such arguments are either largely naive about how doctors are trained and how drugs are approved, or sucking up because medicine is a higher-status profession than education is. Let's all pretend we are neuroscientists. Let's pretend that reading instruction is a health issue. Let's pretend that the learning disabilities/dyslexia gurus know something about the nature of good classroom reading instruction.

But pretending doesn't make you a neuroscientist if you earned a doctorate in pupil personnel services. Literacy is a social activity more than it is a neurological event. Yes, the brain is involved. But it is also involved in singing and dancing, and no one is suggesting that singing off-key or having only limited mastery of the polka is primarily a neurological or medical problem. There is no need to pathologize reading difficulties. In fact, we should consider it normal that some children find learning to read more difficult than other children. In every human capacity, people differ in the effort needed to develop proficiency. We should expect that some children will need more expert, more intensive, more extensive instruction in order to develop proficient reading. There is no need to suggest difficulty in acquiring reading proficiency is abnormal or evidence of some personal deficiency. Instead, policy makers should be figuring out how to fund the needed expert, intensive teaching that some kids need to become readers. The current "blame and penalize the victims" approach to reading difficulties is both wrongheaded and counterproductive.

Evidence and Politicians

I've already noted that I am a skeptic when it comes to believing that politicians really, really want to know what the research says. I've written about the research the politicians in Texas and California ignored as they implemented their ideologically based reading programs (Allington, 1999b). You read the paper that Haley Woodside-Jiron and I developed on the single issue of decodable texts (Chapter 9), and if you read *Put Reading First*, the NIFL booklet that summarizes the NRP's findings, you will find virtually identical assertions about what the research supposedly says about decodable texts. Never mind that the NRP report said *nothing* about decodable texts. Never mind that no research anywhere supports the use of decodable texts. Ideology trumps evidence.

But what about the scientific evidence on class-size reduction (Achilles, 1999; Finn, 1998)? That evidence is clear and it is scientific. Smaller primary grade classes produce better achievement and lasting improvements, especially for poor children. Yet the new education bill eliminates federal funding for class-size reduction.

What about retention in grade versus social promotion? Again, the research is clear and scientific (Denton, 2001; Heubert & Hauser, 1999; Holmes & Saturday, 2000; Shepard & Smith, 1989). Flunking does not improve academic performance, but it does increase the likelihood of dropping out. And it is expensive, costing the equivalent of a full year's additional schooling per child. But the U.S. House of Representatives passed House Resolution 401 urging states to "end social promotion," and politicians of every stripe have campaigned on that theme.

Even if flunking was a positive educational treatment, using a single standardized achievement test to make the decision would be bad science. The National Academy of Science, the American Educational Research Association, and the American Psychological Association all agree on that point. Is it possible that no one in the U.S. Department of Education (or the many state education agencies) has heard about this? Is it possible that no one has actually read the manuals that the test publishers provide? Is it possible that none of the president's education advisors have heard about it either? Are federal education bureaucrats psychometrically challenged? Did they read the test manuals accurately, but fail to comprehend them?

What about book access? The *Put Reading First* booklet says that teachers should encourage students to read outside of school in lieu of allocating instructional time to independent reading. Is it possible that no one at NIFL is aware of the research of Assistant Secretary of Education Susan Neuman? The evidence she presents on just how unlikely it is that poor children, the kids supposedly targeted by the No Child Left Behind legislation, have any access to books outside of school (Neuman & Celano, 2001)? It's bad enough that the Bush administration's original education budget eliminated funding for Reading Is Fundamental (RIF) and that Secretary Paige indicated that his department is about "reading instruction" not "mere exposure to books" (Henry, 2001). Luckily, legislators reinstated the RIF funding and so some poor children will get books to read. Is it possible that the Secretary of Education, once superintendent of one the nation's largest urban school districts, is unaware of the research showing how limited the supply of books is in urban schools and how limited poor children's access is to even those few books (Guice, Allington, Johnston, Baker, & Michelson, 1996; McGill-Franzen, Lanford, & Adams, 2002)?

What would lead the NIFL to produce the self-contradictory *Put Reading First*, which on the one hand indicates that extensive reading is not a scientifically valid practice, but on the other hand recommends that teachers have children read at home, noting that most vocabulary is developed during extensive independent reading? Naivete? Ideology? Bad editing?

The Problem of the NRP Report and the Plain-Language Summaries

If you read this book from front to back, you've read the several papers that critique the NRP report and Elaine Garan's incisive critique (Chapter 4) of the distortions of the original findings in the Summary of the NRP report that was produced for wide dissemination. I can think of no explanation that adequately accounts for that distortion of the findings. Even NRP panel member Tim Shanahan (2001) acknowledged that the NRP report's Summary contains substantive discrepancies.

> *Dr. Garan notes the unfortunate mismatches between the NRP report and its Summary. The report is more than 500 pages long, has lots of detail about how the analysis was conducted, and provides specifics on what we found out about instruction. The Summary, on the other hand, is only twenty-six pages long. I would agree that it is an imperfect and incomplete representation of the report. The Summary is a bit ragged at times and it is of minimal use to teachers because it doesn't contain some of the meaty specifics. . . . I fear that it conveys the idea that good, older readers should be taught phonics, something neither stated nor implied in the report. The best antidote to this problem and the ones noted by Dr. Garan would be for more teachers to read the report itself. (Shanahan, pp. 70–71)*

So the Summary is not a reliable expression of the Panel's findings. And the best solution is to have teachers read the 500-plus page report. Why not pull the Summary from distribution and issue a rewrite that does not distort the NRP's findings? Why not produce plain-language documents that are sophisticated and reliable summaries of what the evidence—even the NRP evidence—actually tells us about effective reading instruction?

Given the attention to potential financial conflicts of interest involved in selecting members of the NRP, why did direct-instruction entrepreneurs play such a seemingly large role in writing the *Put Reading First* document? Why have so many McGraw-Hill authors been involved in shaping both state and national reading policies (Allington, 1999; Garan, 2002; Metcalf, 2002)?

Conclusion

I wish I had a grand plan for stopping this ideological federal freight train, loaded as it is with unreliable evidence. I don't. As I note in the Preface, I've pulled this book together because it's important that we consider what the research says and whether the reports summarizing that research—even the narrow subset of experimental research reviewed by the NRP—are reliable. The articles in this book document substantive difficulties with the procedures used by the NRP, procedures that proved to be both inadequate and inconsistent. But more troubling for me is the rampant distortion of the NRP's findings in the plain-language summaries. It's more troubling because there are probably not more than a handful of people who have actually read the complete NRP report (and several of them are represented in this volume). In other words, it isn't the NRP that is being widely read or quoted, but the plain-language summaries.

It would have been more difficult, though more honest, to prepare summaries that simply acknowledged that the research did not provide clear guidelines on what sort of phonics instruction works, in what amounts, for what sort of kids, at what developmental stages. It would have been honest to report that the evidence only points us in a general direction and provides no detailed prescription. It would have been honest to tell readers that the NRP studied only a few of the important aspects of beginning reading because of time and financial constraints. But the authors of the NRP report Summary, the NIFL's *Put Reading First* booklet, and the LFA's *Every Child Reading: A professional development guide* elected to follow a different course. Ideology trumped evidence again and again and again.

These are troubling trends and troubling times. As a researcher, I believe that the evidence does provide us with useful direction. But the research has its limits, even when it's considered broadly. I must conclude that the research evidence is being distorted and purposefully misrepresented in ideologically consistent ways, in politically consistent ways, in reliably profitable ways. Reading researchers have remained silent for too long. Reading professors, too. Reading professionals in the schools seem to be more often resisting these ideological mandates, but

P. David Pearson, dean of the College of Education, University of California at Berkeley and former director or codirector of two national reading research centers, discussed the potential unintended consequences of national "consensus" reports:

"However, if the recommendations get picked up by policy makers and transformed into legislative mandates that tell schools and teachers to teach in particular ways because of their presumed evidential superiority, then I fear that all of that energy, which could go into new research and development initiatives, will be channeled into new policy battles over curriculum control. . . . Let me be clear. I do not like mandates; I see little evidence of their overall positive impact, and I have serious questions about their legitimacy in professional matters." (Pearson, 1999, p. 245)

they are under enormous pressures to conform to inventions about what the research says. Schools are under substantial pressures to accept the NRP's findings because they desperately need the funds that the federal legislation provides. That legislation requires that reading instruction programs be research based, but distortions of the research are driving the evaluative criteria for what qualifies as research based.

I have no simple answer or action plan. But we cannot continue to sit by while ideology trumps evidence. Tip O'Neill, the venerated longtime speaker of the U.S. House of Representatives, said, "All politics is local." I agree. I suggest that local action is the only likely path to follow to halt the ideological freight train. The stakes are huge. The money is huge. The needs are huge. But the National Governor's Association has already managed to get concessions on testing mandates from the U.S. Department of Education (Toppo, 2002). Several state commissioners of education have indicated that they will not implement the federal plan, as have several local school system superintendents. Their resistance stems from the deep flaws in the federalized testing and accountability mandates. Perhaps we can convince more of those who lead state and local education agencies that the science behind many of the reading mandates is flawed. Maybe we can convince federal policy makers that ideology, not evidence, is driving many of the mandates. Maybe not. But if we don't out the ideologues, who will?

Changing the larger course of educational policy making will be even more difficult than changing the direction of reading policy making. The strength of American education has been its historical reliance on local control. This, of course, produced an enormous diversity of educational policies and practices. But this is hardly a homogeneous society, and we are becoming more diverse every decade. One-size-fits-all classroom instruction violates virtually everything we've learned from a hundred years of educational research. I cannot imagine that federal one-size-fits-all educational policy making will improve U.S. schools.

The federal push for a national reading curriculum is simply part of a much larger and much more dangerous attempt to shift control of public education from those who are closest to it—local taxpayers and teachers—to those who sit in bureaucratic offices far from the classrooms they are attempting to control. I also worry that Gerry Bracey (2002) and others just might be correct—that the real goal is to undermine the public and political consensus that supports a public education system.

There is much at stake here. The ideological push for a national reading curriculum is just the tip of the iceberg.

References

Achilles, C. M. (1999). *Let's put kids first, finally: Getting class size right.* Thousand Oaks, CA: Corwin Press.

Allington, R. L. (1999a). *Big claims, little evidence.* Paper presented at the National Reading Conference. Scottsdale, AZ.

Allington, R. L. (1999b). Crafting state educational policy: The slippery role of educational research and researchers. *Journal of Literacy Research, 31,* 457–482.

Allington, R. L. (2001). *What really matters for struggling readers: Designing research-based programs.* New York: Allyn & Bacon.

Allington, R. L. (2002). Research on reading/learning disability interventions. In A. Farstrup & S. J. Samuels (Eds.), *What research says about reading instruction, 3rd ed.* Newark, DE: International Reading Association.

Allington, R. L., & McGill-Franzen, A. (1992). Unintended effects of educational reform in New York State. *Educational Policy, 6* (4), 396–413.

Armbruster, B., Lehr, F., & Osborn, J. (2001). *Put reading first.* Washington, DC: National Institute for Literacy.

Bracey, G. W. (2002). *The war against America's public schools: Privatizing schools, commercializing education.* Boston: Allyn & Bacon.

Carnine, D. (1998a). A report on reading initiatives and their implementation. In P. D. Pearson (Ed.), *New York State Reading Symposium: Final report* (pp. 107–118). Albany, NY: New York State Education Department.

Carnine, D. (1998b, June). *The metamorphosis of education into a mature profession.* Paper presented at the meeting of the Society for Prevention Research, Park City, UT.

Coles, G. (1987). *The learning mystique: A critical look at learning disabilities.* New York: Pantheon.

Cunningham, J. W. (2001). The National Reading Panel report. *Reading Research Quarterly, 30* (3), 326–335.

Denton, D. R. (2001). *Finding alternatives to failure: Can states end social promotion and reduce retention rates?* Atlanta: Southern Regional Education Board.

Fine, L. (2002, March 6). Special education advocates hail graduation test ruling. *Education Week,* pp. 1, 27.

Finn, J. (1998). *Class size and students at risk: What is known? What is next?* Washington, DC: U.S. Department of Education.

Garan, E. (2002). *Resisting reading mandates: How to triumph with the truth.* Portsmouth, NH: Heinemann.

Grossen, B. (1996). Making research serve the profession. *American Educator, 20* (3), 7–8, 22–27.

Grossen, B. (1997). *30 years of research: What we now know about how children learn to read: A synthesis of research on reading from the National Institute of Child Health and Development.* (www.cftl.org): The Center for the Future of Teaching and Learning: Santa Cruz, CA.

Guice, S., Allington, R. L., Johnston, P., Baker, K., & Michelson, N. (1996). Access? Books, children, and literature-based curriculum in schools. *The New Advocate, 9* (3), 197–207.

Henry, T. (2001, June 11). Lawmakers move to improve literacy, the "new civil right" goal: All 3rd-graders read at grade level, using newest methods. *USA TODAY,* p. A.1.

Heubert, J. P., & Hauser, R. M. (1999). *High stakes: Testing for tracking, promotion, and graduation.* Washington, DC: National Academy Press.

Hitt, J. (December 9, 2001). Evidence-based medicine. *The New York Times Magazine,* p. 22.

Holmes, C. T., & Saturday, J. (2000). Promoting the end of retention. *Journal of Curriculum and Supervision, 15* (4), 300–314.

Jauhar, S. (2001, September 11). Life and death stakes in the numbers game. *New York Times.* www.nytimes.com/2001/09/11/health/policy/11ESSA.html

Kavale, K. A. (1988). The long-term consequences of learning disabilities. In M. C. Reynolds, M. C. Wang, & H. J. Walberg (Eds.), *Handbook of special education research and practice: Mildly handicapped conditions* (pp. 303–344). New York: Pergamon.

Kolata, G. (2002, February 10). The painful fact of medical uncertainty. *New York Times,* p. A5.

Krashen, S. (2001). More smoke and mirrors: A critique of the National Reading Panel report on fluency. *Phi Delta Kappan, October,* 119–123.

Learning First Alliance (2000). *Every Child a Reader professional development guide.* Washington, DC: Author.

Lyon, G. R. (1995). Toward a definition of dyslexia. *Annals of Dyslexia, 45,* 3–27.

Lyon, G. R. (2001, September 6). Letter to the editor. *New York Times.*

McGill-Franzen, A., & Allington, R. L. (1993). Flunk 'em or get them classified: The contamination of primary grade accountability data. *Educational Researcher, 22* (1), 19–22.

McGill-Franzen, A., & Goatley, V. (2001). Title 1 and special education: Support for children who struggle to learn to read. In S. Neuman and D. Dickinson (Eds.), *Handbook of Early Literacy Research* (pp. 471–483). New York: Guilford.

McGill-Franzen, A. M., Lanford, C., & Adams, E. (2002). Learning to be literate: A comparison of five urban preschools. *Journal of Educational Psychology.*

Metcalf, S. D. (2002, January 28). Reading between the lines. *The Nation.* Available at: http://thenation.com.docprintmhtml?:=20020128&=metcalf

National Center for Improving the Tools of Educators (1996). *Reading: The first chapter in education.* Eugene: University of Oregon.

Neuman, S., & Celano, D. (2001). Access to print in low-income and middle-income communities. *Reading Research Quarterly, 36* (1), 8–26.

New York State United Teachers (April 21, 1997). Inclusion raises questions on testing. *NY Teacher,* 23.

Parker-Pope, T. (2002, February 8). Women are still urged to get mammograms despite controversy. *Wall Street Journal,* p. B1.

Potter, D. C., & Wall, M. E. (1992, April). *Higher standards for grade promotion and graduation: Unintended effects of reform.* Paper presented at the American Educational Research Association, San Francisco.

Scarr, S. (1985). Constructing psychology: Making facts and fables for our times. *American Psychologist, 40,* 499–512.

Schemo, D. J. (2002, January 19). Now, the pressure begins for Bush's reading expert. *New York Times,* p. A12.

Shanahan, T. (2001). Response to Elaine Garan. *Language Arts, 79* (1), 70–71.

Shaywitz, S. E., Escobar, M., Shaywitz, M., Fletcher, J., & Makuch, R. (1992). Evidence that dyslexia may represent the lower tail of a normal distribution of reading ability. *New England Journal of Medicine, 326,* 145–150.

Shepard, L. A., & Smith, M. L. (Eds.). (1989). *Flunking grades: Research and policies on retention.* Philadelphia: Falmer.

Snow, C. E., Burns, M. S., & Griffin, P. (1998). *Preventing reading difficulties in young children: A report of the National Research Council.* Washington, DC: National Academy Press.

Sternberg, S. (2000, January 19). Drug firms spend big bucks on doctors, get results. *USA Today,* p. 7D.

Strope, L. (2001, December 26). Financial conflicts pose threat to research. *Albany Times-Union,* p. A4.

Toppo, G. (2002, February 24). Governors seek flexibility on tests. Associated Press (Downloaded on Feb. 25 from www.nga.org).

Vergano, D. (2000, March 9). Who's teaching the doctors? Drug firms sponsor required courses and see their sales rise. *USA Today,* p. D1–2.

Wasson, D. (2002, March 2). Publishers agree to train teachers on phonic method. *Tampa Tribune.* (Available at http://www.tampatribune.com/MGA9XF8WAYC.html).

Bibliography on the Confrontation Between Ideology and Evidence

Allington, R. L. (2001). *What really matters for struggling readers: Designing research-based programs.* Boston: Allyn & Bacon.

Baumann, J. F., Hoffman, J. V., Moon, J., & Duffy-Hester, A. (1998). Where are teachers' voices in the phonics/whole language debate? Results from a survey of U.S. elementary teachers. *Reading Teacher, 50* (8), 636–651.

Bracey, G. W. (2002). *The war against America's public schools: Privatizing schools, commercializing education.* Boston: Allyn & Bacon.

Coles, G. (2000). *Misreading reading: The bad science that hurts children.* Portsmouth, NH: Heinemann.

Garan, E. (2002). *Resisting reading mandates: How to triumph with the truth.* Portsmouth, NH: Heinemann.

Moffett, J. (1988). *Storm in the mountains: A case study of censorship, conflict, and consciousness.* Carbondale, IL: Southern Illinois University Press.

Morrow, L. M., & Tracey, D. H. (1997). Strategies used for phonics instruction in early childhood classrooms. *Reading Teacher, 50* (8, May), 644–653.

Rothstein, R. (1998). *The way we were? The myths and realities of America's student achievement.* New York: The Century Foundation Press.

Routman, R. (1996). *Literacy at the crossroads.* Portsmouth, NH: Heinemann.

Sacks, P. (2000). *Standardized minds: The high price of America's testing culture and what we can do to change it.* Cambridge, MA: Perseus.

Shannon, P. (1998). *Reading poverty.* Portsmouth, NH: Heinemann.

Spring, J. (1997). *Political agendas for education: From the Christian Coalition to the Green Party.* Mahwah, NJ: Lawrence Erlbaum Associates.

Taylor, D. (1998). *Beginning to read and the spin doctors of science: The political campaign to change America's mind about how children learn to read.* Urbana, IL: National Council of Teachers of English.

Bibliography on the Politics of Reading Instruction

Allington, R. L. (1999). Crafting state educational policy: The slippery role of educational research and researchers. *Journal of Literacy Research, 31,* 457–482.

Allington, R. L., & Woodside-Jiron, H. (1999). The politics of literacy teaching: How "research" shaped educational policy. *Educational Researcher, 28* (8), 4–13.

Altwerger, B., & Strauss, S. L. (2002). The business behind testing. *Language Arts, 79* (3), 256–263.

American Educational Research Association. (2000). *AERA position statement concerning high-stakes testing in preK–12 Education.* American Educational Research Association. Available: http://www.aera.net/about/policy/stakes.htm.

Berliner, D. C. (1997). Educational psychology meets the Christian Right: Differing views of children, schooling, teaching, and learning. *Teachers College Record, 98* (3), 381–416.

Berliner, D. C., & Biddle, B. J. (1996). *The manufactured crisis: Myths, fraud, and the attack on America's public schools.* White Plains, NY: Longman.

Bracey, G. W. (1997). *Setting the record straight: Responses to misconceptions about public education in the United States.* Alexandria, VA: Association for Supervision and Curriculum Development.

Calkins, L., Montgomery, K., Santman, D., & Falk, B. (1998). *A teacher's guide to standardized reading tests: Knowledge is power.* Portsmouth, NH: Heinemann.

Carnine, D. (1999). Campaigns for moving research into practice. *Remedial and Special Education, 20* (1), 2–6.

Coles, G. (2002). *Great unmentionables: What national reading reports and reading legislation don't tell you.* Portsmouth, NH: Heinemann.

Dressman, M. (1999). On the use and misuse of research evidence: Decoding two states' reading initiatives. *Reading Research Quarterly, 34* (3), 258–285.

Ellis, L. (1998). We'll eat the elephant one bite at a time: The continuing battle for control of literacy education in Texas. In K. S. Goodman (Ed.), *In defense of good teaching: What teachers need to know about the reading wars.* (pp. 87–105). York, ME: Stenhouse.

Garan, E. M. (2001). What does the report of the National Reading Panel really tell us about phonics? *Language Arts, 79* (1), 61–70.

Heubert, J. P., & Hauser, R. M. (1999). *High stakes: Testing for tracking, promotion, and graduation.* Washington, DC: National Academy Press.

Kozol, J. (1991). *Savage inequalities: Children in America's schools.* New York: Crown.

Lieberman, T. (2000). *Slanting the story: The forces that shape the news.* New York: The New Press.

McGill-Franzen, A. (2000). Policy and instruction: What is the relationship? In M. Kamil, P. Mosenthal, P. D. Pearson, & R. Barr (Eds.), *Handbook of reading research, Vol. 3* (pp. 891–908). Mahwah, NJ: Erlbaum.

McQuillan, J. (1998). *The literacy crisis: False claims, real solutions.* Portsmouth, NH: Heinemann.

Metcalf, S. (2000, October 2). Remedial ed: Bush saves a department to destroy it. *The New Republic,* 21–23.

Metcalf, S. D. (2002, January 28). Reading between the lines. *The Nation.* Available at: http://thenation.com.docprint.mhtml?i=20020128&=metcalf

Moats, L. C. (2000). *Whole language lives on: The illusion of "balanced" reading instruction.* New York: Thomas Fordham Foundation.

Neuman, S. B., Celano, D. C., Greco, A. N., & Shue, P. (2001). *Access for all: Closing the book gap for children in early education.* Newark, DE: International Reading Association.

Pearson, P. D. (1999). A historically based review of Preventing Reading Difficulties in Young Children. *Reading Research Quarterly, 34* (2), 231–246.

Pearson, P. D. (2001). Learning to teach reading: The status of the knowledge base. In C. Roller (Ed.), *Learning to teach reading: Setting the research agenda* (pp. 4–19). Newark, DE: International Reading Association.

Pellegrino, J. W., Jones, L., & Mitchell, K. (1999). *Grading the nation's report card.* Washington, DC: National Academy Press.

Pressley, M. (in press). Effective beginning reading instruction: A paper commissioned by the National Reading Conference. *Journal of Literacy Research.*

Pressley, M., & Allington, R. L. (1999). What should educational research be the research of? *Issues in education: Contributions from educational psychology, 5* (1), 1–35.

Stahl, S. A., Duffy-Hester, A., & Stahl, K. A. D. (1998). Everything you wanted to know about phonics (but were afraid to ask). *Reading Research Quarterly, 33,* 338–355.

Strauss, S. L. (2001). An open letter to Reid Lyon, director, Human Learning and Behavior Branch, National Institute of Child Health and Human Development, National Institutes of Health. *Educational Researcher* (June/July), 26–33.

Valencia, S. W., & Wixson, K. K. (2001). Inside English/language arts standards: What's in a grade? *Reading Research Quarterly, 36* (2), 202–211.

Index